D0374847

"A must-read for anyone who wants to unleash the power of personal calling. Reading and heeding the message of this book can make your career come alive and revitalize the institutions shaping our society. Trust me, you've got to read this one."

—Dick Staub
Host, The Dick Staub Show

"I am excited about the guidance and direction for staff and students provided by Miller's process. We expect to make use of it throughout the world in the teaching of students, career counseling of staff, and in job-match issues."

—Loren Cunningham,
Director, Youth with a Mission

"Arthur Miller claims that we were made for joy, that our Creator has fitted us for a life purpose, for life work and life fun. This book is winsome, illuminating, and faith-evoking. Read it, no matter what age you are!"

—R. Paul Stevens,
Professor of applied theology, Regent College

"The interview and analysis Art provided gave a different look at myself and my team which was much needed in our high-tech aerospace industry."

—John Capellupo
Former president, McDonnell Douglas Aerospace Company

"In this book, Art and Bill have directly addressed the central issue pressing every major organization to the wall. Their articulation of the path to full engagement of the heads, hearts, and hands of people in a way that recognizes each individual's inherent dignity and uniqueness is an imperative for those who wish to rise above the din of relentless competition."

—Fred Harburg
Director of Education, Training, and
Organizational Development General Motors Europe

"This book is provocative. It is a formidable assault on the assumption of the person underlying modern psychology. The education profession, business leaders, and politicians are each in turn humbled by the relentless application of the author's insights on giftedness to their own particular fields. It is also provocative in that it contains a worldview which has roots deep in Judeo Christian theology."

—The Right Honorable Lord Griffiths of Fforestfach
Economic advisor to former British Prime Minister Margaret Thatcher

"I have found the description of my motivated abilities from the SIMA® assessment process to be encouraging and practical in helping me judge good job fit. We used People Management and their consulting to select key staff and found the insights very important. As I have moved from my U.S. Senate career back to private life, the information has been clarifying and significant to me personally."

—David Durenberger
former U.S. senator

"We have used the SIMA® process and People Management's application consulting over 350 times to gain insight into job fit and team performance at the Fairview Health System. Motivated ability and the understanding of high performance job fit are building blocks for continuous business process improvement and effective management."

—Richard Norling
CEO, Fairview Health System (Minneapolis)

Why You  Can'tBe anythingYou WanttoBe

arthur f. miller jr.
with William Hendricks

ZondervanPublishingHouse
Grand Rapids, Michigan

A Division of HarperCollinsPublishers

To Ralph Mattson and the late Tom Marshall of New
Zealand, whose gifted teachings have been foundational
to our faith, and nourishment to so many, many of us

Why You Can't Be Anything You Want to Be
Copyright © 1999 by Arthur F. Miller Jr.

Requests for information should be addressed to:

📖 ZondervanPublishingHouse
Grand Rapids, Michigan 49530

Miller, Arthur F.
    Why you can't be anything you want to be / Arthur F. Miller, Jr., with William
Hendricks.
        p.   cm.
    Includes bibliographical references.
    ISBN 0–310–22647–3 (hardcover)
    1. Ability. 2. Ability—Religious aspects—Christianity. 3. Motivation (Psychology) 4.
Motivation (Psychology)—Religious aspects—Christianity. 5. Individuality. 6.
Individuality—Religious aspects—Christianity. 7. Self-actualization (Psychology) 8.
Self-actualization (Psychology)—Religious aspects—Christianity. I. Hendricks, William,
1954–   . II. Title.
    BF431.M475 1999
    153.9—dc21   99–18579
                                                                                         CIP

This edition printed on acid-free paper and meets the American National Standards Institute
Z39.48 standard.

Interior design by Sherri L. Hoffman

Printed in the United States of America

00 01 02 03 04 05 /❖ DC/ 10 9 8 7 6 5 4

Contents

Acknowledgments

The writing and rewriting of this book would not have been possible without the support of our network of Partners: Steve Darter (Northeast); Rob Stevenson (Mid-West); Nick Isbister (UK); Peter Stork (Australia); Tommy Thomas (Mid-South) and John Samuels (Singapore) and Affiliates: Anton Philips (Benelux); Ken Johnson (Seattle); Marlys and Meryl Hanson (Livermore); Bill and Lynn Banis (Chicago); Thom Black (In-Genius Center); Sharon Daugherty (North Jersey); The Hendricks Group (Dallas); Paul Lewis (Family University); Jonathan Ladd (Baltimore, MD); Rick Wellock (Pittsburgh); Ruth Lewis (Madison, WI); Johann Primloo (South Africa).

Special thanks go to Art Miller III, and Kim Miller, keeper and trainers of our technology, and to our other veteran case writers: Don Kiehl and Lisa Villesvik* who serve the network in need, as well as those who serve their local clients throughout the world. And the third generation is in hot pursuit: Julie Goldsmith, Mark Stevenson, Kevin Stork, and Joshua Miller.

It is so typical of one's progeny and why so many businesses don't survive the heirs of the founder. One of my sons wants to move toward more systemic applications of our technology, using archetypes as normative targets. The other son wants to go deeper and broader in our work with individuals, encompassing the entire family. I prefer to see this development as desirable complementarity, because it does provide a rich diversity of service to our clients. Time will tell.

In thinking about thanks due to those who have made personal contributions to my life and work, I want to mention just a few stars whose giftedness wonderfully matches their calling. Each has made a significant difference in my life:

Erick Kaardal, my attorney from Minneapolis—a brilliant lawyer—practical; innovative; passionate about justice, politics, debate, virtue, and his Catholic faith. He has been a rock for me.

---

* Example of Lisa's work is on pp. 50–51.

Roger Park, my daughter Elizabeth's husband, strong and gentle. More than anyone I know, Roger has sought, through trial and great effort, to be true to his giftedness, and he has succeeded wonderfully. They live their faith fully.

Mark Scholtz, who leads a small choir in which I sing, is the quintessential organist-cum-director in our small gem of an Episcopal church: demanding, but forgiving, he selects mainly English choral music that, at its best, hovers between pure worship and the ineffable beauty of deeply experienced human emotion (always controlled of course).

Gary and Betty Cobb, who run a fishing and hunting camp with such concern for guests and long-term quality of the sport, and amidst such beauty that people return year after year, even with the next generation, even when they are near the end of their lives. It seems almost a foretaste to many of us.

My next to last star is Linda Spak, a realtor in our area. Linda is direct, thorough, fair, probing, honest, and concerned about all parties. She has been an example to me of how it all ought to work.

Finally, there is Niles Golovin, who produces chewy-crust hearthbaked bread in a local bakery that feeds my soul, even after freezing it (the bread) and letting it thaw a week later. How many ways we can love one another!

I would give very special thanks to the women who have labored throughout this decade (Connie Cather), and more recently (Iola Held), to produce what I trust will be of value to the present age.

Sandy Vander Zicht, my editor at Zondervan Publishing House, has been my lifeline through the often turbulent waters of publishing. Her vision and guidance at every stage have been invaluable to me. I would surely have been "lost at sea" if not for her.

And of course, to Bill Hendricks, who transformed a less-than-sparkling manuscript to one that is eminently readable. I bow to his giftedness, with thanks. A man of sound judgment, Bill was so impressed with the value and usefulness of our work that he joined the family!

Foreword

I always look for the man behind the book. If he is a good writer, the man is the book. The distinction between them is seamless.

I remember the first time I saw Arthur Miller. It was at a Washington, D.C., hotel in 1977, where we both were attending a counseling convention. Over the phone, we arranged to meet. As he came striding toward me, I was impressed with his stature and his regal bearing; he looked like a born leader.

Since 1977, I have found out he is: a leader in the realm of new ideas, new ways of looking at each individual's potential, and discovering that individual's unique "gifts."

What I like about Arthur is that he is very gifted himself in many ways, but above all in seeing patterns within people. How our age needs that! We are bombarded with so much information, so many little bits and pieces every day that we wander—as David Shenk has said in his book—in a Data Smog.

That is true of all our information about the world out there. But it is true also of what we know about ourselves. Bits and pieces. Self-awareness smog!

We need organizing principles to make sense of all the smog. That is Arthur's unique contribution to career counseling. More than any other person in the field today, Arthur has a gift for seeing patterns in the way you and I relate to the world—and to our gifts. And he has a gift for teaching us to do the same.

I have, in my own work with job hunters and career changers, been able to use his insights in so many ways.

I think you will too.

Richard Bolles
What Color Is Your Parachute?

Preface

Perhaps you are unaware of the fact that you are the customized expression of a loving God. He has wired you through some genetic mechanism we do not as yet understand. You have been endowed with a unique mix of competencies and the desire and drive to use them in pursuit of an outcome of unrivaled personal importance. Your life has meaning built into it. Effectively, you have an exciting, challenging, and achievable destiny if you will but discover and embrace who you are designed to be.

Once through the discovery process, the main obstacle between you and your fulfillment lies in the society you inhabit. The institutions of education, work, and religion are not interested in your giftedness and passion except in regards to what it can do for them. Which is, as we say, the way it is in this life—at least for now.

Don't let this fact frustrate or paralyze you. Implement the suggestions that make the most sense to you. Then let your teacher or boss, and your clergy as well, know that you will give them what they want from you, as they give you what you need—the chance to be who you were designed to be.

Introduction

A Tale of Two "Illuminations"

During World War II, I served on a Landing Ship-Tank (LST) in the Pacific. On this night, as on every night, the ships moved without lights to avoid attracting enemy attention. Suddenly we realized that we were on a direct collision course with a darkened, fast-moving hospital ship. Immediate action was required, but the engineering officer in charge of our ship, as it speeded through the dark night toward a likely disaster, froze up. The skipper was called and arrived on the conning tower just in time to take evasive action.

Weeks later, our LST was literally stuck on a beach during the invasion of Zamboanga in the Philippines. We were under heavy shelling and took a hit amidships, which started a fire directly over large quantities of high-octane fuel and ammunition. With the noise of a shell hitting steel, the shouts of "Fire!" and the sight of smoke, those of us near the opened and lowered bow began to stream out (actually running like rabbits!), trying to escape from the danger of a massive explosion. I was not at the front of those seeking a safe harbor, but I wasn't among the stragglers, either. In the face of widespread panic, the same engineering officer who had been immobilized earlier now resolutely led a small crew toward the fire to save the ship and our collective skins. (Oddly enough, when the shell hit, it burst a water pipe, which put the fire out in a few minutes.)

Later I wondered about the apparent paradox of the same man choking in one emergency situation and performing heroically in another, even more threatening, one. I began to realize that the two responses—inability to act versus heroism—were not contradictory but rather reactions to two very different situations.

Why does a person who is useless in one emergency perform heroically in another, even more threatening one?

The first emergency involved abstract radar data, great risk to several hundred lives, the necessity of an immediate reaction, vector force analyses of options, and speed. In the second situation the site of the problem could be visually determined, the nature of the problem and the likely solution were reasonably clear, the risk was limited to the engineer himself and his team of volunteers, and there was time to make and correct decisions.

The apparently contradictory responses began to make sense. The engineer froze in the first situation, not because he was a coward or a weakling, but because there was a mismatch between the demands of the situation and his natural abilities. He performed heroically in the second emergency because the situation demanded precisely those skills and reactions that he possessed.

Why does a person who is useless in one emergency perform heroically in another, even more threatening one?

As for my own performance—I didn't have to abandon ship with the other rodents—I could have stayed to help fight the fire, yet I ran. On the other hand, I later disarmed a crazed sailor—twice the victim of torpedoed ships in the North Atlantic—who came at me with a .45 while I was burning confidential documents that he thought were his personal papers. Again, different situations drew different reactions. In one, I was unmistakably cowardly. In the other, I took immediate action based on my read of the situation, effectively unaware of any personal risk. (Actually, I think I thought he was kidding!)

These events in the Pacific turned out to be the seeds of the first of two "illuminations" that have unfolded into a destiny I have followed and continue to follow more than five decades later.

The next time I encountered dramatic evidence that we each have certain strengths and motivations and not others was when our firstborn boy was six months old and suffering with a high fever and a bad cough. We lived in a garret apartment on the third floor of a home. When the pediatrician arrived at our door, more than a little winded, I shook hands with the original wimp. Fishy grip, suit that seemed several sizes too large, eyes that wouldn't meet yours, pasty complexion—this man had come to doctor my sick son?

But a transformation occurred when he instructed us to put the baby on top of the bathinette. In no more than a few minutes, through a series of decisive actions of physically feeling and listening and observing that baby, he diagnosed the problem to be a form of pneumonia, wrote out a prescription—and became the wimp again. I still marvel when I recall the beauty and grace exhibited by that doctor, functioning in his strengths to bring healing to our son.

As I write this ancient memory, I am reminded of another episode. My wife was hospitalized for several weeks. During the daytime she was usually attended by a floor nurse who never seemed to know how to locate the source of blood in the human body, much less withdraw the needed amounts without causing undue bruises and pain. Besides leaving her patients in a mess, she was actually seen walking into a wall while doing late-night rounds!

Imagine my wife's reaction when she came out of the six-hour operation and was wheeled into intensive care. Who appeared to nurse her back to the land of the living? Yes, it was! But before my wife had the time or strength to panic, the nurse put a lit flashlight in her hands to connect her to the living world and proceeded to comfort her, ease her pain, distract her from the terror that was assaulting her. Here was the quintessential intensive care nurse—the same person who was virtually useless when doing routine, mundane duties! It was a question of motivation and job match.

I think you begin to see the pattern in these stories. It took several more years of experience with myself and other people before this pattern really took shape for me. I studied law, and as a young lawyer joined the University of Chicago's Argonne National Laboratory. But instead of pointing out in lawyerlike fashion the potential difficulties in a position or proposed language, I found myself consistently drawn to finding a way of resolving the problems that were brought to me or that I encountered. On reflection, I realized that I had shaped the job around "what came naturally to me," that which I was instinctively motivated to do, that which drew on my natural abilities. Such

> We instinctively shape a job around "what comes naturally to us"—around that which draws on our natural abilities.

behavior by a lawyer was greeted most positively by those I served, and within two years I was asked to leave lawyering and take over the personnel department.

As the newly promoted head of personnel, I remember my shock when the head of our physics division, Lou Turner, asked a newly hired Ph.D.

what he would like to do now that he had settled on Argonne Laboratory as his home. I was bothered by the apparent permissiveness and lack of direction, but I soon came to realize the wisdom behind it. Lou's approach tapped into the young scientist's natural, preexisting motivation to pursue discoveries that were of personal significance to him.

It was a lesson I learned well. Bob Starrett, the man in charge of recruiting technicians at Argonne, had been on the verge of being fired by my predecessor because, as I recall, he didn't follow the rules and procedures. Though not a college graduate, Bob was extremely well-read, managerial, analytical, an excellent conversationalist, and he truly liked the "skunk-works" atmosphere and mind-set—even the difficult personalities encountered in the world of research.

I was realizing more and more that the conventional way of evaluating people—looking at where they were educated, for how long, and what related experienced they had—was flawed. I had already begun to look at each person as an individual who had something unique to give, something that was expressed in his or her thinking and speaking and actions. So, rather than firing Bob, I promoted him to run all recruiting for professionals in every field of science and engineering represented at Argonne. He turned out to be spectacular in supporting R&D, a function deemed by many knowledgeable recruiters to be the most difficult to staff. One year, as I recall, his highly personalized but efficient process resulted in the hiring of around one hundred Ph.D.'s and several hundred people with bachelor's and master's degrees!

Of course, there were failures. People who required ongoing supportive supervision didn't do too well under my management. As a manager I could open doors for people who were able to make the most of the opportunity. I was not able, and have not been able in the forty-plus years since, to provide continuing management, even when I was responsible for managing several hundred persons. I found that I am good at leading but not at managing. Ongoing supervision is not one of the things that come naturally to me.

THE FIRST "ILLUMINATION"

These experiences and many others like them lodged in my memory. But it wasn't until 1958 that they all surfaced one beautiful morning. I had invited Bernie Haldane, a pioneer in job hunting, to speak at a seminar on self-development sponsored by the American Management Association about *building résumés on the basis of successes one has experienced.*

What he said about focusing on positive past experiences brought together a number of latent observations I had made over the years about the way people are put together. All of a sudden I heard something that I *knew* was the truth. I saw a new paradigm, a better, more elegant and useful way to read a person than what is found in college textbooks or in conventional academic wisdom about the psychology of human beings.

Most psychological theories perceive people as evolved animals without a unique makeup or willpower. Psychology looks for general principles that explain how people function. The study of individuals as such is seen as of little value, because it cannot yield general, governing principles. Apparently, no one figured out that if each person's behavior is uniquely motivated, you can't find any general principles that can predict future individual behavior or explain *why* an individual behaves in a certain way.

> **The new paradigm focuses on the *uniqueness* of individuals—not on general principles or traits.**

The paradigm I suddenly saw come together focused on the uniqueness of individuals—not on general principles or traits. It involved studying individuals to determine *what uniquely motivates each one*, what their personal "motivated behavior" is, what makes them who they are in all their individuality and giftedness. I realized that if this paradigm were true, the implications were enormous. It would open up new ways to help people understand what makes them tick and how they can become free to live out of their true strengths and their true motivations.

In the four decades since, I have systematically studied (first alone, and since the '70s with my colleagues at People Management) what is going on in folks that drives them toward certain pursuits, things that allow them to function in "full flight" with passion and commitment, pouring their hearts and minds into something that to them seems natural and that gives them great satisfaction. We estimate that we have studied more than fifty thousand people. Our staff has spent as much as forty hours with a single individual in the process, which has become increasingly detailed and documented.

A person's pattern of giftedness emerges in early childhood and *remains fundamentally the same throughout life* in its essential content, structure, and dynamics.

Central to all of these efforts is a phenomenon that many others have recognized as well: The past is the best predictor of the future.

As we investigated this phenomenon (to my knowledge more extensively and in more detail than anyone else), we saw emerging what has turned out to be essentially a law of human behavior:

Every time people do something they experience as satisfying and as done well, they are in fact repeating part or all of a recurring pattern of specific competencies and motivations.

After forty years we have never encountered a person whose behavior fell outside this law. And this consistency has been true regardless of culture, environment, gender, race, or national origin.

Here are some of the characteristics we have found in this pattern of specific competencies and motivations. (Incidentally, the key terms I use—*giftedness*, *pattern of giftedness*, *design*, *motivational pattern*, and *Motivated Abilities Pattern* or *MAP*—are slightly different ways of describing the same thing. For all practical purposes we use these terms interchangeably.)

- Giftedness is universal. *Every* human being appears to be endowed with a unique design or Motivated Abilities Pattern (MAP).
- One's pattern of giftedness functions *regardless* of whether an individual is aware of it.
- A person's pattern of giftedness emerges in early childhood and *remains fundamentally the same throughout life* in its essential content, structure, and dynamics. It is *not* the result of a developmental process.
- The pattern of giftedness captures the *essence of the person*, how any job or role will be attempted, and effectively how the person "sees" reality.
- *Learning* and other mental activities are effectively determined by one's pattern of giftedness. Not only *what* a person is motivated to learn, but *how* (whether alone or with others, with or without a teacher) and *why* are determined by this pattern.

We have found many more characteristics of the pattern of giftedness or MAP over the years. In part 1 I'll explain in some detail (with real-life examples) not only what giftedness is and what a MAP looks like, but also how you can begin to find your own giftedness. (In appendix D you'll find a set of simple forms that will help with the basic process.)

THE SECOND "ILLUMINATION"

It happened late in the winter of 1958–59. As is my wont (that is, my MAP), I had been driving hard, working late, and partying a bit much for ten years. I had suffered under a lousy job fit for a year, where I developed an ulcer, was in a new job where I was taking some cutting-edge risks in staffing and organizational structures, experienced a full load of stress from two moves in three years, all with four kiddies and a beautiful wife who wanted to be and was gifted as an actress. Not much different from the scenario of other ordinary people's lives. Nor was the fact that I began to develop psychosomatic problems like dizziness in a crowd, anxiety attacks, chest pains—classic symptoms of stress. Irritating at first, I was able to shake them off and plunge ahead. However, they became more severe and, to my active imagination, life threatening. I was near a breaking point.

One evening, I was driving slowly on the back road between Wayland and Harvard, Massachusetts, where I lived, when I was overcome by my fears and cried out to God to help me. I've often wanted to be able to describe what happened to me in those few minutes, but it is beyond my power and language to do so. All I can say is that I experienced violent wave after wave of a love so passionate it took my breath away and left me a sobbing heap at the side of the road.

Even now, forty years later, I fight back tears at the memory of the time God touched me and removed all symptoms threatening my life. The love of God I experienced is beyond comprehension and description. But you will understand when I say that in these forty years since, I have never, ever questioned the reality of a very personal God or his love for us.

Within days of "recovering" from this encounter, my thoughts were that I should move toward action (again, an expression of my MAP, of course). Now that I knew God is real and I had been graciously deposited into the kingdom of God, my question—or rather, my statement—was, "Let's go!"

In the next weeks and months—years in fact—I asked all the authorities I knew about what you did with your life after you came to faith. No one had any answer, beyond seminary, "full-time Christian service," or evangelizing the lost. No one seemed to know what the after-conversion life looked like. No one.

Attempts by other groups of believers to bridge the gulf between the secular and the sacred turned out to be an attempt to return to first-century Christianity, communal living in the inner city, or a collective attempt to live by Christian principles, whatever they were understood to be. Our bunch went for retreats and ultimately established a day school. But none of these thrusts made any difference when it came to what people should do, working day-to-day in the "world."

> After my conversion I asked all the authorities I knew what you did with your life after you came to faith. No one seemed to know what the after-conversion life looked like.

I attended "Faith-at-Work" conferences (big at the time), gave my testimony, and heard others tell of how they came into the kingdom of God. (Still no help on what came after that.) Over the months and years I did all the things you were supposed to after a "born-again" experience: lots of Bible study, solid teaching, fellowship groups, sharing personal difficulties, darkness, and victories. I read scores of books about one or another aspect of the faith walk. I experienced accurate personal prophecy. I witnessed discernment and foreknowledge of future events. I viewed exorcisms taking place, apparent miracles being performed, glossolalia being spoken and interpreted, and I experienced the intimate actions of God in the deep details of my life that only I could recognize. In and through it all, I fell deeply in love with Jesus Christ.

But the question remained and haunted my seeking after a faith that would invade and conquer all my life: What did such a life look like? I remember giving a keynote address at a conference in Hartford nine years after my conversion experience, titled "Now What?" (I didn't provide the answer, only the question.)

However, because God is always faithful, I began to find some answers. I ran into the tiny book by Brother Lawrence called *Practicing the Presence of God*. He describes his life with God in the kitchen where his faith was exercised in the process of preparing meals and cleaning up (as I recall). Back in my own church after a long absence, I sat under the teaching of Ralph Mattson, who spoke of God as the author of joy and of life-giving pleasure. Since I was coming from a series of experiences that explored the deeper life in Christ and focused on the importance of suffering and travailing in our spiritual growth, his insight into the nature of God fell like a spate of summer showers on a dry and thirsty land.

It was not long after those teachings that Ralph and I slowly figured out that the answer was in front of my nose. It lay in what I had been doing for over ten years—exploring the joy people experience when their giftedness is engaged. Over time (I'm a slow learner!) we realized what lies at the heart of a seven-days-a-week faith: *It is using one's endowed giftedness to serve the world with excellence and, through that service, to love and honor God!* The calling that fully engages what God has given you is a holy task!

> **The heart of a seven-days-a-week faith lies in using one's endowed giftedness to serve the world with excellence and, through that service, to love and honor God!**

In part 2 I'll talk about the answers to my question: How can I find and follow God's will and plan for my life? My meager attempt to describe a life rooted in Jesus Christ is based on my experience with God and seeks to open up practical Christian living to fellow believers. It is not an attempt to evangelize. Besides, I'm not very good at winning souls.[1]

THE TRANSFORMING POWER OF HUMAN DESIGN

But if I am right, and every person has been given the means of living a rewarding, productive, richly satisfying life, what is wrong with the people around us?

- Why are seven out of ten teachers, managers, ministers, sales representatives—in short, seven out of ten people—neither motivated nor competent to perform the basics of their jobs?
- Why can't between fifty and eighty percent of all workers use their talents on their job?
- Why don't people pursue the life and career for which they are eminently suited?
- Why is school such a drag and so ineffective for most students?

---

1. Because my experience and faith revolve around the triune, Christian God, I ask the forbearance of readers of other faiths. Each of us has to make our own deal with whatever and whoever has captured our trust about this life and what awaits us beyond. I cannot judge your judgment. I only know in whom I believe.

- Why don't people concentrate on what they do best?
- Why do so many millions of Americans spend their working lives in what bores them, stresses them, or fills them with self-hatred?

The key problem is the Myth of "Becoming"—the mistaken notion that we can become anything we want to be. (I talk about it at some length in chapter 6, at the end of part 1.) It is a myth

The key problem is the Myth of "Becoming"—the mistaken notion that we can become anything we want to be.

that our culture simply assumes to be true, and it underlies most of our business, educational, and (dare I say it) religious institutions—even our evangelical churches.

What can we do about it?

In part 3 I suggest substantial changes on the *institutional level*—in our institutions of work, education, and religion—if we are to rebuild a society that enables life, liberty, and the pursuit of happiness for all of its people.

The recommendations in part 3 would, if followed, lead to

- businesses that employ people in accordance with their motivated strengths, and a system of capitalism that recognizes and rewards as equal partners the giftedness of employees as a renewable and critical source of wealth generation.
- education that equips students to find and prosper in a calling suitable to their endowments.
- religion that encourages believers to serve the world through their endowments. (To be honest, I am trying to pry religious experience out of the church's grasp and into the fresh air of faith lived out in real life. I'm trying to encourage [goad, cajole, shame] our churches to lift their sights and to minister to their flock for a life in the world God gave his Son to save—and redeem through his working saints.)

As you read through this book, look at the extent to which my statements and observations are supported by your own experience—you may be surprised! Feel free to disagree, argue with me, write to me, or interact with this material in any way that comes naturally—and watch your MAP in action!

Part One

Giftedness and Human Design

Giftedness is the only means I know of for the ordinary person to make sense out of life. Each one is given a purpose and the drive and competencies to achieve that purpose. Meaning is thereby built into the adventure of living for everyone.

Chapter One

Giftedness: Seeds of Destiny

Come with me, quietly, to a kindergarten classroom. Slip in unnoticed during one of the many eruptions of noisy activity, when the children are lost in the moment, immersed with total abandon in what they are doing.

If we observe carefully, we will see each child reveal something unique and special about himself, some essential element of her person.

Here, for example, we find a little girl absorbed in finger painting. Look at her eyes, the way they light up at the vivid colors she selects. Look at her hands, how they squeeze and glide and press and test the tempera that oozes between them. She delights in these materials. She extends for as long as possible the time allotted to work with them.

Over there are two boys building a tower with blocks. Notice how one piles them up in random, rapid order, showing little care for the finished product. It is his partner who takes pains to adjust and straighten the assembly and who makes suggestions for what to do next. Completely captivated by each other's company, these playmates require no supervision.

Out on the playground we find the class tease. He runs here and there among the groups of children, stealing the boys' ball, chasing girls around the jungle gym, kicking sand in the sandbox, nattering like a blue jay. His whole game seems to be to provoke a response—*any* kind of response. More often than not, he is shooed away with the refrain, "Leave us alone!" But usually it sounds like an invitation more than a protest. As a result, he is certain to be back.

Finally, off to the side we see a child sitting by herself. Is she sad, or bored, or just shy? We cannot tell by looking. The only thing we can see is that she is detached, apparently by choice. The activities of the others seem to hold little interest for her. She seems content in a world of her own.

THE CHILD IS FATHER OF THE MAN

Are these scenes merely snapshots of random play? By no means! The poets tell us that "the child is father of the man."[1] And so it is. Whenever we observe a child freely and spontaneously involved in an activity, we are peeking into the future—if the child grows up and lives true to his or her giftedness. In such a case, we are not guessing at the future—we are witnessing it. All of which is true of your kids, if you will but watch and wonder.

The same delight and intensity that the little girl showed for finger paints will reappear later, when as a full-grown woman she works as a buyer of textiles for a clothing manufacturer. Her eyes will still light up over colors and patterns. Her hands will still seek the feel of the material against her skin. Meanwhile, at home, her children will sense her tingle of joy whenever she takes their hands in hers to shape a lump of clay or knead a ball of dough.

> The poets tell us that "the child is father of the man." And so it is.

Likewise, the two boys building with blocks will, as men, exhibit their respective patterns. The one will still be clamoring for results, a drive that suits him well as a salesman bent on meeting or exceeding performance goals. The other will always be a refiner, straightening things up, maximizing their effectiveness—the perfect match for his job as a manager in a retail store. And whether at work or in their personal lives, both men will still be pairing themselves with others who supply strengths they do not possess.

Meanwhile, does it surprise anybody that the teaser turns out to be a superb talk-show host? His native talents at turning heads and drawing attention to himself and his opinions will gain him a hearing in ways that are hard to resist. Even in private he will express these gifts through his hobby of playing the piano and "MC-ing" noisy games, to the delight of family and friends.

---

1. William Wordsworth, based on Milton's lines from *Paradise Regained* (I.220),

    The childhood shows the man,
    As morning shows the day.

And what of the girl with a preference for solitude? She will continue to nurture her inner life, storing up observation and reflection. No wonder that, as the acquisitions editor for a major publication, she will enrich everyone around her with perceptive insight into the potential of an unknown author-to-be.

TURNING BACK THE CLOCK

Now, what about you? Suppose we could turn back the clock to your childhood. What would we have seen you doing?

What do you remember you did when you could do what you wanted to do? Play with friends? Go fishing? Build something? Sing a song? Train your dog? Draw a picture? Write a poem? Imitate a comic? Play house? Play cowboys and Indians? Take a hike? Win at games? Throw a ball against the steps? Make a new friend? Read? Imagine a story? Talk to the birds? Watch a plant grow?

I remember working with Marshall, who recalled how, as a very young child, he accompanied his mother to gather blackberries and spent his time inspecting the *underside* of leaves on the blackberry bushes. He is now a research scientist who made an important contribution to solving the problem of material used on the surface of spacecrafts "burning up" when reentering the earth's atmosphere.

Most people's memory of childhood experiences does not go back farther than when they were five to eight years of age, but some, like Marshall, remember events from when they were two to three years old.

I recall two separate but similar examples of these very early recollections. Both people started their story with how they were looking out at their world from inside a playpen. One remembered lifting up the floor of the playpen—which was next to a fence, bordering a road—and digging a tunnel under the fence so he could get on the road and get on with his life. He was retrieved a half mile down the road in his diapers! Jack is now a nationally known trial lawyer, frequently employed as a "hired gun" by other law firms facing difficult opponents.

The other person remembered being in his playpen on the locked porch of a summer cottage that overlooked a small boat on a small pond that was bordered on the far side by a grove of trees. He remembered spending several days "figuring out" his escape and, at some point, got out of his playpen, unlocked the porch, got down to the boat, and somehow propelled it across the pond and into the woods, which apparently was his objective. Dr. Litzke ended up being a metallurgist, consulted by scientists from many lands about intractable welding problems.

In the early days, upon hearing such childhood achievements, my reaction, probably like yours, tended to be rather dismissive—"charming, but probably a random and irrelevant bit of personal history." But we learned rather quickly that *the behaviors manifested in childhood were literally precursors of what was to come.*

We've looked at these seeds of destiny in childhood achievements hundreds upon hundreds of times. Take Merwin, the president of a health services firm, known for his ability to turn around faltering businesses or to extract the potential from promising businesses. At the age of six, he "borrowed" his little sister's red wagon and converted it into a fire engine for himself and his friends to play with, at some cost to his back end. He saw what was but also had the imagination to see what might be and the drive to implement it.

> **The behaviors manifested in childhood are literally precursors of what is to come.**

Or take Stan, the kid raised in Brooklyn, whose early achievements were clever, but illegal, ways of beating the subway turnstiles and retail toy stores out of paying for goods and services received. Stan became a professor. But he is still "beating the system," though now by going after certain established systems of interpretation of the Scriptures as wrong or badly flawed.

Wonder at the minority child, Vanessa, who remembers giving shows to family and friends in spite of extreme poverty and hardship. She was the only one of her siblings to escape a life of drugs and crime, and made it through to star on Broadway. (Don't try to tell us that the kids just copy what they see and hear at home or on TV. If so, why are brothers and sisters so different?)

Or Juanita, whose earliest recollection was of a business she concocted in her head, with named employees who did named jobs, with whom she held regular communications, including disciplinary actions. She is now an entrepreneur who runs a successful catering business.

Finally, a childhood memory *about* someone, written by a cousin:

> [He] was a large school boy when I was still in the nursery. He had a disconcerting way of looking at me critically and saying nothing. He filled me with awe. His playroom contained from one end

to the other a plank table on trestles, upon which were thousands of lead soldiers arranged for battle. He organized wars. The lead battalions were maneuvered into action, peas and pebbles committed great casualties, forts were stormed, cavalry charged, bridges were destroyed—real water tanks engulfed the advancing foe. Altogether it was a most impressive show, and played with an interest that was no ordinary child game.

One summer the [family] rented a small house in the country for the holidays called Banstead. [He] and Jack, his brother, built a log house with the help of the gardener's children and dug a ditch around it which they contrived to fill with water, and made a drawbridge that really could pull up and down. Here again war was proceeded. The fort was stormed. I was hurriedly removed from the scene of the action as mud and stones began to fly with effect.[2]

Here the child was clearly the father of the man. This boy ended up changing history. He became arguably the greatest leader of Great Britain in this century, possibly of any century. A strong case could be made that were it not for Winston Churchill, England would have fallen to Nazi Germany in World War II, Europe would have been lost, and the map of the world would look far different today.

This reminiscence is striking. It tells us something of what the boy Winston would do when *he* could make the choice, freely and spontaneously. The account approaches the exercise with which I began this chapter, of visiting a class to watch children engaged in play. In observing her cousin's battles—which to him were "no ordinary child game"— she was peering, as it were, into his future, glimpsing the fire within him that would burn brightly fifty years later.

THE SIREN SONG OF SUCCESS

However, there is a danger in pointing to prominent figures who are so looming and inspiring that it is easy to be seduced by their greatness, so that we start to wonder: "How could I become like that?" Or, "How can I be like Michael?"[3] There are plenty of books that promise to give you the answer.

---

2. Clare Sheridan, *Nuda Veritas*, as cited in Virginia Cowles, *Winston Churchill: The Era and the Man* (New York: Grossett & Dunlap, 1953), 32.

3. Jordan, Jackson, or Angelo (a.k.a. Michelangelo), depending on your MAP.

Every season seems to bring a new crop of "success titles" purporting to show the remarkable secrets of *Peak Performers*, or how to get your life on track by adopting the *Seven Habits of Highly Successful People*, or how to practice *The Psychology of Winning*, or how to become a super-competitor by learning to *Swim with the Sharks*, or how to get what you want by acquiring *Unlimited Power*.[4]

> The idea that we can choose to become what the world values is as misguided as the alchemist's ancient promise to transmute lead into gold.

Books and related audio/videotapes like these have limited value and major drawbacks. They imply that success means greatness, and that it comes to those rare individuals who are shrewd enough to acquire a handful of attributes that confer the Midas touch. "You, too, can be a Churchill, an Edison, a Bill Gates, a Marc Andressen (the twenty-four-year-old cofounder of Netscape) if only you buy this book and take its message to heart." It's a siren song that many find irresistible.

But resist it we must! For *the idea that we can choose to become what the world values is as misguided as the alchemist's ancient promise to transmute lead into gold*. If we really want the fullness, the richness, and the joy of life, if we want genuine significance and true success, if we want to find our meaning and purpose, then we should not look at others and try to copy what has been given to them. Rather, we need to consider: *What has been given to me? What endowments do I possess?*[5]

"DOING YOUR THING"

One standard approach is to take a series of psychological tests. You fill out questionnaires of several dozen or several hundred items, it is scored, and you now have a report that supposedly summarizes your personal-

---

4. I do not mean to imply that these books (or books like them) are wrong (though some are). But the belief that we can become a visionary leader, or a financial success, or a supersalesman, or anything else we want simply by applying the "right" principles is flat-out wrong. We cannot, and it is foolish to believe otherwise, as I will show in chapter 6.

5. Oddly, in a society where "becoming" is the mantra of self-improvement, people rarely stop to identify their natural strengths. In the '70s, I estimated that less than 1 percent of the people I and my colleagues worked with had ever made a serious study of what they already had to offer.

ity. In all fairness, you have probably learned something about yourself, but are you any closer to knowing how you operate in the real world?

The acid test of the value of any inventory or test is not whether you learned something about yourself. All of the popular assessment tools can do that. The real test is whether or not it describes you as a unique being and accurately captures how you behave—how you learn—how you reason—how you decide—how you act—what motivates you. Can you rely on the test results to make a decision about your life?

> **For a test to be of value, it must describe you as a unique being and accurately capture how you behave— how you learn—how you reason—how you decide—how you act— *and what motivates you*.**

Almost all of these tests depend on statistical norms to develop your "profile." They yield a picture of how you compare with the rest of the population. Say that on a scale of dominance versus passivity you score in the seventy-eighth percentile. Is that enlightening? Not exactly. It suggests that in a given situation, the odds are better than even that you might be inclined to take charge. But then you can recall other situations where you had no interest in being in charge. So you've not really gained very much.

Personality tests and interest inventories do not, contrary to popular belief, yield answers to questions about individual makeup and behavior. At best they provide comparative data about more or less pronounced traits, sometimes gathered into types. But traits and types have little meaning in and of themselves. Unless tied into motivation and competence, they are essentially meaningless in predicting individual behavior and makeup.[6]

So if personality tests and inventories can't help us understand who we are, then what can? How can we know ourselves? *The surest way I have found to unlock the essence of a person is to look at what he likes to do and do well.*

As mentioned in the introduction, my colleagues and I at People Management have for nearly forty years been studying individuals in the full flight of their activities, engaged heart and soul in memorable achievements. We have been looking at what goes on when a person is in hot pursuit, completely absorbed, utterly turned on, "doing his or her

---

6. For a more detailed discussion of tests and their limitations, see appendix A.

thing." Consider our work a form of research around a phenomenon occurring in the life of every person. Simply stated, every time a person does something that he experiences as enjoyable or satisfying and done well, he reveals a certain pattern of behavior. That design is unique to that person; no one else has one exactly like it. It is like a fingerprint.

> The surest way to unlock the essence of a person is to look at what he or she likes to do and does well.

As our insight into this phenomenon deepened, we began to realize two astounding things. First, a person's distinctive way of functioning—what we came to call his *motivated behavior*—gave us access to the very essence of the person. To understand his design was to understand his unique approach to life. In effect, we were finding an answer to the riddle, "Who is this person?"

Hand-in-glove with this idea came a growing awareness that the rich mix of talent and passion was not the result of anything a person had done or acquired or "become," but appeared to be completely inherent in that individual, a natural endowment that the person "just had." This suggested a name for the phenomenon we were observing: *giftedness*.

WHAT GIFTEDNESS IS

Later we'll look at support for the belief that each one of us has unique giftedness. For now, let's be clear on what this term means. Giftedness is the way we are by nature. It's what makes us *us*. It's the way we were designed to function, and therefore the way we actually do function best and with the greatest delight. It includes what we do well and are motivated to accomplish.

Perhaps you've heard the expression that a particular job fits someone "to a tee." The idea is that a perfect match exists between person and task. That's a good illustration of giftedness. Giftedness fits us for certain tasks. In fact, when we function according to our giftedness, the work almost doesn't seem like work; it's more like fun. Incredible reservoirs of energy are released as we "pour ourselves into the task," as they say, and we "put our heart and soul into it."

Perhaps you are already thinking of synonyms and concepts related to giftedness. By our definition, giftedness is bound up with *human design*: who you are as a person is largely expressed through your giftedness. Another related term is *bent*, your natural strength or tendency or inclination, especially in vocational matters. The French have a word, *métier*, that conveys much the same thought. It is the work for which you are especially suited, what we might call your specialty. In slang terms, we speak of someone's *thing*, as in "doing your thing"—the thing that you particularly and authentically want to do, perhaps even *must* do.

> When we function according to our giftedness, the work almost doesn't seem like work—it's more like fun: incredible reservoirs of energy are released.

All of these ideas point to unique self-expression and a sense of destiny, or at least destination. As humans, we have a hunch that our lives have some purpose to them, some end we are seeking to fulfill. That ultimate aim is integrally tied up with who we are. Frustrate us in our pursuit of that mission, and we feel a tremendous sense of injury.

WHAT GIFTEDNESS IS NOT

It is also important, however, to understand what giftedness is *not*. First, *I am not using the term in an exclusive way* in the sense that some schools now designate certain bright students as "gifted and talented." It is hard to pin down exactly what "gifted and talented" means, particularly when the criteria for measuring these qualities vary from school to school. But the basic idea seems to be that some students have abilities and aptitudes that go beyond what the normal course of instruction can satisfy. Therefore, they are placed in an enriched setting where their "gifts and talents" will be nurtured.

Without commenting here on the wisdom of that approach, let me state clearly that *giftedness* is not limited to school smarts, genius-level intelligence, or precocious musical talent. If a child is "gifted" in the eyes of the schools, very well; that tells us more about the limited understanding and reach of the schools than it does about the child.

Second, *giftedness is not a personality type or trait*. Certain assessment models, such as the Myers-Briggs Type Indicator, classify people into categories of shared traits, or "types." But "traits" say nothing about the essential nature of an individual, even when bundled together into "types," and cannot accurately identify the gifted elements of any one person's makeup, much less the outcome that drives their behavior (i.e., motivation).

Finally, *giftedness is not some quality that can be acquired*. You either have whatever "it" is, or you don't. Every person has a particular mix or design of giftedness.

Don't make the mistake of assuming some people just haven't had the opportunity to so express their giftedness. Untrue. Because it is like breathing, *every* person has used their giftedness throughout their years, be those years long or short.

To illustrate that the expression of a person's giftedness has little or nothing to do with opportunity or supportive parents, let me give you a couple of examples from our files.

> **Because it is like breathing, *every* person has used their giftedness *throughout* their years, be they many or few.**

Here was Sligh, an only child being raised by working-class parents on a marginal farm, who exhibited entrepreneurial and management abilities in developing an egg business, raising and selling heifers—making enough money to support himself into and through college.

Or Melinda, a nine-year-old child of a bottom-line yuppie CEO, who spent hours counseling her friends about problems with their parents or their friends.

Nothing in these kids' environments or in the type of support their parents were able to give could have predicted either their giftedness or the particular way in which that giftedness found expression.

FOLLOWING YOUR DESIGN

What happens when a person possessing certain giftedness approaches each day? A typical scenario would be that when one wakes up in the morning, one starts thinking about some person or problem or situation of motivational interest.

For example, say that you are motivated to deal with money issues. If so, don't be surprised if your first thoughts have to do with the financial implications of recent tax legislation or rumored interest rate moves by the Federal Reserve. Or say technical issues are of consequence to you. In that case, your mind will likely be filled with thoughts about a nagging valve at a customer's factory, or maybe some unexpected results in a research project.

Of course, you may not be a morning person. Just finding a cup of coffee may be a major accomplishment at that hour! But once you are awake and facing the day, your giftedness really comes alive. As you tackle the range of activities that comprise your "occupation," you find yourself concentrating on the tasks that hold the greatest motivational value to you.

For example, if your bent is for tasks that are new to you, you may see what new tidbits showed up overnight in your e-mail. If you thrive on projects that you can complete in a few hours, you'll probably be mapping out your schedule from now until lunch. If you crave the especially difficult problem, you'll be sizing up the giants in front of you to determine which one to slay first. If your way is to respond to the clear requirements of others, you'll enjoy reading the company newsletter until your supervisor rushes in with the day's assignments. The point is, *your agenda will be driven by your design.*

> **Your personal agenda is being driven by your design.**

Furthermore, not only will you focus on what *you* value most, you'll *avoid* things that hold little motivational value for you, or the things you don't do well. For instance, if you lack an interest in details, it's unlikely you'll reread a letter or check your arithmetic. If what the customer says has little meaning for you, you won't bother calling or checking before going ahead with your own understanding of what is needed.

"Wait a minute, Art!" I can imagine someone saying. "It sounds like you're sanctioning sloppy work by ignoring details, or encouraging people to ignore their customers!" If you are thinking that, I encourage you to reread the previous paragraph—and take it seriously. People will be who they are—who they were made to be. You cannot fundamentally change them. You should not even try. Instead, you should place them in the areas where their strengths will be best employed and where their lack of competence or motivation has no significant bearing on the outcome.

If a position demands a high attention to detail, then put a detail person in the position; if you need someone to service the customers, then assign someone motivated to do that. But by all means, don't try to force someone who is gifted in other ways to function outside his pattern. To do so is to set things up for failure and frustration.

Can you see that giftedness is all-encompassing? *There is no escape from being who we are.* And why should we ever want to? There is no point

There is no escape from being who we are. And why should we ever want to?

in seeking fulfillment and sustained excellence outside of that which engages our essential motivational makeup. Our lives would be richer, our work more productive, our selves more authentic if we deliberately built every thought and work on the foundation of our inherent giftedness. So how do we discover the real you? How do we find out all that wonderfully rich information about how you have been designed? Stay tuned.

Chapter Two

Discovering Your Giftedness

Have you ever thought of your own life as a story in which you are the main character? William Kirk Kilpatrick, professor of educational psychology at Boston College, says that these wishful instincts do not mislead us, because "a life *is* a story. That is the proper way to look at it. The best way to interpret and explain a life is in a narrative way. No other way will do."[1]

That is certainly what I have found. Virtually every time I have asked someone, "Tell me about some of the things that you have done in life that you enjoyed doing and believe you did well," a story begins to unfold. It may begin with just an incident, or just the snatch of a distant memory. But if I probe for more detail, invariably I get a remarkable tale that reveals profound truths about the person—about the essence of who he is and how he functions.

THE STORY OF BILLY JOE

For example, a man whom I came to know well and whom I'll call Billy Joe, recalled a summer job that he had had as a teenager. "I remember how much I enjoyed working at a summer fruit market and gas station," he told me. "You know, meeting and dealing with people."

I asked Billy Joe to tell me more about working at the fruit market. He thought for a moment, nodding. Then he said, "There was a guy who ran a fruit market at a resort north of our town. There were maybe

---

1. William Kirk Kilpatrick, "Why Secular Psychology Is Not Enough," Hillsdale College *Imprimis*, vol. 15, no. 4 (April 1986).

two hundred cottages up there, plus a motel. Anyway, we'd stock this thing with fresh fruit and vegetables, chicken, eggs, that sort of thing."

It was clear from his expression that he was enjoying the memory of this experience. I asked him to tell me how he went about his work.

"It was a lot of fun, I'll say that," he remarked, lighting up with a smile. "There were a lot of people around—a *lot* of people! So many, they'd have to take a number. You see, I fixed up these numbers on little cards. Then when their number came up, I'd wait on them."

"What do you mean, you'd 'wait on them'?" I asked.

"Well, by adding up their purchases, you know, and taking their money. I'd do that all morning and through lunch. Then I'd go off in the afternoon and buy the stuff we needed for the next day. When I got back, I'd run the thing through the late afternoon, and then close up.

"That was a lot of fun," he remarked again, almost glowing with satisfaction. "I really enjoyed that."

"What was so satisfying to you?"

"Just the people coming up and greeting them. I mean, it gave me a feeling of importance. Plus, I got really good at adding figures." He laughed. "I remember one time I challenged this guy that I could add up the figures faster than he could punch them into the cash register!"

"You mentioned something about a gas station," I said. "Tell me about that."

"Yeah, the gas station," he replied, warming to this part of the story. "Well, you see, I always worked at gas stations. I had all kinds of odd hours doing that. I really enjoyed meeting with people. You know, people would ask you directions—like where is a good place to eat. I used to pride myself on that, that I could give good information." He was nodding in self-affirmation.

"I worked for several gas stations. I'd figure out what the boss wanted, and then I would do it. I remember this one real grumpy old owner told me, 'I like you! You do things the way I want.'" He was imitating the old man's voice.

"I guess he had gotten some good reports from customers. Plus, he had these oil cans stacked right on the edge of the shelf, so you could run your finger along them and just touch the can." He was using his hands to show me what this must have looked like. "That's the way he wanted it, so that's the way I did it."

"Anyway, I liked to meet people when they would come in. There was just something about that contact with people that I liked—going out there and seeing them. I thought it was just kind of exciting. I know I did, because I worked a lot of hours."

ACHIEVEMENTS DRIVEN BY PASSION

I daresay this fellow could have gone on for hours telling me about that summer job. You may be inclined to regard his conversation as just a trivial, albeit pleasant bit of reminiscing, the sort of innocuous chit-chat that a stranger might engage in to pass the time of day. But if you are thinking that, think again! For what this man said reveals volumes about his fundamental makeup, his giftedness—if we bother to pay attention.

> **Giftedness is more than a mere inventory of talents. It's the lifeblood of a person, the song that her heart longs to sing, the race that his legs long to run.**

Our first clue that something is up is the *passion* with which he retells these events. You have only his words to read; I had the benefit of listening to him in person. And I can assure you that he became quite lively in recounting these memories.

The reason why is that giftedness goes beyond a mere inventory of talents. It's the lifeblood of a person, the song that his heart longs to sing, the race that his legs long to run. It's the fire in his belly. It's his reason for being. So any time you tap into giftedness, you hit a nerve that runs right to the core of the individual.

I tapped into Billy Joe's giftedness by asking him to tell me about his summer job—an achievement that he enjoyed doing and did well—and then probing the details of how he went about doing that job and what he found so satisfying in it. I and my colleagues call this Achievement Interviewing®.

When taking an achievement history, it is quite common for the person being interviewed to become highly animated, maybe even transported back to the moment—feeling as he felt at the time, speaking as he spoke, moving as he moved. A man who rarely laughs can suddenly start chortling loudly over the recollection of a teacher's reaction to his mischievous boyhood scheme. A woman's voice can rise almost to a shout as she describes her response to a risky challenge. Tears can begin to fall as someone mentally and emotionally revisits the warm, redolent workshop where a father patiently explained a deft technique of woodworking.

There's an electricity associated with giftedness. Give a person the chance, and he'll jolt you—and maybe himself—with the power and passion of his pattern. That's what makes our work so thrilling . . . not people in the abstract, but with real, live, flesh-and-blood *persons*—persons in their full humanity.

Every one of them has a story—a complete story that connects all the significant achievements in their life. Billy Joe went on to tell me about quite a few of his achievements—activities such as delivering papers, helping his uncles on the farm, building model airplanes, working as a night watchman, working to put himself through school, developing curriculum as a teacher, organizing a system that puts retirees in a position to do volunteer work.

His list of achievement activities was not a random collection of everyday events. They might appear that way to others. But all the incidents were scenes from a unified story—a true story. They represented the seamless, lived experience of one human being. If we were writing Billy Joe's life into a novel, these episodes would form the plot, and his actions would reveal his persona as the main character. (In appendix B you'll find more of Billy Joe's story.)

WHAT MIGHT HAVE BEEN

Asking people about what they did well and enjoyed doing is like tapping into the mother lode of their soul. If you give them the time, it is not unusual for two or three hours of stories to come gushing out like water from a broken dam. Quite often, this is exactly what is happening, because *no one has ever asked them for their "story."* It's their secret story, in fact it's so secret, they don't even know it until they write and talk about it.

> In many people, gifts have been virtually unrecognized and vastly underutilized, for years or even a lifetime— to everyone's loss.

In other words, no one (including themselves) has ever tapped the wellspring of their giftedness. What an utter tragedy! Gifts that have been crafted into these individuals may have been sitting there for years, maybe for a lifetime—virtually unrecognized and vastly underutilized, to everyone's loss.

When I say "to everyone's loss," I am not just being dramatic. Do you realize what we are missing when we fail to engage even one person's giftedness? The question bears down on us: What else *could* have happened *if* more people had been awakened to their destiny? What discoveries could have been made? What victories could have been won? What inventions could have been produced? What art could have been created? What treaties could have been signed? What cures could have been found? What ideas could have been thought? What joys could have been shared?

These questions are not mere speculation, for history is a book with too many pages torn out. Characters who ought to have played a significant role are missing. And too many others are "out of character"—not at all what the Author intended.

No one can rewrite the past, but the present and the future are another matter. To a large extent, our destiny is written on our hearts. If we wish to take hold of that future, we must become literate in the structure, components, and language of giftedness.

THE ACHIEVEMENT STORY

When we asked for detailed, written descriptions of what people did and what they found satisfying, it usually took about six hours (sometimes longer) for them to recall and write down their recollections.

As the next step in Achievement Interviewing, we went back over their statements and asked them to tell us more about their accomplishments. We wanted to hear all of the *action* details and the *actual mechanics* of how they did what they did. Our goal was to exhaust the achiever's memory, to hear about every detail, no matter how "minor." We discovered that none of our interviewees had ever probed their memories with such precision. In fact, few had ever described their enjoyable achievement experiences *to anybody*, at least not in any detail.

As the years went by, these achievement interviews became more probing, more insistent, and more carefully documented. We went from using reams of yellow legal paper to taping the interviews, and even to videotaping some of them. In the end, everything of substance the interviewees said was transcribed. At one point, we were producing between twenty and forty typed pages of these recollections, editing out only extraneous material that we learned from experience merely added to the number of pages.

Our rules for interviewing were severe: no leading, no summarizing, no judging, no editorializing, no building relationships, no seeking of causation, no playing psychologist. *Just the facts of how the person did what was done.*

Whenever our interviewees spoke in abstractions or generalities, we asked for illustrations to specify exactly what they did—their *actions*.

For example, if someone said, "I just did it," we might ask, "When you say you 'did it,' what would I have seen you doing if I had been standing there?" Or if the person said, "I started working on it," we might ask, "Can you tell me the things you did when, as you say, you started 'working on it'?" Again, our aim was to probe objectively for the mechanics involved in people's actions, perceptions, thoughts, and words when they were engaged in a time of satisfying achievement.

Let me show you just one example of the amount and quality of facts generated when you probe into the detail of what a person loved doing, and did well. When I met Alex, he was pursuing a career in training and development and had recently left a clinical psychology practice working in a mental hospital with seriously disturbed adults. He had achieved some remarkable breakthroughs in communicating with several of the psychotic patients, but ultimately found this field of work unrewarding.

Here is the revealing account of one of his early achievements; before age ten, as I recall. (It is a "shorthand" summary of the interview.)

ALEX
Childhood

Raised, saddle broke, and trained a stallion Tennessee walking horse from its birth. It was the second colt that I raised; he was the finest that I've come in contact with—right from birth, you're in the stall and you're making a lot of hand contact with the animal—getting them very familiar with you so they're not afraid. This horse had tremendous high spirit and line. Spend a lot of time with a horse—touching it, walking it, talking to it.

As the horse begins to strengthen physically, sometimes you have to help it stand up initially—help it wobble around. As horse begins to grow, then you move into currying it and cleaning it. Little by little you throw a blanket on its back—walk it with a blanket—talk to it while it has the blanket on its back—take it away from the mother—mother is nearby but you tether her nearby and walk the colt away—as a few weeks go by you may throw on very light saddle—without cinching it—just put weight on its back or I would take a bag of grain, ten to twenty pounds—keep increasing it over time—let him feel the weight of that on his back—then move to a saddle—use lighter saddle first—move to heavier saddle—move to cinching saddle so they feel that tension—doing this without any bit in their mouth—just walking them with a halter—then start working with a very soft rope bit in their mouth—then move to leather one—then move to regular steel bit so they get the feel of working that in their mouth—get it under their tongue. Ultimately, take small child—younger than I—put them in the saddle so they feel that weight in the saddle—then put myself in the saddle after a period of time—horse is going to buck and kick initially—they're not very comfortable with that—they want to get it off—I've been thrown more than a few times—get back on and do it again.

I lived in a semi-rural area and you'd watch the other people and other kids who were raising horses. Pick it up by osmosis—had grandfather who knew something about horses—he gave me some pointers—kind of picked up the information—very rewarding—nobody ever rode that horse but me until I sold it—that horse and I were like one—I'd get in the saddle and that horse was so attuned to my actions—take that horse out and you'd be walking—that horse would be so ready to respond ... horse was ready to gallop and I wasn't giving it any signals that I was aware of until I paid attention to what I was doing—I was clearing my throat—to the horse that's "Let's go"—we were really a unit so I had to be careful—then you did give the signal and that horse took off like the wind—was really just a tremendous animal.

Did you see the parallels with the movie *The Horse Whisperer*? Did you notice how gentle, yet firm and entreating the child was; how wise; how he built the relationship; how he respected the object of his caring; how he somehow saw into the mind and heart of the horse and knew what to do, and what would likely happen? Notice how he observed detail; how he built a regimen; what a natural trainer he was; how incremental he was in dealing with fear. Amazing grace bestowed on a child.

YOUR STORY

All of this leads to the question: *What is your story?* What activities have you done in life that you enjoyed doing and believe you did well?

I invite you to at least taste the process right now by setting aside this book for a while and taking out a legal pad or sitting in front of your computer. Jot down as many incidents as you can recall that satisfy the two criteria: things you enjoyed doing, and things you did well.

Don't be shy about putting items on the list. The more you write down, the more memories you'll likely have involving incidents of enjoyable activity. And don't minimize a memory's significance. If the achievement was important *to you*, add it to the list.

> No matter how impoverished, sterile, dysfunctional, repressive, or even abusive the conditions, people can remember at least a handful of satisfying achievement experiences, despite the sadness of their early lives.

Perhaps it was a bloodied assault on the neighborhood bully; beating the boys in a foot race (and you were a girl); locating a rare stamp; entering a pig in the county fair and feeling the pride of winning second place.

Let your mind hark back to the days before your life became so governed by societal expectations: secret memories of books read, glens explored, courage displayed, poetry memorized, rocks collected, pictures painted, animals befriended, victories secured.

How far back in your memory should you go? As far back as you can recall. By the way, don't assume that if you grew up in difficult circumstances, you won't be able to recall any meaningful activities. We have interviewed people from every conceivable background. We've discovered that no matter how impoverished, sterile, dysfunctional, repressive, or even abusive the conditions, people can remember at least a handful of satisfying achievement experiences, despite the sadness of their early lives. It may take some prompting and probing, but the giftedness is there; it was there even when things seemed at their worst.

A LIFETIME OF ACHIEVEMENT ACTIVITIES

But don't stop with childhood memories. What did you do in your teen years that you found enjoyable and meaningful? Did you put on a magic show for your neighbors? Write a poem that was published? Play a duet in a band concert? Hike the entire length of the Appalachian Trail?

And then there are the activities from adulthood. These may come from your occupation in the workplace, your efforts as a parent, your activities as a parishioner, or your service in the community. Whatever accomplishments have held enjoyment and significance for you, put them on the list.

Maybe you invented a special process for mixing paints and had it patented. Found an old house and restored it to its original condition. Ran for the school board and lost—but raised issues that led to change. Made all the arrangements for placing your elderly parent in a retirement home. These are illustrations of the kind of activities we are looking for.

> **Giftedness expresses itself in achievements rather than successes, in activities rather than experiences.**

I call these "achievement activities" because they describe achievements, and because they are activities involving specific, identifiable things you did. Ideally, we want people to tell us about *achievements rather than successes*. For example, "I was named Miss Cauliflower" tells us little about the person. We'd rather hear about what she did to be granted that honor (if it had meaning for her). For instance: "I lost twenty pounds, memorized a song, and sewed my own gown in order to compete in (and win) the Miss Cauliflower contest."

Likewise, we want people to tell us about *activities* rather than experiences. "I heard President Kennedy give a speech when I was nine years old" is a lovely memory; unfortunately, it tells us nothing about the actions of the nine-year-old. A true achievement activity would relate something like, "I skipped school, took the bus downtown, and wormed my way to the front of the crowd in order to hear President Kennedy give a speech when I was nine years old." Now we know something about the achiever—what he *did* to gain such an impressionable experience.

For now, keep writing for as long as you need or want. Only when you're done should you go to appendix D, where you'll find what to do with all the sheets you filled with your achievement story.

In the next chapter we'll move from *giftedness* as revealed in one's life story (achievement story) to finding the *pattern* of that giftedness—the Motivated Abilities Pattern or MAP.

Chapter Three

Patterns of Giftedness: The MAP

The rigorous but enjoyable exercise of writing down one's history of achievements—those things the individual enjoyed doing and did well—yields reams of raw "data." But what can we do with all this information?

Following a standard scientific method, we began to analyze the data to find recurring themes or patterns.[1] Did the person repeat certain words or phrases of identical or closely similar meanings? We were not disappointed in this inquiry. In *every* case, the data showed that *people had invariably reverted to the same pattern of functioning whenever they had done something they enjoyed doing and did well.* This unique behavior was like their signature, their theme song, their own patented process.

THE MOTIVATED ABILITIES PATTERN OR MAP

Detecting a pattern is one thing; describing it is quite another. In the early days, our reports on each person were almost as idiosyncratic as the person's particular pattern of functioning. Meanwhile, our clients (largely in the corporate world) needed convenient ways to compare people with people, and people with jobs, so they put pressure on me to develop a system that would do just that.

---

1. Our process is an evidential one, not a playground for the creative mind. We look at data and what they tell us, not at an analyst's interpretations. Admittedly, this makes the process quite pedestrian and not of much interest to those who want to give free reign to their theories and beliefs. But the additive nature of the process makes it extremely powerful in its explanatory and predictive ability, and essentially impregnable from the influence or attacks of anyone who might have a vested interest in obtaining a different outcome.

So, to bring some consistency to our reporting and to make the results easier to understand and use, we pored over hundreds and hundreds of pattern reports to create a "taxonomy" that would classify the various elements that people talked about. Thus we developed a system for describing people's patterns, based on the many patterns we had identified.[2]

We found that all patterns of giftedness have five dimensions:

Abilities—the natural competencies a person uses to accomplish the results he wants (for example, study, experiment, analyze, persuade, strategize, teach).

Subject Matter—the objects or subject areas to which a person is naturally drawn and in which he achieves his most productive and fulfilling achievements (for example, numbers, concepts, people, tools, machines, color).

Circumstances—the ideal conditions in which a person functions (for example, structured, visible, competitive circumstances) and the factors that "trigger" his motivation, (for example, needs, problems, and potential for measurable results).

Operating Relationships—the way a person interacts with others in order to accomplish meaningful results (for example, team member, individualist, spark plug, facilitator, coordinator).

Payoff—the singular, characteristic outcome a person seeks in order to feel a sense of accomplishment and satisfaction (for example, excel, overcome, meet requirements, gain response, acquire goods and status, pioneer).

> Our data show that whenever a person does something he or she enjoys doing and does well, the individual invariably reverts to the same pattern of functioning—a unique pattern that is like the individual's signature.

The general pattern of giftedness is the *Motivated Abilities Pattern*, or MAP. We'll look at these five dimensions of the MAP in more detail in the next chapter, but first I want to stress three vital points.

THE MAP IS ORGANIC

First, the MAP is not a random, arbitrary construct that someone made up. It was suggested by the data themselves. It came out of a carefully

---

2. We call this SIMA®: the *System for Identifying Motivated Abilities*.

controlled regimen of letting people recall and describe in great detail their achievement experiences, followed by a careful analysis of their statements to detect repeated themes and threads. In this process of factor analysis, which correlated the data from thousands of people, the five dimensions listed above recurred time and again. Thus the MAP and its five dimensions are essentially organic: they naturally and inevitably occur as people experience and recall their achievements. No other template is imposed on the achievements.

We have consistently sought to avoid a fundamental mistake made by many people who come up with schemes for understanding and describing human beings by imposing their own theories or constructs on their subjects in a way that leaves little room but for the subjects to verify their theories.

THE MAP IS SYSTEMIC

This brings us to a second vital point: the MAP is a *system*. To be more precise, an individual human being is a system—a unified, integrated whole. Therefore the individual's MAP must be seen as a whole, not just a collection of five "parts." Each element of the MAP functions in relation to *all* the other elements.

For example, say that one of your motivated abilities is to evaluate by appraising worth. You have an instinctive knack for sizing up value. This skill will always operate *in concert with your other motivated abilities*. (Most people have about five to seven primary strengths, or motivated abilities.)

In applying your evaluative ability, you will be motivated to use it on particular *subject matter*—say structural objects and money. Thus you consistently find yourself appraising the worth of things like buildings or factories, and the financial implications involved. This comes naturally to you. Whatever technical knowledge and skills are needed you acquire with ease and delight.

However, in using your evaluative skill with structural objects, you will always seek to operate under certain *motivating circumstances*—perhaps situations that involve competition and the need for an immediate response. Thus it is not surprising to find you scrambling to put together bids for various properties in a town where real estate is booming.

As for your *operating relationships* in this go-go environment where you are using your worth-appraising skills on structural objects and money, you will relate to people in a way that uniquely suits who you are.

Perhaps it's as a Lone Ranger as you ride around town, seeking to make a profitable deal.

All of these elements—motivated abilities, subject matter, circumstances, operating relationships—will serve your drive for a particular *payoff* that you find incredibly satisfying. Perhaps it's to meet requirements established by others. So when an agreement is inked up, your greatest joy comes when your prime investor says, "This is great! This is perfect! You got me exactly what I wanted!"

Can you see how all the elements of a MAP operate together as an integrated system? Every element enables but also constrains every other element.

EACH MAP IS UNIQUE

You may be wondering how "unique" a person's MAP can actually be, given that it is comprised of only five dimensions. In a world with seven billion people, wouldn't the potential combinations be exhausted fairly rapidly?

The answer is no, for two reasons. First, each of the five elements of the pattern has a rich variety of possible expressions, as we're going to see. To give but one example, we have cataloged some fourteen different categories of motivated abilities, with about eighty-four subcategories. Consider that people express these abilities working with certain subject matter, within certain circumstances, and with all manner of variation in emphasis and combinations, and you begin to realize that there are probably endless possibilities for the expression of motivated abilities.

So even if someone's ability is teaching, he will teach in a way that is manifestly unique and different from any other teacher. Think about all the teachers you have had—especially the really good ones, the ones who actually knew how to stimulate learning—and you can see what I mean. They were all teachers, but each one taught with his or her own special flair.

Look at the following example in the box, which illustrates these last three qualities of the MAP: organic, systemic, unique. This is a teacher, a woman we were asked to evaluate for an open position. Our response includes the MAP and a narrative describing the unique organic, systemic way she would perform the position in question.

APPLICANT FOR TEACHING POSITION

MOTIVATED ABILITIES PATTERN SUMMARY

A. *What Are Her* Motivated Abilities?
Investigating: by interviewing, inquiring
Evaluating: by analyzing
Developing: by refining, clarifying, modifying
Overseeing: by facilitating, providing a way
Influencing: by involving, getting participation
Teaching: by tutoring, guiding

B. *What* Subject Matter *Recurs in Her Achievements?*
Knowledge
Materials
Individuals
Mechanisms: Methods, Steps

C. *What* Circumstances *Does She Find to Be Satisfying?*

What Triggers Her Motivation?
Problems
Needs

What Factors Keep Her Motivated?
Opportunity To Impact Effectiveness

What Results Does She Seek?
Application Involved

What Degree of Structure/Definition Does She Need?
Instructions, Specifications Available

What Environment Motivates Her?
Growth, Developing Situation
Project, Program

D. How Does She Work Best with People?
Enabling, Coaching, Facilitator

E. What Is the Payoff She Wants?
Improve/Make Better/Enhance

NARRATIVE

Applicant for Teaching Position is driven to improve virtually everything and everyone around her. To that end, she constantly searches for needs and problems which she can address. She will view her students as individuals who need her assistance in order to improve their understanding, competence, and effectiveness. Each person will become almost a project for her—something to take from state A to state B.

Because she is inherently driven to work with people as individuals—not as groups—she will not use a lecture format or other group instruction methods. Rather, she will structure her classroom and projects to facilitate one-on-one tutoring. Her compulsion to improve will drive her to invest the bulk of her energy in those students who appear to have special needs or potential. If students are timid or disinterested, she will strive to engage them in the class activities.

She naturally functions as an enabling, coaching facilitator. As such, she will labor to provide the materials, opportunities, and guidance necessary for each individual to enhance his or her academic performance. It is essential that she is continually able to identify specific areas of improvement which are clearly the result of her impact. In the absence of any meaningful needs or problems, her efforts, energy, and enthusiasm will wane. It is quite likely that she will "invent" problems to solve—and she will strive to make improvements even in those situations which others regard to be quite acceptable. She will resist considering anything as "finished"—she will continue to refine and modify it, believing it must somehow be better than it is.

Her motivation to have an impact and to make improvements will be manifested not only in her teaching, but in her relationships with her colleagues, in her preparation of materials, in her scheduling, in her own professional growth—indeed, in virtually everything she does.

In order to assure herself that her efforts are appropriate, she will actively search for instructions, specifications, or rules she can follow. She will look to experienced instructors and to relevant resource materials for proven methods to use in the classroom. This applicant must not be expected to develop her curricula from scratch or to personally create innovative materials, projects, or strategies; rather, it is essential that she is provided with clear instructions and procedures. The order inherent in well-defined methods gives her the security of knowing that her efforts are not the product of random reactions to unpredictable situations, but are based on well-researched techniques. True to her nature, she will refine and improve those procedures. When situations arise for which she has no tested approach, she will likely be hesitant to take action. Positions which demand that she work creatively within a fluid, flexible environment will soon undermine her effectiveness and erode her enthusiasm.

The beauty of a MAP and one of the things that makes it fundamentally different from most other ways of understanding people is that it gives a fair and accurate representation of who you have been manifesting yourself to be throughout your life. In the language of a music metaphor, when we come up with your MAP, we are not writing a tune for you to sing; we are trying to capture on paper the tune that *you are already singing*— and have been singing throughout your life!

> **When we come up with your MAP, we are not writing a tune for you to sing; we are trying to capture on paper *the tune that you are already singing*—and have been singing throughout your life!**

LEARNING TO READ THE MUSIC

Wouldn't you like to know what that song is? Wouldn't you like to know what songs the people around you are singing, especially those whose lives are influencing you and who are being influenced by you—children, parents, spouses, students, teachers, employees, bosses, and the like? If you really want to understand what they are singing, you need to study their song.

That's where a MAP comes in. To use a simple, whimsical illustration: "I designed and built a thirty-foot dory to cross a very rough sea by myself in order to hear my true love say yes to my proposal for marriage sent six months before by carrier pigeon."

Quite a touching song! But like every other "song," or motivated achievement, it can be represented in terms of the five dimensions of the Motivated Abilities Pattern:

- *Motivated Ability:* I designed and built
- *Subject Matter:* a thirty-foot dory
- *Circumstances:* to cross a very rough sea
- *Operating Relationships:* by myself
- *Motivational Payoff:* in order to hear my true love say yes to my proposal for marriage sent six months before by carrier pigeon.

We will look at each of these five elements in more detail in the next chapter.

Chapter Four

The Details of Our Pattern

The purpose of the Motivated Abilities Pattern is not to pigeonhole people or to identify specific "types." It is the opposite—the Motivated Abilities Pattern is a tool that allows us to ask the right questions, and that keeps us from overlooking one or more dimensions of a person's giftedness. In this chapter I'm only scratching the surface of the possibilities. Allow yourself to marvel at the almost infinite variety of giftedness and thus of people.

MOTIVATED ABILITIES THAT COME NATURALLY

Motivated Abilities are those natural, God-given competencies that a person uses to accomplish desired results. The woman whose baked beans win first prize at the county fair each year, the man who turns a nondescript, weed-grown lot into a landscaped marvel, the teenager who can solve complex math problems in her head, the little boy who amazes his relatives by his talent for rhyming or rapping almost any word or phrase—these are everyday expressions of motivated abilities.

It is not that motivated abilities must necessarily be impressive or outstanding. Sometimes they are not. The person who has an intuitive grasp of how a trout "thinks," the child with a knack for spelling, the waiter who handles effortlessly and efficiently large numbers of orders from customers in a crowded restaurant (and actually

> Motivated abilities often stand out, not because of what they accomplish, but because *they accomplish so much with so little effort.*

enjoys his work)—these are all examples of motivated abilities. Motivated abilities often do stand out, not because of what they accomplish, but because *they accomplish so much with so little effort*. They stand out because they come naturally and effortlessly. They are the skills that make people who can't tell a trout from a bass, or who can't spell a word the same way twice, or who by the time they reach the kitchen can't remember whether the visiting couple wanted tea and ice water or lemonade and coffee shake their head and ask in amazement, "How do you do it?" And the answer is invariably, "I don't know—I just do it."

This *naturalness* is one of the hallmarks of motivated ability. These are primary, inborn strengths. The person doesn't really have to think about using them, much less try; he or she just uses them. He may have to learn the mechanics of the activity and possibly develop certain motor skills. And he may cultivate his strengths through practice and training. But he doesn't have to "acquire" them; he is *born* to them, as a bird is to flight. Furthermore, he is naturally *motivated* to use them. That is, he never tires of them. Day in and day out, year in and year out, we find him turning to these skills to accomplish his ends—throughout his life!

So the various motivated abilities we possess cover essentially everything we do in the course of a day. They determine how we

- perceive our world
- acquire and assimilate knowledge
- evaluate the soundness or rightness of things
- conceive and develop anything new
- organize and plan our activities
- take action
- inform and influence others

MOTIVATING SUBJECTS THAT "TURN US ON"

Motivating subjects are the topics, objects, or areas of life in which an individual is naturally inclined to function—in which his or her motivated abilities find natural expression. If the hallmark of motivated abilities is *naturalness*, the hallmark of motivating subjects is *passion*.

People become passionate about subject matter that engages their MAP. If you ever doubt that, just look into the eyes of a championship athlete. You'll find fire there, if she truly loves her sport. You'll see passion in almost everything she does—how she trains, how she competes, what she eats, what she reads, even whom she associates with.

It's not that sports don't include some people solely because of ability rather than motivation. But athletics, perhaps more than any other field, tends to "qualify" people through a grueling, long-term process of competition. The system favors passion as well as performance because it is such a long way to the top. Few people get there unless they truly love what they are doing.

> **The hallmark of motivating subjects is *passion*. People become passionate about subject matter that engages their MAP.**

That's why we sometimes hear professional athletes saying things like, "I can't believe they pay me to do this!" Their sport is not just a "job" to them—they are having fun! They're operating within their motivated subject matter. Of course, it's not just athletes who demonstrate this sort of passion. I've seen it in secretaries, doctors, preachers, Cub Scouts, restaurateurs, gardeners, and homemakers.

There's a man who runs a fruit and vegetable stand near my office—Henry Balsamo. Henry not only knows his products, he's downright passionate about them. He starts his day in the middle of the night at the wholesale market, buying only high-priced, very good quality produce. He will not buy the ordinary. It is why people come from long distances, and sometimes in chauffeured cars, to tap Henry's passion. His wife says he is a "maniac" about his work. I'll visit Henry to buy a couple of melons, and lightly squeezing a couple of dandies ask, "Are these ripe?" "Not yet!" Henry declares. "Gotta wait until tomorrow." Then he adds, mischievously, "About three o'clock!"

I think he's only half kidding. I think Henry and Frank, his brother, have been working with produce for so long—maybe five or six decades—that he really does know almost the exact instant when a piece of fruit becomes perfectly ripe! That's the kind of expertise associated with a motivating subject!

Imagine if everyone could find the same intensity as a dedicated athlete or as a vendor of fresh produce like Henry Balsamo. Imagine what could happen in the workplace, in schools, in religious institutions, or in community services if people in those spheres were as passionately involved in what they are doing!

EVERYONE HAS A PASSION—ABOUT SOMETHING

Is that really possible? Of course. *Everyone* has certain subjects or objects on which their motivation thrives. It's not that a few lucky people in this world have areas of unusual interest while the rest of us must resign ourselves to tedium. *Everyone* is motivated by certain subject matter.

But unfortunately, many people spend their most important hours working on other subjects. For instance, a woman will put in her eight hours working as an accountant, getting by with satisfactory results. It's a job. But then she comes home to her garden. Suddenly, reservoirs of energy are released as she tends each plant as if it were a member of the family. Whereas an hour or two earlier she was straining to focus her mind on ledgers and balance sheets, now she becomes delightfully lost in processes of pruning, aerating, composting, and watering.

When you see that, you have to wonder—what could happen if we placed that woman in a position where others could benefit from her passion for growing things? Might her life become more productive for society and more fulfilling for herself?

How many people do you know who, upon retirement, or after being "downsized" late in their career, have made radical shifts in vocation? The father of a good friend of mine spent his "working career" as a parish priest in a number of small towns. After he retired he began building homes for needy families—happily and seemingly twenty years younger!

MOTIVATING CIRCUMSTANCES IN WHICH WE THRIVE

People use their motivated abilities and apply them to motivated subject matter—but they do so best when they can function in motivating circumstances. Motivating circumstances are the ideal conditions for an individual, where he or she can function best.

Let me detail several ways in which circumstances are critical in engaging people's motivated behavior.

What Starts Your Engine?

One of the most frequently asked questions by employers and managers today is, "How can I motivate my people?" They are asking what it takes to get people started, to get them "off the dime," as the saying goes. Often, in the same breath, the manager will add, "I'm looking for go-getters—people who can see a need and then meet it."

But that betrays a *fundamental misunderstanding about how people are motivated*. Some people are self-starters. They do well in situations where no one can or will give directions, and they don't need any. But many people require someone else to get them started. *That's not a weakness, that's a request for leadership*.

> A person who does not respond may not be indifferent at all—just unmotivated. There's a vast difference.

What triggers a person's motivation? Have you ever been in a meeting where someone laid out a critical need and made an impassioned plea for help? Perhaps a handful of people leaped up to volunteer. But others hung back. Some people would interpret this seeming lack of response as indifference—which is again a fundamental misunderstanding. These people are by no means inherently indifferent—just unmotivated. There's a vast difference.

Some people are motivated to respond to need. But others are motivated, not by needs, but by problems. Unless they perceive a problem to be solved, they remain unmotivated. Others respond to competition, or to opportunity, or to an emergency, and so forth. The more precisely we understand what ignites an individual's involvement, the more accurately we'll be able to say, "This is a job for him!" And the more we understand what triggers our own enthusiasm, the more accurately we'll be able to say, "This is the job for me!"

I know a woman, Anne, who is highly creative, opinionated (again, "highly"), extremely independent in her desire to do things her way, perceptive, and a rich source of wisdom and insight for those with personal or artistic problems. She has a demonstrated ability to spark individuals and organizations to new levels of understanding and accomplishment, but she is unable to get started in a new endeavor on her own. She needs to be invited into something that exists and has potential for growth and new expression if she is to function optimally. Period.

What Keeps You Running Hard?

Getting started is one thing, keeping at it is another. Here again, it is common to blame people who lose motivation in the midst of a task. They are "slackers," they "lack commitment," they "failed to count the cost" before they jumped in. Such are the accusations.

But MAPs reveal that when people stop putting their all into a task or activity, *it is usually not a matter of character but of motivation*. The circumstances have changed, and with it, their energy level. For just as circumstances are crucial in triggering people's involvement, so they are critical in sustaining it as well.

> When people stop putting their all into a task or activity, it is usually not a matter of character but of motivation.

Some people thrive in the pressure cooker. As long as the press is beating down their front door, or the customer has doubled his order but must have it tomorrow, or the patient's life hangs in the balance, they are supremely focused and intent. The best of their energies are devoted to the situation at hand. But once the story breaks, the package is in the hands of FedEx, or the patient is out of danger, the person's motivation quickly evaporates.

For others, it is the opportunity for personal growth that keeps them driving hard. While they are being mentored by a senior executive, while they are mastering the routing system, while they are perfecting their cake-decorating technique, they are like dogs on a hunt. But force them into a routine maintenance mode where they do the same old thing in the same old way, time after time, day after day, and they'll start checking out emotionally and begin chasing rabbits.

You want to manage your life a bit more effectively? Then find out why and when you run out of motivational gas!

The research head of a very large petrochemical firm located in the Midwest asked if we could find out why the research efforts of a particularly creative scientist gave the company such little return for its considerable investment in him. Our motivational study of him revealed that once he "saw" the likely conceptual solutions of a problem, he stopped pursuing it—even though six to twelve months more of work could have paid off handsomely for all concerned.

Results—Specific or General?

Motivation is closely tied to results or to some other sought outcome. Some people are driven to obtain a measurable, quantitative result or a product: a bottom-line profit, a done deal, a win-loss record, a prize. But others are process-oriented and spend years of effort on outcomes that are much less defined or even obscure. For instance, a professor puts his heart into adding to existing knowledge—perhaps knowledge that only a handful of people in the world care about and that has no practical implications. An inventor gives his life to creating a new process for measuring moonbeams. A teacher dedicates herself to improving the reading skills of her students.

How do these folks know when they are achieving what they want? The question is almost meaningless when applied to them, for their joy comes in the doing of the task as well in its completion. The gains come day by day: as long as the articles keep getting published, as long as the underlying technology is becoming clearer, as long as students keep progressing from book to book, motivation stays high.

If you want to manage your life a bit more effectively, find out why and when you run out of motivational gas!

Place people where they are most likely to experience the outcome they seek. If the satisfaction of solving problems is what drives them, steer them toward a problem-ridden environment. If quality is what they long for, then put them where they can refine to their heart's content. If their longing is to create something completely new, then take away the barriers to their creative vision. If profitability is in their heart, make them the boss. ← ? NOT GOOD A LOT OF TIMES

Structured or Open-ended?

One of the most important elements of motivating circumstances is the way in which tasks are defined and structured. There tend to be two poles: highly structured environments, where the ground rules and methodology are clear; and open-ended, fluid environments where the way forward is full of uncertainty. Obviously, there are many possibilities in between.

People are naturally drawn to certain kinds of structure. Contrast the relatively well-scripted tasks associated with playing baseball, writing computer code, baking an apple pie, or tearing down a motor, with the more fluid dynamics of making a complex investment decision, counseling a pregnant teenager, playing jazz, or defining new goals for an organization.

Know how much or how little structure one requires before offering or taking on an assignment. A person who is not given the amount of definition that he or she needs may feel like a ship at sea without a rudder. Secretaries have been known to make inquiries of Chicago sources (my hometown) about putting out a contract on their boss because he drove them nuts with not enough (or too much) structure and direction. A mismatch can turn a good job into serious and destructive stress!

Conditions of Work

Close on the heels of structure are the working conditions under which people prefer to operate.

Next time you are in a major metropolis, walking in the canyons between towering skyscrapers, look up and see if there are any window washers perched dozens of stories above the street. Then ask yourself: what sort of motivational pattern does it take to work on an eight-foot ledge dangling from a couple of cables, maybe several hundred feet in the air, against the side of a building? Yet some people thrive under these conditions.

> Every person requires particular conditions for his giftedness to thrive.

Contrast that with the policy analyst who beavers away in a think tank. Left alone to do his research, he quietly and methodically builds his case for a particular point of view that he hopes will influence decision makers. He requires a stable, unpressured environment where he can sift through the nuances of a thought without the distractions of tension and worry.

The point is that every person requires particular conditions for his giftedness to thrive. Unfortunately, too many people today are trying to operate outside of their domain. The results can be as absurd as a polar bear on a tropical beach and as tragic as a fish out of water.

The conditions within which we work or live can be utterly destructive—or encouraging and life-giving. A typical death march is the transfer of a highflier who moves from a results-oriented field operation, where everybody's on the same team, to a headquarters operation where politics reign supreme.

Or, on the home front, a demanding, authoritative, "I know best" father or mother can be good for a child who wants a lot of direction and clarity of expectations, but pure hell for the child who is a dreamer, inclined to experimentation and independent thought and values.

Or take competition as a condition of work in which people shine or wilt. Cal Ripkin Jr. and his record streak of playing consecutive games without missing one, is a case in point. From Cal's autobiography, we learn this about his desire to compete and win:

> I was so competitive and annoying that Elly and Fred tried to keep me out of these games at times, but I usually managed to bully or beg my way into the action. In cutthroat Hearts, they tried to

stick me with the queen, and I tried to take them out with a show of disgust, then shoot the moon. One year in Miami, my competitiveness caused a trip to the emergency room. I'd been teaching a friend how to play checkers and lured her into some wrong moves that set up a quadruple jump for myself. When I leaped up in joy after that triumph, I slammed my head against the windowsill. Five stitches, according to Ripkin lore.

I was a bad loser and a bad winner too, and I got what I deserved. During all the coverage of the streak, someone in the family circulated the story that I cheated my own grandmother at Canasta. I don't remember that, but I might have occasionally drawn too many cards on her, because I did cheat on everyone else. For years I kept detailed statistics on all these family games, for the sole purpose of trying to prove that I was the best. The only positive note here is that I finally figured out that the only proof of how good you are is if you play within the rules.[1]

The Place of Recognition

Earlier I said that motivating circumstances are like the stage on which we act out our achievements. That's a useful metaphor, because it raises the issue of recognition. Who sees us perform our function, and what response is important to sustain our motivation?

Many people assume that everyone likes to have their moment in the spotlight, their round of applause. But that's not true. MAPs show that some people must have recognition, while others genuinely do better behind the scenes. Those who delight in visibility might seek it through acting, sports, modeling, singing in a choir, or even leading a rebellion. Meanwhile, those who prefer to stay in the background would rather paint the scenery, take the tickets, sew the garments, tune the piano, or pass out the handbills.

What is most critical to understand is that if motivationally you crave recognition, and your work excludes it as a practical reality (you work, for example, in the boiler room or on the third level in the library), you will seek recognition somewhere else in

> **Some people must have recognition, while others genuinely do better behind the scenes.**

---

1. Cal Ripkin with Mike Bryan, *The Only Way I Know* (New York: Penguin, 1997).

your life, where your desire to be noticed can be achieved in proper ways (e.g., amateur dramatics) or in ways you will end up regretting (e.g., frequent confession of sin before the church fellowship).

Pavarotti, the glorious tenor, is unabashed about his desire for notoriety and renown, which emerged at age five, loudly and clearly:

> I was only about five or six when I discovered I had a voice. It was a fine alto voice, but nothing sensational. Even though my voice was only average, I used to love to sing. I used to go into my room and close the door and, at the top of my lungs, sing "La donna é mobile"—in a child's voice, of course. Of the sixteen families in the building, fourteen of them would yell at me to shut up. That's funny, because when I was very small—about five—I had a toy mandolin. I would take it into the courtyard behind our building where there was a fountain. I would carry a little child's chair and set it up by the fountain and serenade all the apartments. The neighbors used to love these concerts—maybe I didn't scream so much—and would toss candies and nuts to me.[2]

The New or Different

Some people actively seek out situations where something must be done that no one has ever done before, or at least that they have never done before. This quest for newness can range from a discoverer's journey into a new emerging technology to a neophyte cook's efforts to produce a perfect lobster à la Newburgh.

Something similar is found in those who always do things differently from what everyone else is doing: adopting an avant garde haircut, wearing outrageous fashions, driving a one-of-a-kind car, working in an offbeat career. They instinctively stand out from others and march to a different drummer. And then there are those with an insatiable appetite for continued personal development, which is also a hunger for the new.

But at the other end of the spectrum we find people who require the known in order to function. Their achievements need prerequisites. Rather than discovering a lost planet, they would rather build on the world as it already exists. Many who operate franchises display this pattern. Routine and predictability are what matter.

---

2. Luciano Pavarotti, *Pavarotti: My Own Story* (Garden City: Doubleday, 1981).

This enthusiastic response to the new or unexpected on the one hand, and the need for the old or routine on the other is a major consideration in assuring job fit. For the world is in a constant tug-of-war between change and stability, chaos and predictability, innovation and preservation. By placing people in circumstances that fit their level of flexibility, we could reduce a great deal of human stress. And by accepting people's preference for either painting freestyle or by the numbers, we could assure a high level of productivity.

> Some people seek out situations where something must be done that they have never done before. Others require the known in order to function.

Examples abound of the good and the bad being visited on folks through new or different circumstances. I was asked by a large parachurch organization to diagnose the decline in performance of Anton, a man whose lengthy career had been filled with heroic, risky thrusts into parts of the world new to any significant missionary work.

There he had built schools and hospitals, using native tools and local materials—really incredible feats. As a reward, he had been given a cushy staff job in a large office overlooking a little pond, inhabited by Canadian geese. Guess what the problem was?

Or, moving in the other direction, a large insurance company promoted Rick, a very successful manager of a large office that sold individual insurance, to head up new product development. The field where Rick had built his outstanding sales record is a bit like organized sports where the ground rules, the products to be sold, the skills needed, and the objectives and quotas to be reached are well-defined and clearly stated. In his new assignment—which involved researching, developing, and selecting products that would be profitable and could be sold by the sales staff—everything had to be done from scratch. His performance in new-product development was notable for starting and stopping and starting again. Ultimately, he came out with an individual life insurance product (oddly enough) for the group-life-insurance people to sell—which they couldn't, because they were good at technical presentation, not selling.

MOTIVATING RELATIONSHIPS WE SEEK

A dominant element in the MAP is the way in which a person interacts with other people to form his operating relationships.

What is striking about these relational dynamics is how clearly they can show up in a person's achievement history. For instance, one fellow rattled off a list of thirteen achievement activities from throughout his life. In every single one he revealed himself as a team player. From his boyhood romps with his buddies, to his days in the military with "the guys," to his joint efforts with his wife to fix up their apartment, to his career achievements with a committee—*all* of his significant accomplishments occurred when he was part of a team. Something about engaging with other people stimulated his best energies.

At the other end of the spectrum is the individualist who either wants to operate alone or, if in a group effort, wants a defined role that contributes to the group objective but that he can accomplish alone. In contrast to the team player, the achievements of an individualist are obviously individualistic in nature: e.g., sports such as hiking, skiing, golf, swimming, fly-fishing, and so on.

How a person wants to operate with others, whether as a team member or as an individualist, star, coach, or spark plug, or in any of a host of other ways I could enumerate, usually becomes quite evident when you examine a person's achievement experiences.

> "Climb as high as you can" is a philosophy that not only ruins lives and careers but is equally destructive of corporate health and profitability.

Yet even though motivating relationships can be so obvious from one's achievement history, they are the part of the MAP most often violated. Our society venerates leaders and managers, and equates these roles with control, success, and prosperity. As a result, there is tremendous pressure on people to "rise to the top."

"Climb as high as you can" is the prevailing American philosophy of success. It is a philosophy that not only ruins lives and careers but is equally destructive of corporate health and profitability. And it is not only stupid, it is also unnecessary. People who are leaders and true managers will crawl through ground glass to get into an executive position. You do not have to encourage them to climb.

To show how this idolatry works to everybody's harm, let me give you what I suspect is a typical example. Probably on the advice of some consultant who believes you develop executives by assigning them to positions drawing on their weakness, the CEO of a large client of ours announced that four high-potential middle-management individuals would be auctioned off for assignment to those divisions offering the most attractive and challenging positions. As a result, three of the four experienced a major disruption in their career progress (euphemistically speaking). One who was brilliant in planning, analysis, and experimentation was assigned an operating job, running a group of facilities in the Pacific Rim. Another prize was a capable operating executive who needed a well-defined game plan and minimum ambiguity in direction and priorities but was assigned to a politically sensitive role between a CEO and the operating heads of a major division. The third was a cheerleader type of manager over a small operation where he could direct and control others through his personal interaction with them. He was assigned to manage a relatively large operation with widely dispersed facilities.

> **The real bottom line is: Become who you are!**

So, what is the lesson you should learn from this pitiful batting average? Be prepared to defend yourself against destructive career moves. Know how you relate to others. Stay your course. *Become who you are.*

THE MOTIVATIONAL PAYOFF WE SEEK

Some folks find their greatest fulfillment in pursuits outside of work. For example, the skipper of a sailboat who is driven to beat the competition lives for the weekend when he can bring his intense focus and determination to a Sunday afternoon regatta. The young hot-rod enthusiast on a never-ending quest for the perfectly running engine thrives in the heat and noise of the drag strip. The musician determined to reproduce the bright canzones of a Gabrieli or the lyrical concerti of a Corelli schedules his life around the practice sessions of the ensemble at the summer institute.

The passion with which people often pursue avocational interests like these suggests how extraordinarily satisfying they can be. Naturally, industry leaders are prone to wonder, "How can we tap that energy and bring it into the workplace?"

The answer is, by understanding the fifth and central element of people's giftedness—*motivational payoff*. Payoff is the singular, characteristic outcome a person seeks in order to feel a sense of accomplishment and satisfaction.

In the popular film *Chariots of Fire*, Olympic runner Eric Liddell is implored by his sister to give up running and fulfill his vow to become a missionary to China. Liddell replies, "Jenny, Jenny, you've got to understand. I believe that God made me for a purpose—for China. He also made me fast, and when I run, I feel His pleasure!" Motivational payoff is the *pleasure*. It's the *enjoyment* in the question, "What have you done that you *enjoyed* doing and feel you did well?" At the core of every person's motivation is a drive to experience personal joy, significance, and meaning.

Let me be clear: this payoff is not just a self-seeking pleasure for the sake of having a good time. It's the pleasure of living with and for a *purpose*. When someone does the thing he or she was born to do, there is an instinctive experience of fulfillment. It's not something she is *supposed* to experience—it's what she actually *does* experience. That joy is the hallmark that one is in fact using one's giftedness.

Payoff is uniquely personal and tied in with all the other MAP elements. Each of us is wired differently—which means that my payoff probably would hold little interest for you, and vice versa. The rush you may feel in tackling a crisis, the puzzlement and ultimate sense of resolution in solving a mathematical equation, the aesthetic "rightness" you sense about a work of art that you have fashioned—none of these will make much sense to someone else. It is to you, uniquely, that this joy is given. It is a gift to you.

> The motivational payoff is not just a self-seeking pleasure for the sake of having a good time—it is the pleasure of *living with and for a purpose.*

For example, a man with a knack for gardening tells of planting eighty-eight caladiums along the front of his house one spring. "In what way was that enjoyable to you?" I ask. He replies, "It just brought the whole landscaping together. It was exactly like the picture I had cut out of the magazine. My yard looked like that picture—and it was gorgeous! I felt, 'At last! I'm home! This is the way it's supposed to be. This is the look I've always wanted.'"

Another person, a union boss, describes an incident in which she stayed up for two nights in a row to negotiate a labor contract. "You really liked that," I'll say. And she responds, "I loved it! It was knowing that I had outlasted them. There was no way I was going to back down. Everybody in the union was depending on me—and I was determined to see this thing through. When I finally walked out of that bargaining room, and everyone standing outside was clapping when I came out, I realized I had done it. I had stared 'em down. I sat there and looked them in the eye until they blinked—and we won!"

Joys like these are simple enough, but they are also powerful enough to drive a person's achievement. The experience of that joy, that pleasure, that payoff is what keeps one coming back for more. Indeed, we discover that it has *always* been a central, primary force in the person's life. The gardener who planted caladiums to bring his yard together has *always* acted out of an urge to make things aesthetically "right." The union negotiator who outlasted her counterparts has *always* strove to prevail.

> **Never assume that because people share in the same activity, they all share the same desired outcome.**

Never should we assume that because people share in the same activity—say, gardening or negotiations—they all share the same desired outcome. Nowhere is this more dramatically proven than in sports. We assume that all athletes want to win. In a sense that is true, but in a more accurate sense, winning may or may not be the personal prize that turns the second baseman on or brings out the best in the catcher.

Look at examples from Little Leaguers, whom we have worked with after they became adults, to get a sense of the range of motivating circumstances critical to each player.

Don Kiehl, one of our premier case writers and a baseball nut, gathered together the motivational payoffs for a number of former Little Leaguers. And you thought players of the same sport all walked to the same drummer!

- *Be unique*: "I was the only kid on my team who wore a real pro-back felt cap instead of those cheap nylon caps we were supposed to wear."
- *Gain recognition*: "I loved the night they announced the all-star game and they used a real spotlight for the first time—I felt like every eye was focused on me."
- *Be key*: "If I hadn't talked my coach into letting me play catcher, and if I hadn't done so many little things well that most fans never noticed, this team would never have gotten to the championship game."
- *Realize a dream*: "I had so much fun imagining I was Ricky Henderson; I copied his batting stance and slid into base just like he

did. I also remember when I finally hit a home run—it was just like I always dreamed it would be."

- *Become proficient*: "I liked getting good at all the different positions. I was able to play first base pretty good, and then my coach wanted me to be the shortstop the next year. I got my dad to work with me one night and I improved rather quickly. Knowing I'm a good baseball player gives me a lot of confidence. I like to get together with my cousins and prove to them that I can throw a pretty good knuckleball."

- *Advance*: "I just liked the natural progression of starting in T-ball, spending a year in Farms, another year in Minors, and then making the Majors. I also remember the day my dad bought me my first real glove—and I can't wait to move on to football now that I'm bigger and my parents will let me."

- *Plan and produce*: "I remember when it was our day to clean up the field. I divided up all the tasks among my teammates, phoned every one to make sure they'd be there on time, and saw my plans work perfectly; the field was spotless after two hours of work. I also liked planning out how to make a perfectly round on-deck circle with the little machine that drops chalk as you push it."

- *Bring to completion*: "I liked those games when the starting pitcher would get tired and the coach would bring me in from left field to pitch. I always was able to get the game over as quickly as possible. I liked being the closer."

- *Make the team*: "My older brother played on the Little League Dodgers seven years ago, and ever since, all I ever dreamed about was being a Dodger. I got to know the coach's son, I made sure I learned how to bunt because I knew that would please the coach, and I'll never forget the day he called me to announce he'd drafted me, and I was finally a Dodger."

- *Meet needs*: "I really liked our coach. I enjoyed getting to know him and doing whatever I could to help around the field—run bases during practice games of pickle, pick up bats and bases, warm up relief pitchers, and do whatever I could to assist the team."

- *Improve*: "I fiddled with my batting stance the whole time, having my dad take videos of me and figuring out constantly ways to get better."

- *Exploit potential*: "I was good at figuring out ways to win. I'd love watching the other catcher during warm-ups and thinking, 'Here's a guy we can run on all day.' To be honest, I also figured that playing baseball would help me be more popular at school with girls and stuff. I was good at taking advantage of every situation presented to me."

- *Gain response*: "I was really good at getting other players to react to me. I'd yell at the opponents and distract them—get them so mad at me they'd do stupid things. I could also get my teammates all revved up, and we'd play more intensely as a result."
- *Be in charge*: "I loved playing catcher because all the players on the field would have to obey me when I'd tell them to back up or move over. My coach called me his manager on the field, and I took that seriously. When I walked out there, I was in control—I loved that feeling."
- *Master*: "Ever since third grade I worked on throwing a curveball. I worked on it constantly, throwing over and over with the same motion until I could throw it for strikes in any situation, on any count. I perfected that pitch."
- *Acquire and possess*: "I have an entire shelf of trophies, ribbons, hats, programs, and baseballs signed by my teammates. I love to look at them, sometimes pick them up; they bring back so many good memories. My mom even started a scrapbook—I know I'll keep that forever."

A Way to Say "Yes" or "No"

This brings us to another way in which payoff is a gift: it lends tremendous perspective on what we should be doing with our lives. By knowing our purpose, we have a basis for evaluating the various opportunities that come our way.

Several times I've mentioned the pitfalls of blindly accepting a career promotion. A respect for motivational payoff can help us look before we leap. First we must look at ourselves and consider what drives us. Then we must look at the proposed position or role and ask, "Would I do it really well? Would this really prove satisfying? Will it pay off emotionally and spiritually, given the way I am put together?"

If not—and this can be very, very hard to do—we must turn down the offer. We *must!* Because to accept, knowingly and willingly, a position that requires someone driven by a purpose that is not our driving purpose shows a total lack of integrity. It is unfair to the position, to the people offering the position, to those affected by the position, and above all, to our own self, our own personhood. It makes no sense.

But by the same token, knowledge of one's payoff can lead to exciting new ventures and meaningful, productive outcomes. Think about all the important things that need to happen in the world. Who better to accomplish these tasks than people intrinsically motivated to accomplish them? Who better to increase yields than the person driven to extract potential? Who better to conquer diseases than the person obsessed with combating and prevailing? Who better to negotiate treaties than the deal maker? Who better to compose poems than the person longing to express life's experiences in a fresh way? Who better to educate children than the person excited about building and developing young lives?

> To accept, knowingly and willingly, a position that requires someone driven by a purpose that is not our driving purpose shows a total lack of integrity.

All the energy is there. What is needed is the wisdom to put it where it will do the most good, to harness people to the tasks that suit them. There is no drudgery in that. People never weary of doing what they enjoy. Indeed, they cannot, because they are constantly rewarded by the fruit of their labors. That payoff is food for their souls. That, too, is a gift.

(If you are interested in the genesis of our MAP technology, I've enclosed in appendix B excerpts from a MAP produced some years ago, when we included all of the evidence from the person's achievements that supported conclusions we reached. The MAP Report is about Billy Joe.)

Chapter Five

The Characteristics of Our Giftedness

We have examined the five dimensions of the Motivated Abilities Pattern (MAP)—abilities, subject matter, circumstances, operating relationships, and motivational payoff. We have asserted that every human being has a unique pattern. We have insisted that this way of looking at persons is not artificial or imposed, but that it is rather an objective summary of what people themselves display organically through the things they enjoy doing and do well. Furthermore, we have stated that each person is a whole—not a random collection of unrelated parts or "traits," but an integrated, unified *system*, if you will.

The purpose of this section is to outline the characteristics of our design (MAP), as a whole, so that you can see the striking ways in which our design by its very nature impacts how we think, speak, and act.

OUR DESIGN APPEARS TO BE INBORN

No one yet knows with certainty all that is "hardwired" into newborns, but people appear to possess their giftedness from the womb. This conclusion seems likely, based on the growing knowledge we have today about human development.

If you are familiar with that field, you know of the ongoing debate concerning how much people are the product of their genes and how much they are the product of their environment. Nature *versus* nurture, as they say.

Evidence does not support the popular myth that "who" people are is primarily a function of the environment in which they grow up.

A growing amount and quality of evidence does not support the popular myth believed and proposed in the middle of this century by major psychologists that "who" people are is primarily a function of the environment in which they grow up.

One particularly useful article on the subject had these observations to make, based on a number of research studies.

> .... most major personality theorists inhabiting the pages of major personality textbooks, emphasized child-rearing styles as formative of adult personality traits.
>
> If parental treatments are in many ways similar in their environmental effects on their children, how can the children be so different?
>
> We now have extensive evidence for genetic influence on normal personality traits—intellectual traits—and externalizing disorders. Although this evidence comes from a variety of research designs, the most convincing one is the adoption study in which adopted children are compared to their biological parents . . .
>
> For most personality traits, adoptive family members resemble one another no more than individuals raised in different families . . .
>
> In these studies, the adopted siblings showed no more resemblance to one another than do individuals in the general population.
>
> A list of shared family environmental factors . . . is really a list of variables without much effect on the development of traits.[1]

The article then lists the following "Family Environmental Variables Without Effects on Personality Development," noting that "these experiences tend to be shared by children in the same family":

Social class	Father's absence or presence
Home features (number of books, number of rooms)	Religiosity
	Diet and nutrition
Parental values	Parental modeling
Child-rearing styles	Family size
Divorce	Maternal employment

---

1. See David C. Lowe, "As the Twig Is Bent: The Myth of Child-rearing Influences on Personality Development," *Journal of Counseling and Development*, (July/August 1990) for an excellent summary of evidence denying the power of "nurturing" to shape people.

OUR DESIGN MANIFESTS ITSELF IN INFANCY

There are other reasons for believing that giftedness is inborn. One of the most compelling is the inescapable fact of precociousness in young children, before any training or other attempts to influence behavior. As any mother knows, every infant displays its own remarkable personality. And as the child grows, it builds on its distinctive repertoire of behaviors. By the time for school, the child manifests a distinct modus operandi or M.O.

No one really teaches the young child how to "be." Sure, parents say words and play games and do other things with their little ones to bring them along (as well they should). But they do not—*can*not—shape the child into whatever mold they want. They may scold him a hundred times for getting into the mud—but what causes him to keep seeking that mud in the first place?

> **Parents cannot shape a child into whatever mold they want. They may scold her a hundred times for getting into the mud—but what causes her to keep seeking that mud in the first place?**

They may weary of answering little Susie's endless questions. But what is it in Susie that causes her to ask questions in the first place—especially when older brother Johnny *never* asked, but merely observed?

It is the easy naturalness of the child's behavior that strongly suggests innate giftedness. The child is just naturally "good" at certain things. Almost from the crib, each child has a knack for something. Going back to where we started in this book, just sit for a while in a nursery or kindergarten class. If the children are allowed to function spontaneously, you will see that each one has a distinctive style. Since each child's highly personal style emerges so early and so dramatically, it is hard to believe that it is the result of background and environment. A more plausible explanation is that the child is already living out who he or she was born to be.

This hypothesis is further bolstered by the fact that once a child establishes a distinctive pattern of behavior, he or she will not easily depart from it. I'm not saying that children don't change. One morning Timmy *demands* sugar and cinnamon on his toast; the next morning he *insists* on jelly; the next morning he *absolutely* will have no toast at all. Erratic behavior? Only to his mother. For Timmy, it is three mornings in a row of exercising a budding proclivity for *being in charge*.

Unfortunately, parents not only love predictability, they love to decide *what* will be predictable. So Timmy's mother may "decide" for Timmy what he will and won't eat, touching off a battle of the wills with her son. She can try a variety of ways to "break him" of his "erratic behavior," from the creative to the manipulative to the abusive. She may temporarily prevail. But her "victory" will be short-lived. At the earliest opportunity, Timmy will quickly revert to pattern. For example, after breakfast, his mother will suggest, "Timmy, get dressed," and pull out his blue shorts. But Timmy will grab his red shorts instead, and defiantly insist, "No, Mommy, *these!*" Timmy is not trying to be difficult; he is trying to be who he was made to be. Isn't giftedness wonderful!

OUR DESIGN IS ENDURING

One final piece of evidence that we are born with our patterns is their enduring nature. I'll say more about this in a moment. Of all the tens of thousands of motivated abilities patterns (MAPs) I and my colleagues have assessed, not a single one has shown evidence of essential change during a lifetime. This, despite sometimes drastic changes in people's experiences, circumstances, education, values, philosophy, or beliefs.

Circumstances may change, so that an individual is better able to express his or her pattern, but *the elements of giftedness remain stable*. This remarkable resiliency makes it hard to believe that either environment or life circumstances have any causative effect on giftedness. It seems as permanent as our facial appearance or the sound of our voice. It appears early. It remains stable throughout life. It operates naturally, spontaneously, and almost unconsciously. Our days do have an inherent destiny to them—a destiny that is ours from the womb.

> **Despite sometimes drastic changes in people's experiences, circumstances, education, values, philosophy, or beliefs, *the elements of giftedness remain stable*.**

The pattern holds up and hangs on no matter what. Despite society's strident and never-ceasing attempts to influence, shape, coax, coerce, manipulate, cajole, trick, deceive, threaten, punish, or even *pay* people to change—*they don't!* At least not in terms of their motivational makeup. Even the best efforts of mother and father, ers, spouses, peer groups, teachers, scoutmasters, Sunday school teachers, coaches, lovers, army drill sergeants, employers, judges, pastors, and motivational speakers are to no avail. People keep living out their patterns! *No one* appears to have any impact on the fundamental shape and nature of a person's pattern.

Please do not misunderstand: I'm not saying that these influencers have no affect on a person. They obviously do. They can profoundly affect the direction of one's life, the quality of it, the habits, excesses, style, and values one embraces or leaves, and probably the level and intensity of one's achievement. But what they do not change is the *design of the person, his or her giftedness.*

The little girl who is absorbed in repairing a robin's wing at age six can still be found forty years later preoccupied by giving intravenous injections to her diabetic husband. The kid who enjoys hawking magazines door-to-door when he is seven will still enjoy winning national sales honors when he is thirty-seven. The toddler who is a natural performer at age three will gladly show you a scrapbook of his publicity photos at age sixty-three.

Based on nearly forty years of achievement data, I have concluded that the MAP is fixed, apparently for life. Elements of the MAP emerge in rudimentary form in early childhood, and by the mid-teens all of the important particulars are fleshed out.

OUR DESIGN REMAINS STABLE YET CONTINUES TO DEVELOP

From then on, the motivation plays itself out again and again—*over a lifetime*. The builder builds. The entrepreneur starts new enterprises. The comprehender keeps learning. The refiner keeps improving.

All that really changes is the maturity of the functioning as the person develops through more complex and demanding achievement experiences. But the essential nature of the giftedness remains constant: it keeps seeking the same basic payoff; it keeps relating to others in the same idiosyncratic way; it keeps working with the same basic subjects, using tried-and-true abilities; it keeps seeking the same conducive circumstances. A person does not do this because he or she is boring or unimaginative or lazy or resistant to growth, *but for the same reason that hawks keep flying and whales keep spouting and beavers keep damming up streams. It is their nature. They know no other.*

"But Art," someone may be saying, "I've changed dramatically over the years. I mean, when I was in high school, I loved gymnastics and marching in the band. But I haven't done a cartwheel or picked up my instrument in thirty years. So how can you say people keep doing the same basic things over and over?"

The answer is that your love of gymnastics and marching in the band is now expressed elsewhere. One would have to look at your pattern to say exactly where. But suppose that you are fundamentally motivated to do things exactly right. "Rightness" is what you are all about. In that case, the data might show that your performance on the gym floor and in the band was a quest to perform a flip at a "10" level, or to stay in perfect formation. In later years, the same motivation might have been expressed through your amazing attention to detail in your job as a software programmer, in the neat, trim lawn in front of your house, and in your urgency to attend a marriage seminar with your spouse in order to learn the "best" ways to build a relationship. The expressions change, but your motivation toward "rightness" remains the same.

> **People express their giftedness for the same reason that hawks keep flying and whales keep spouting and beavers keep damming up streams. It is their nature. They know no other.**

So it is with every pattern. Apparent departures from the pattern are merely surface changes. If you perceive a discrepancy, it is not because you have actually changed, but because you are not aware of the common denominator in your pattern. The surface of the sea changes constantly, but the nature of the ocean is a constant. So with giftedness. It remains stable throughout one's life.

There is a simple test of whether or not this is true: ask someone to describe his achievement history, then go back to him several years later and ask him to describe it again. I have found that in the second assessment, people invariably describe many of the same achievements they detailed in the first, *often using the exact same words!* Of course, they often recall some achievements in the second go-around that they left out in the first, and they may add a few recent achievements. But an examination of these new memories shows that the *pattern is still the same!*

To close this part on the stability and yet growing complexity of a MAP, reread the childhood achievement story of the "horse whisperer" on pages 42–43. Now, read the adult achievement of the same person, twenty-five years later, as a clinical psychologist. See how many consistencies you can pick up.

I had a female patient who was very seriously disturbed. Talked only in rhyme. The traditional therapeutic approach—individual or group therapy—tell me about what your problem is. This lady responds in a rhyme that seems meaningless, and ticks off everybody in group therapy. So I butted my head up against the wall for a while.

One day she was in the day room—kitchen area—doing her rhyming. So I listened to her rhyme for a little bit. I rhymed back. I made a rhyme and talked back to her. She rhymed back to me. Her rhyme started to make sense.

You've got to get to where the wire is exposed. All of a sudden I started being able to understand the messages that were in her rhymes. Really, what her rhymes were about was that she was feeling tremendous pain and fear of her children, being abandoned ... so I rhymed back in a way that would respond to that. Encouraged her to do more. That was a real breakthrough. After a while she felt comfortable enough that she didn't need to rhyme. She could sit down and talk about it. The fear of what she was facing—she was defending against that by not wanting/dealing with it. The rhyme was a way of separating. That breakthrough allowed her to trust that somebody wouldn't think she was a terrible person.

Satisfying: the discovery that I found another alternative—another way to get there. I'm a pragmatist—trying different options to reach somebody.

Another lady on the ward kept stealing all the linen from everybody's room, the linen closet, everywhere. She'd take it in her room and defend it. Tug of war. Staff would try and take the linen back and people would complain because they didn't have any sheets. I watched that for a bit and then did a 180—OK, from now on, we encourage her to have all the linens she wants. In fact, we are going to deliver linen. She won't have to steal it—had the staff bring in her linen. We put it on her bed, dresser, floor, until there was no room to live in the room because there was so much linen. I said, pay attention. The first time she throws linen out, don't bring her anymore.

The room was unlivable. She started throwing linens out. The staff stopped bringing her linens. She cut it out. When she saw that she could get what she wanted—in fact, more—it was the end of her behavior.

Satisfying: I worked with a lot of hard cases and I reached some. The satisfying moments were when I recognized that I got through and they recognized that they were making some progress.

OUR DESIGN IS IRREPRESSIBLE

Have you ever tried to keep a half-dozen ping pong balls under water? You keep pushing them down and pushing them down, but inevitably they slip away and resurface. This is a good analogy for the idea that giftedness is *irrepressible*. No one can keep giftedness from bobbing up and expressing itself in an individual's life. It will always surface. The truth about a person will out, as they say.

Let me give you several examples of the irrepressibility of our design. They are from real people and their real lives, like you and your life.

The first case was a guy from upstate New York by the name of Hal, who evaluated things by trial-and-error experimentation, as opposed to analyzing, comparing to a standard, or assessing the value of a proposed action. Hal had taken a number of flying lessons, gotten a license, and was soloing when he encountered severe winter weather conditions that closed down the ceiling and visibility to a few hundred feet. With plenty of gas left in the tank, what do you think his MAP would "compel" him to do? Right. He intentionally force-landed his small plane (fortunately in the trees on top of a hill) because trial-and-error experimentation was how he approached new situations. Having landed, he removed his seat and got down from the tree. And using his seat as a sled, he slid down to the bottom of the rather high hill and flagged a ride home. I kid you not.

Gasp at five-year-old Dianne, whose motivational payoff was to beat the system, who took money from her mother's purse, ran down to the local convenience store, and returned with a loaf of Wonder Bread, just as her mother was taking several loaves of freshly baked bread out of the oven.

Or check out Molly, motivated to build relationships, whose new apartment is filled with unpacked boxes six months after a move because she has spent her available time making friends in the new neighborhood.

Contrast Molly with Glen, motivated to organize things by classifying and categorizing them, whose apartment was in shipshape, perfect condition one week after his move—but whose neighbors still haven't met him one year later (no "people" in his motivating subject matter).

Your behavior, judged a bit odd in spots by those who know you, is probably due to some part of your pattern. Similarly, those close to you who do things that seem a bit bizarre or extreme to you, are likely acting out *their* MAPs.

OUR DESIGN EXPLAINS WHAT WE *DON'T* DO

Because you do or try to do what you are competent and motivated to do, your MAP also explains why you do not (from the perspective of a boss, spouse, friend, child, parent) do what it would be nice for you to do, such as any of the following.

Make a Decision

1. *Situation:* Your living room and your family need a new couch.

- *Problem:* You can't decide between the green, the mauve, and the charcoal one.
- *Reason:* You don't have color sense, or anything else visual (texture, forms, etc.), in your MAP.

2. *Situation:* You have been invited to open a new office a thousand miles from home to test-market a radically different product line.

- *Problem:* The boss wants a decision by Friday, and you are sweating because you don't know what to do, and your future may be at stake.
- *Reason:* You are not motivated to take risks or to pioneer anything; you are the fourth generation to live in the Boston area and you are highly relational; you make decisions by "doing the numbers," and here you can't quantify anything.

3. *Situation:* You are in a Thai restaurant (for the first time) with a first-time customer you want to impress.

- *Problem:* You are uncertain about what to order.
- *Reason:* You are motivated to evaluate by comparing what is in front of you to a standard of previous experiences, plus you are motivated to cause a response (positive).

Plan to Meet Future Needs

1. *Situation:* Four dinner guests are due in three hours and you don't have enough food of one kind to feed six people.

- *Problem:* They are relatives from your husband's competitive, judging family, and he is going nuts over the situation.
- *Reason:* You have no—none—planning marbles in your MAP or, for that matter, any interest in food or serving. Besides you've been working on a report for your boss and you thought that you had some chickens in the freezer. And after all, you are motivated to overcome impossible situations. Surprise!

2. *Situation:* You were scheduled two months ago to give a presentation to the brass. You come to the meeting needing to make several new visuals and copies of your agenda. Plus the bulb in the overhead projector burned out two days ago.

- *Problem:* You are being considered for a position in long-range planning and your potential future boss appears impatient.
- *Reason:* Your MAP includes planning by setting goals and big-picture conceptualizing, but no rehearsing and no details.

Keep Promises

1. *Situation:* You promised to get involved (time, talent, money) in the Southport project once it got off the ground.

- *Problem:* The project got off the ground and is waiting for your support, but you have in the meantime thrown your energy into the Northport project.
- *Reason:* You are motivated to make money and exploit potential, and as things shook down, the Northport project had much greater potential for a dollar return than the Southport project.

2. *Situation:* You promised your son you would attend as many of his soccer games as you could.

- *Problem:* The season is half over and you haven't gone to one yet.
- *Reason:* You are motivated to have an impact on your client's quality practices, and you are in the middle of a major effort generating a substantial change in level of quality and customer satisfaction.

Get the Job Done

1. *Situation:* Harry reports to you and has a performance record of few hits and many, many errors. He needs to be confronted and terminated.

- *Problem:* Harry's wife has been ill, and Harry has been moonlighting, so you have failed to lean on him.
- *Reason:* You are not motivated by results, or by managing, or by solving problems. Furthermore, you *are* motivated to facilitate and empower others.

2. *Situation:* The drawings are due by Monday and a pilot model is to be built based on these drawings by the end of this month.

- *Problem:* The drawings won't be ready for two to three weeks.
- *Reason:* Your MAP is heavily influenced by your innovative activities and your desire to develop an object beyond the normal expectations for it.

Be Intimate and Relational

1. *Situation:* You and your spouse are on a long walk in the woods and remote fields of grass and he/she wants to make some "wild splendor."

- *Problem:* You are not prepared for the same and resist his/her spontaneity.
- *Reason:* You are motivated to follow methods and procedures, want time to get ready for any activity, and are motivationally concerned about appearances and image.

2. *Situation:* Your ten-year-old daughter asks you about sex and drugs.

- *Problem:* You are unable to be straightforward and open, so you lapse into abstract generalities.
- *Reason:* You are not relational, and when you communicate you need to be extremely well versed and knowledgeable or you are not comfortable. Communication is not interactive with you but explanatory.

Please note:

"My MAP made me do it" is not a valid excuse!

Make your own list. What you do well and what you don't do, or don't do well, is traceable to your MAP. Please don't get the wrong idea—"My

MAP made me do it" is not a valid excuse! It merely explains why some things are more difficult for some people to do than for others.

OUR DESIGN ACTIVELY SEEKS EXPRESSION

I find it fascinating—and it is a further clue that the MAP is irrepressible—that people oftentimes instinctively and actively *seek out* whatever it is that gets their motivational juices going. It's as if they have a homing device within them that locks onto the "right" situations—right, that is, for their particular bent.

I remember Dr. Neullo, a Ph.D. chemist working for a large chemical company in the Midwest, who was motivated to meet requirements. As a basic researcher he was not very fruitful, because what he needed was the opposite of what the work needed—which was someone who could explore scientific "hunches" with a large and likely payoff. Instead, he remembered doing a lot of crossword puzzles and taking additional courses at the local community college—both of which had requirements for him to meet.

> **There are literally millions upon millions of us who use only some of our giftedness on the job and then seek other outlets for our talents.**

For each of us, motivation is sensitive to the climate around us. Unfortunately, the climate may be arid or even hostile to our giftedness. As a result, many of us do the best we can "under the circumstances." Like plants in the desert, we wait for that rare thundershower that waters our natural inclinations. Then we burst into bloom—albeit briefly.

I shudder to think how many people are toughing it out in occupations that actually prevent them from using their patterns. Fortunately, many of these folks have other options. For example, the CEO of a small electronics company was motivated to build and develop, but his company was in a maintenance mode, nursing a static operation, waiting for an upturn in their market.

This went on for ten years. During that time, he added a recreation room to his house, then a patio, then a whole new extension. In addition, he built a cabin in the mountains, helped get a scout troop going, and worked with a community group to put a new wing on the local hospital.

There are literally millions upon millions of us who use only some of our giftedness on the job and then seek other outlets for our talents. It is one reason why America's largest "employer" is not industry or even the government, but the nonprofit sector, where fully one half of all American adults spend at least three hours a week serving as volunteers.[2] For many, serving food in a soup kitchen, mentoring a child in an inner-city school, writing articles for a monthly newsletter, or chairing a membership committee are the only outlets they have to express their motivation. Denied that opportunity where they work, they are more than happy to pursue it in a volunteer setting.

OUR DESIGN SHAPES OUR PERCEPTIONS

We see life in terms of what has meaning for us, that is, in terms of whatever has significance in light of our motivated abilities, motivated subject matter, motivating circumstances, operating relationships, and especially our motivational payoff. *We actually interpret reality in a way that suits our motivational makeup.*

Illustrations of this law abound. Consider a banquet that brings together a vast diversity of individuals. The master of ceremonies, who happens to be driven to gain recognition, sees an audience. The speaker, who is a politician compelled to be in charge, sees votes. The guest soloist, who is exercised to impress others, sees a roomful of critics. The professor at Table 29, who is all about shaping students, sees a potential pupil in the fellow seated next to him and begins to bend his ear. The social butterfly, who has to be at the center of the action, sees a room of dignitaries to glad-hand and remind that she was the one who funded the event. The event planner, meanwhile, who is concerned about making everything work just right, sees a room full of problems waiting to happen.

> **We see life in terms of what has meaning for us, that is, we actually interpret reality in a way that suits our motivational makeup.**

Perception and motivation go hand in hand. This is crucial to understand in the workplace. An employer or supervisor may define a task in terms of a job description and a set of performance expectations. But the

---

2. Peter F. Drucker, *Managing the Nonprofit Organization* (New York: HarperCollins, 1990), xiii.

employee will look at the job through the lens of his MAP, and perform according to pattern. If he is motivated to innovate, he will try to innovate; if to control, he will set up controls; if to overcome, he will find something to overcome; if to build relationships, he will seek them out; if to pioneer, he will expand the boundaries; if to perfect, he will look for the rough edges.

Never mind that an "objective" assessment of the job might call for a different approach. The worker will try to do it "his way"—the way in which he naturally perceives the task. He will meet the requirements of a job description only insofar as they match his pattern. That is why it is so important that both employer and employee understand the MAP of the employee, as well as the nature of the position.

Take José, for instance. He is hired with the famous line, "We're going to make a salesman out of you." By "salesman" José's employer means someone who overwhelms the customer with a "winning" personality and a razzle-dazzle presentation. But that's not José's motivational pattern. He's more low-key.

For a while José does his best to master his boss's "patented sales system." He dutifully attends the company's training classes. He goes through the motions of role play. He learns a few corny jokes the trainer says are "guaranteed" to break the ice. He even tries to mimic the voice and style of the trainer.

And just as a monkey can be dressed up to look like a human, so José makes a decent imitation of a "salesman" (as defined by the company). But ultimately, that's not José. José has ability to influence, but it's through the plodding, methodical persuasion of piling up technical facts. He doesn't try to overwhelm people; he coaxes them to his point of view. His style is to sit down with a customer and hold a conversation about the customer's needs and how his product can meet those needs.

We could debate whether that style is suitable for the company's product and its market. The point is that José is going to be José, no matter what. His pattern will express itself regardless of the company's demands. Any attempt to conform José to the company's image of a salesman is like a man with a 38-inch waist trying to squeeze into a size 32 pair of slacks. The slacks obviously don't fit, but if he's forced to wear them, he'll suck in his gut and stretch and pull until somehow he's got them on. But it won't last. Sooner or later, the buttons will pop and the seams will rip out, and everyone will see that it was a poor fit to begin with.

Likewise, as long as José is in that sales job, he will stretch and twist and make alterations in a valiant effort to fit it to his pattern. He may or may not succeed. Regardless, he himself will not change.

Some may find this behavior selfish or manipulative. It can be that. But the larger lesson is that people redefine their tasks not because they are rebellious or stubborn or self-willed, but because they cannot do the task well any other way. They are driven to express their giftedness, striving to do the thing to which they were born. Circumstances can encourage that or impede it, but they cannot stop it.

That is why it is so important to match people with situations that best suit them (something José's employer would have been wise to do). Otherwise they will resist demands that conflict with their pattern. They will distort tasks and expectations to make them conform to their agenda. They are liable to flare up in anger if unduly frustrated. They will slump into despondency if, over time, they are prevented from exercising their motivational bent. And when a given task or role has been played out and its motivational value exhausted, they will seek out a new direction and focus where they can once again seek their motivational payoff.

OUR DESIGN COLORS OUR EMOTIONAL RESPONSES

A great deal of psychotherapy today appears to be rooted in the belief that human behavior is based on emotion. As a result, treatment tends to concentrate on helping people come to terms with their feelings—to know what they feel and, on the basis of some personality theory, where those feelings are coming from.

Emotional reactions are often traceable to a person's MAP. Not that the MAP is concerned with psychological causation. The MAP doesn't consider whether your consuming interest in butterflies owes to some formative experience in your youth. What is significant, from the standpoint of human design, is that color and shapes and delicacy have been part of a lifelong pattern of motivated achievement—a pattern that consistently brings you enjoyment.

Joy

Joy is one of the most striking emotional tie-ins of the MAP. Joy and a sense of meaningfulness are the telltale signs of gifted activity. Indeed, without in any way discounting the intense emotional pain that wracks so many people, I feel certain that many of their troubles would lighten if their giftedness were more engaged. I have seen too many cases of people coming alive to their patterns to believe otherwise.

Conversely, I have seen too many cases where the *failure* to follow a pattern has produced what might be called "negative" emotions. For example, put someone in a situation that will test areas falling outside his strengths—such as being forced to give a "down and dirty" thumbnail report when he is motivated to do everything comprehensively. Suddenly he is sweating bullets of anxiety, wondering how he's going to fit everything in.

Anger

Another negative reaction tied to the MAP is the anger and even outright belligerence that people display when the remarks or actions of others appear to attack their motivational treasures. For instance, the manager who is passionately possessive of a project will dig in for a fight when the company shows signs that it may cancel or diminish "his" project. Or you convince the other team members to back your idea, and Charlotte chills the idea by raising the issue of how busy we already are, or who's going to pay for it. Or you are producing a piece of work of (to your eyes) ineffable beauty and the foreman tells you to hurry up and get it done by the close of the shift.

Depression

Motivational factors can also play a part in depression, which is a growing problem in our society. There seems to be a chemical basis for some depression. But an often overlooked source is any combination of circumstances, especially at home and at work, that makes motivated activity impossible.

For example, here is a woman working for a government agency. Her boss, who is new to the position, is a hands-on, look-over-the-shoulder sort of micromanager. He gives her the task of revising an old manual, a job that ends up requiring two months of her time—largely because he keeps butting in. This situation goes directly against her MAP. She requires a collaborative style of management that provides support only when it is asked for. And the kind of meticulous detail required to rewrite this particular manual is not found in her pattern.

Meanwhile at home, circumstances are just as odious. The woman's husband is in graduate school, so he has precious little time to listen—

something her pattern desperately needs. And not only is she the main breadwinner, she is also the main parent for a child who needs a lot of help with homework—a responsibility that, again, demands detailed attention from Mother, which, of course, she is not gifted to give. Aaarrgh!

Is anyone surprised that in short order this woman feels seriously depressed? It's depressing just to read about the weight she is carrying! But the source of her funk is that *she is trying to carry a load for which she was not designed*. Meanwhile, nothing in her world seems to be making use of that for which she was designed.

Frustration

For her—for all of us—frustration is perhaps the most common experience when we can't accomplish what is motivationally significant. If joy is the low hum of fully engaged energy and passion, frustration is the blue smoke warning that our motivational engine is melting down.

The classic illustration of this is the boss who won't listen to our ideas. Few things are as demotivating as an unresponsive boss (or, if one is a child, an unresponsive parent). Why? Because quite apart from the merit of the idea itself, the fact that we present the idea in the first place and the way in which we present it speak volumes about how we are motivated. In effect, we are saying, "This is what turns me on. This is how you can get my best effort." For someone to ignore us at that moment is like draining oil out of our crankcase. Pretty soon, our gears are grinding and our valves are smoking with white-hot friction.

OUR DESIGN AFFECTS OUR SOCIAL BEHAVIOR

By now you have probably guessed that just as giftedness heavily affects what goes on inside people, it affects what goes on between them as well. In communication, for example, the person motivated to excel will be found steering conversations toward a subject or issue where he or she can exercise preeminence. The person motivated to make an impact on others will hold them spellbound by reliving the drama of his recent trip to a war-torn city. The person motivated to meet needs will adroitly coax another individual to reveal some problem that he is currently facing, and then proceed to offer counsel. The person motivated to prevail will instinctively seize on the soft places in another's position.

One of the most helpful benefits of knowing one's MAP is the insight and perspective it lends to conflict. All of us face conflicts. Most of them can be explained and often resolved by *recognizing that motivation, rather than emotion or character, may be driving the situation*.

> **Conflicts can be explained and often resolved by recognizing that motivation, rather than emotion or character, may be driving the situation.**

For example, an individualist wife marries a team-member husband. Is it any surprise that his constant appeals to "help me with this" drive her up the wall? Or there's the young employee who wants a supportive boss who gives clear and constant directions. Could this have something to do with the rage he feels toward his supervisor, who hands out instructions in the morning and then closes his door because he is not motivated to work with people?

Conflicts still have to be worked out. But knowing the motivational roots of conflict can help immensely. If I know what matters to you, I can arrange things so that you achieve some, perhaps even all, of what you are seeking, and vice versa. In fact, together we may be able to turn a conflict into a coordinated, complementary effort that uses the best of what we both have to offer.

OUR DESIGN LIMITS THE EFFECTIVENESS OF EXTERNAL MOTIVATORS

Suppose I had the power to double your salary. Would that double your productivity? Would it double your satisfaction with your work? It might make you very happy for at least a week or two. But an increase in pay does not fundamentally change a person's productivity or attitude toward work. Not unless one's giftedness happens to involve money, as such.

In a way, that's too bad. If all it took to raise productivity and employee morale were a hefty pay increase, I can assure you, employers would have handed out the checks long ago. But years of research have shown that money alone is not enough to motivate most people. Most people are looking for payoffs other than financial rewards.

The same is true of other external motivators. In nearly forty years of patterning people, I and my associates have never seen a case where some influence from *outside* a person, strictly speaking, suddenly brought new motivation. We have heard about strict fathers, overbearing mothers, nurturing grandparents, teachers working their magic, enlightening mentors, peer pressure, inspiring friends, devoted lovers, peak experiences, sensitizing exercises, summer camp, atrocities of war, bonuses, penalties, deprivation, fear, teamwork, conflict, failure, and newfound faith. Factors like these have been profoundly meaningful in people's lives, but in the end, nothing that happens *to* a person seems to create new motivations *within* the person.

Money alone is not enough to motivate most people; most people are looking for payoffs other than financial rewards.

In fact, there is growing evidence that external "motivators" actually diminish the performance one seeks. Creativity is a case in point: if you try to motivate my creativity by promising me a bonus, I'll give you less than if you would simply have let me alone to create.[3]

OUR DESIGN RESPONDS TO OUR ENVIRONMENT

External factors may not play a *causative* role in a person's design, yet they often play a critical role. We could say that giftedness seizes opportunity. One's pattern is always eager to express itself, indeed, always does express itself in some manner.

Consider learning, for example. Everyone learns at some level, but for some people, "learning" is a *motivated ability*—a key strength they naturally possess and are motivated to use. However, some who have that ability require some sort of "teacher" to stimulate their learning. Without a teacher, they are unmotivated. Thus, an external factor—a teacher—becomes the key to their functioning. The (gifted) teacher unlocks the door of opportunity, and the (gifted) learner walks through it.

But note: different learners make use of the teacher according to their different patterns of giftedness. One individual learns as a result of gaining a response from the teacher. Another learns because she meets the teacher's expressed expectations. Another learns as a function of building a relationship with the teacher. Another figures out what the teacher is "about" and then develops a strategy to deal with this authority figure. The different ways in which motivated learners make use of the teacher seem endless.

---

3. See Alfie Kohn, *Punished by Rewards* (New York: Houghton-Mifflin, 1993).

It helps, of course, if the teacher is gifted at teaching—meaning that she has natural, motivated ability to cause learning to take place. If she does, she is quite likely to be as highly motivated by the learners in her class (at least the ones who need a teacher) as they are motivated by her. They will trigger her instinctive powers of teaching, just as she triggers their instinctive bent toward learning. It's a beautiful dance to watch!

Yet having said that, I caution anyone against the temptation to generalize, as so many do, by saying, "You see, the key to learning is a good teacher." That is clearly true for some—but not for all. There are many ways in which people are motivated to learn, and not all of them require a teacher. For example, there are those who learn by doing (which our studies suggest is the dominant way people learn), those who learn on their own, those who learn by reading and reflection, those who must explore or observe.

For these learners, a teacher is less a stimulus or enabling mechanism than she is a resource to be used on an "as-needed" basis. Their motivated learning seizes on other factors in the environment, with or without the presence of a gifted teacher.

What is true of learning is true of many other motivated behaviors—creating, problem solving, decision making, developing, and more. Oftentimes the reason someone fails to exercise one of these talents is not because of lack of ability but of opportunity. The environment, so critical to his behavior, is barren relative to his motivational needs.

But if the conditions ever become ripe, watch out! The exercise of motivated behavior can be spectacular. For instance, one person will remain inert, unmotivated to invest energy until suddenly confronted by a problem or need—a crisis in the office, an accident in the home, a neighbor in trouble, a desperate plea from a community leader. The sudden demand for help can act like a catalyst in a chemical reaction. All the ingredients are present. It just takes the right agent—the introduction of a problem or need—to precipitate the person's response.

But in addition to triggering motivated behavior, environmental factors often *sustain* it as well. Consider Amanda, a civil servant who is motivated to shape situations and make an impact. For a number of years, City Hall is controlled by a series of mayors who are generally similar in focus and direction. As a result, Amanda is able to get her policies pushed through, and she enjoys seeing the results in the life of her community.

But then a radically different administration is voted in. Suddenly, Amanda finds herself losing clout. Her recommendations are questioned, delayed, underfunded, sometimes ignored. Her phone calls often go unreturned.

Programs that she worked hard to implement are canceled. Slowly but surely, her motivation withers as she senses that she is not making any difference. Amanda begins to look for a job in another city.

The question of environment as a stimulus to motivation is particularly relevant to organizations. Industry has long sought the ideal way to deploy its human resources in order to "get the most and the best from its people." It has tried quality circles, self-directed teams, skunk works, entrepreneuring, decentralized management, "upside-down" organizations, and many other approaches. None has been the panacea it was billed to be. Some workers have responded well to these supposedly "state-of-the-art" organizational schemes; many have not.

> There are no generalizations that can be made about "how people work best"—except, perhaps, that people work best when a company organizes them in light of their motivational patterns.

By now, you can see why. Every worker requires different environmental factors to perform well. So there is no single, one-size-fits-all organizational model. There are no generalizations that can be made about "how people work best"—except, perhaps, that people work best when a company organizes them in light of their motivational patterns.

Some workers require triggering circumstances, others don't. Some need structure, others don't. Some have a need for visibility, others don't. Some have to have measurable results, others don't. Some seek out a certain kind of organization, others don't.

Does it sound like a lot of work for management to sort out who needs what? It can be. It will initially cost time, effort, and money. But the payback in money and satisfaction can be awesome. And it is the way forward. Nothing else really works.

Nevertheless, many industrial leaders are convinced that they can somehow "make" or "get" people to do what they want them to do. They search (in vain) for a set of governing principles by which to establish just the right conditions for productive, profitable labor. Workers have an uncanny ability to resist all such principles—not because they are by nature obstinate, lazy, or selfish, but because their innate giftedness instinctively seeks the environment for which it is best suited. Wouldn't it make sense, then, to cooperate with nature, rather than contradict it?

As a society we are slowly learning how to use the earth, its soil-water-flora-fauna, and the atmosphere that surrounds it, without destroying them. When will we get around to using our human resources in a way that doesn't damage them?

Chapter Six

Trading Your Birthright for a Myth

It is difficult to think of a cultural bondage more insidious, more costly, and more destructive of human life and values than the mismatch between people and the jobs they occupy. Studies reporting on the mismatch between employee strengths and job requirements vary—but only in shades of darkness:

- Only thirteen percent of workers studied find their work truly meaningful.[1]
- Only twenty percent of 350,000 employees in 7,000 corporations who were studied over a sixteen-year period were in jobs that made use of their talents.[2]
- Fully fifty percent of the managers hired in a preceding three-year period "had not worked out," according to a survey of fifty-five companies.[3]
- Only one out of every three managers was well-suited to his position, according to assessments done by us over a period of almost four decades.
- To the extent organizations or individuals are infected by job mismatch, they are imitative, lifeless, stressed, and inevitably mediocre in output.
- Job mismatch reveals itself in familiar attitudes: petulance, sullenness, unresponsiveness, lack of alertness or initiative, unthinking indifference.

1. Daniel Yankelovich, "Putting Work Ethic to Work," *Public Agenda Foundation*, 1983.
2. Herbert M. Greenberg, *Report for the Marketing Survey and Research Corporation*, Princeton, New Jersey, 1976.
3. Richard Sampson, *Managing the Managers* (New York: McGraw Hill, 1985), 158.

Regardless of level or function, when work does not engage employee strengths, the employer reaps a litany of problems: productivity problems, emotional problems, morale problems, loyalty problems, conflict problems, troublemaker problems.

THE HIGH COST OF IGNORING HUMAN DESIGN

The problems accompanying job misfit betray a storm going on inside the person. Evidence is growing that job misfit (whether it involves underutilization or an inappropriate use of giftedness) and the stresses it creates contribute directly to heart and other circulatory ailments, marital breakdown, alcoholism, drug addition, and other mental and emotional disorders, premature death, or crippling disability.

> To the extent that organizations or individuals are infected by job mismatch, they are imitative, lifeless, stressed, and inevitably mediocre in output.

Sooner or later the destructive stress that accompanies mismatch takes its deadly toll on physical, emotional, and spiritual health. A well-documented longitudinal study of causes of circulatory disorders found that only twenty-five percent were due to genetic or dietary factors, personal habits, and excesses. *Seventy-five percent were due to what the investigators characterized as absence of job satisfaction.*[4]

Look at those percentages and consider the attention and money and worry devoted to cholesterol levels, exercise, and stress-reduction techniques. Then think of the minimal concern with and investment in job fit.

Whatever the numbers, organizations lose twice. Labor costs are unnecessarily inflated because executives, managers, supervisors, and workers who do not fit their jobs are less productive. And the constant stress that is a direct and proximate result of job misfit[5] results in mind-boggling—and unnecessary—costs.[6]

---

[4] *Work in America—Report of a Special Task Force to the Secretary of Health, Education & Welfare* (MIT Press, 1971), 79.

[5] "Work Environment, Type A Behavior and Coronary Heart Disease Risk Factors," *Journal of Occupational Medicine*, vol. 23, no. 8 (August, 1981).

[6] E. M. Gherman, M.D., *Stress and the Bottom Line*, (ANACOM, 1981), 20–21.

Here are the costs *for a single year:*

- Premature deaths: $19,400,000,000
- Disability payments and medical bills: $26,000,000,000
- Recruiting replacements for those felled by heart disease: $700,000,000
- Heart disease and resultant loss of work days: $132,000,000
- Cost to American industry of alcoholism-caused absenteeism and medical programs: $16,000,000,000
- Percentage of employee emotional problems that are stress-related: 80
- For every death caused by accidents in the workplace, the number of workers who die from cardiovascular disease: 50

The National Science Foundation reported *$100 billion in stress-related costs for a single year*. Approximately seventy-five to eighty-five percent of all industrial accidents are caused by an inability to cope with stress, and in a recent year such accidents alone cost U.S. companies thirty-two billion dollars.[7]

Spending a great deal of money, year after year, to relieve the *symptoms* of stress without resolving its *cause*—job mismatch—clearly does not make sense. What produces this apparent irrationality is, on the one hand, a fundamental misunderstanding of what causes job mismatch and, on the other hand, reliance on a "solution" that ignores the real cause.

> Spending a great deal of money, year after year, to relieve the symptoms of stress without resolving its cause—job mismatch—clearly does not make sense.

THE MYTH OF "BECOMING"

The "solution" is as American as apple pie and the fourth of July. It is the idea, deeply ingrained in the American psyche, that *one can become and do whatever one wants.*

This is without doubt one of the greatest lies ever promoted—this fantasy that one can become and do whatever one wants. "Whatever the mind can conceive, the will can achieve" is how the Myth is often framed.

---

7. Reported in M. T. Matteson, J. M. Ivancevich, *Controlling Work Stress* (Jossey-Bass, 1987).

This widespread belief in unlimited options for personal destiny has to be among the chief deceptions and destroyers of our age.

The truth is, you have exactly one MAP to guide you in life to be the person you were born to be. Whatever your pattern of giftedness is, it defines your options. You cannot operate outside that pattern in any sustained, productive way and experience a sense of satisfaction and meaning from your effort.

> One of the greatest lies ever promoted is without doubt the fantasy that one can become and do whatever one wants.

The tragedy of our age is that we give in to the Myth of "Becoming." Its siren song reaches out to a doleful worker grinding away at his wearisome task or to an ambitious one anxious to get ahead, and says, "Hey, you can become something else, something better!" It's the same song sung to young people: "You can become anything you want!"

The pitch is almost irresistible. In the first place, it is only human to long for something better. And then to think that one has a "right" to this better way of living—why, that's downright American! It's what the country was founded for.

Challenging that thinking is like spitting into the wind, because our culture has bought wholesale into the Myth of "Becoming." It goes back to the frontier days and is passed on by all the important people who influence our lives, from parents and teachers and preachers to employers and scoutmasters. With advocates like these, it's no wonder people everywhere are kneeling down at the altar of "becoming." It's the religion they grew up with. It's why we rarely meet someone who has made a serious study of who they already are.

> "Becoming" is based on someone else's dream and vision, not yours.

But the idea that we can become whatever we want is a lie at its core. It is based on the misconception that people are putty and can be shaped and reshaped to conform to their own wishes, to what employers need, and to what society values. In this model, which is assumed by the world of work and supported by our educational systems, human beings are seen as commodities and interchangeable parts who can be taught to do what is needed and taught to become what is valued.

"Becoming" is based on someone else's dream and vision, not yours:

- "become" the supervisor your company wants;
- "become" the lawyer that your father thought you should be;
- "become" the salesperson as good as your aunt;
- "become" the rabbi your synagogue expects you to be;
- "become" the mother your mother-in-law expects you to be.

No matter whose dream you pursue, there's no escaping the grim truth that "becoming" is all about expectations. It says that you are *not* adequate as you are, but with enough effort you can (maybe) "become" adequate in time. Anyone who believes that will quickly find himself weighed down with expectations. He will always be climbing a mountain, always be "in process," but never be quite "there." What a wretched way to live! This is why I call the Myth of Becoming an evil deception. Under the guise of liberating people, it enslaves them. It puts them under a yoke—or more accurately, under one yoke after another.

One day, out of annoyance at the shell games practiced by those in the "people-changing" business, I prepared a list of twelve principles that are presented as guides for unsuccessful, unhappy people who are trying to become successful and happy. I call it the Dirty Dozen.

> "Becoming" is about expectations. It says that you are *not* adequate as you are, but with enough effort you can (maybe) "become" adequate in time.

1. Ignore signals indicating destructive stress (no pain/no gain principle).
2. Try to become what success requires (Horatio Alger principle).
3. Work hard to improve your weaknesses (educator's principle).
4. Believe you can do anything (if-you-fail-try-again principle).
5. Build goals around careers that pay well (Uncle-Harry's-advice principle).
6. Pretend to go along (what-difference-does-it-make principle).
7. Accept any promotion in order to get ahead (onward-and-upward principle).
8. Cover up your deficits (the-road-most-traveled principle).
9. Believe you control your own destiny (new age principle).
10. Seek behavior you can't sustain (read-my-book principle).

11. Question your values (join-my-cult principle).
12. Develop what you haven't developed yet (you-are-becoming-who-you-will-be principle).

We *cannot* become anything we want. In truth, we cannot *become* anything other than who we already *are*, if we wish to be fulfilled in our lives and vocation. We must stop trying to "become" something else, or to "develop" or "cultivate" some trait that we fundamentally lack, and instead start *being* who we already are by identifying our giftedness and living it out. We could spend three lifetimes developing and exploring who we have been gifted to be.

Now I know, as a red-blooded American, telling anybody that something can't be done is an invitation. So if you haven't tried enough ways to remake yourself, have some more fun. But there will come a day when you will bend your neck and give up trying to "become," and will settle into that most exciting, exhilarating comfort zone called "you." Then you will really start to have fun and begin to make a real difference to others with your life.

WHY DOES THE MYTH PERSIST?

Why then does the Myth of Becoming persist, even though it is as mythical as George Washington's cherry tree and does not produce results? In behavioral psychology, behavior that is not rewarded will "extinguish"—it will disappear. You'd think that if a dog can figure out that a particular behavior is a waste of time because it doesn't produce any rewards, highly intelligent people would be able to figure out that trying to change people doesn't work.

There are several reasons:

1. The Myth of Becoming is democratic and egalitarian—everybody has the same chance of becoming whatever. It is part of the democratic ideal.

2. It has been drilled into us from childhood: "You can become president if you want to."

3. A lot of people have a vested interest in perpetuating the Myth. Not that they consciously perpetuate something they know to be untrue, but it is very useful and potentially very profitable.

- Parents can use it (unfortunately) to spur on their children to "success."
- Dissatisfied workers can use it to maintain a measure of hope that there may be a possibility of a better future.

- Managers can use it as a carrot: "Work hard and you can become as successful as I am."
- Corporations can use it to be more flexible (and less accountable) in the manipulation of human resources and corporate needs.
- Business consultants can use it to show a corporation how to improve the bottom line (by the time failure is evident, a new fad will have come along, and the consultants can start all over).
- Psychologists can benefit from it by treating the symptoms of the failure of the Myth: depression and so forth.
- Gurus can use it to become very wealthy indeed.

Okay, I am being a bit cynical, but you get the point.

4. Theories of personality, personality inventories, and IQ tests generally *fail to distinguish between motivated and unmotivated behavior.* Conclusions drawn from work with animals and extended to apply to human beings as well, as in the case of Skinner's work with pigeons or Pavlov's work with dogs, are good examples of the gross errors committed by *failing to realize that the conditioning principles discovered only apply to human beings when they are not engaged in motivated behavior.*

Behavioral psychology fails to realize that the conditioning principles it has discovered only apply to human beings *when they are not engaged in motivated behavior.*

In other words, when our behavior is not driven by our MAP, we as human beings are subject to general principles of behavior, like other animals.

The failure to realize a duality of behavior in human beings has been a major contributor to forming the models of behavior that support so many wasteful and ineffective practices employed by education and industry.

I'm not saying that you have no choice. You do. The way the world works, you can climb the wrong ladder, but there are serious consequences if you do. You can take a job that is wrong for you. But that means turning to *unmotivated* behavior. Hardly a meaningful choice! Why would anyone want to stop doing the thing he loves, the thing he is passionate about, and the thing he is competent to do, in order to pursue what he doesn't like, feels no affinity for, or has no ability in?

Of course, there are times every day when we are forced to do a task because it just has to be done, and there's no one else to do it. We all have our personal lists of odious or "nothing" chores—perhaps balancing the checkbook, doing the paperwork, the grocery shopping, mowing the lawn, following up, maintaining, you name it. We all have to step outside our motivational domain frequently and regularly.

The tragedy occurs when we spend the bulk of our time there. Yet millions of people do precisely that in occupations that are essentially drudgery. The problem is not the job itself (one person's drudgery would be another's delight), but what I have just said: these hapless people are trying to operate outside their patterns. Consequently, their performance is uninspired; their stomach is grinding; their attitude stinks; their cardiovascular risk factors are soaring.

> Programs based on the Myth of Becoming can genuinely help those people whose MAP is engaged by the program. But this is a relatively small minority.

5. Which leads us to the main reason why the Myth of Becoming is still embraced by almost everyone: The Myth of Becoming does produce some successes and numerous *apparent* successes—enough to keep it alive.

Some people, because of the nature of their giftedness, can adapt to meet new demands. Many grow into new and larger roles that continue to call on their strengths. Programs based on the Myth of Becoming can genuinely help some people whose MAP is engaged by the program. But this is a relatively small minority.

There is another group that shows change—but it is *apparent* rather than *real* change. Their MAP is not engaged, so *what changes is their unmotivated behavior.* The change is due to the adaptability of these individuals to new challenges and requirements within their existing strengths. But their MAP remains unaltered. *You cannot change motivated behavior!*

THE BOTTOM LINE

For nearly forty years we have explored what causes people to pour their hearts, minds, and souls into their work. Some people, because of the nature of their giftedness, can adapt to meet new demands. Many grow into new and larger roles that continue to call on their strengths.

But what we have *not* seen in the thousands of individuals we have worked with is change in fundamental makeup. We look at the experience of those proclaiming the power to cause such change, but we find no compelling evidence that this kind of radical change ever occurs.

Years ago, I challenged a group of behavioral psychologists at a federal institute for executive development in the Southeast to produce *one* case of a person who had undergone a basic change in his motivated behavior.

They leaped to the challenge and offered me Cyril, a person whom I later interviewed. Let me tell you what I found.

As a boy, during World War II, Cyril had gathered a group of his friends and had gone through their neighborhoods, soliciting and gathering up tinfoil until they had a huge ball of foil, which they then offered up to the war effort at a local receiving station.

After the war, Cyril proceeded through a technical education and later worked his way up the ranks with a company until he had arrived at an executive position in charge of manufacturing. At some point, he resigned from the executive ranks (here supposedly was the big change!) and went to work in a community center in the inner city, helping kids.

So, during my interview with him I asked, "What was your next achievement after you left your executive position with the manufacturing company?" It turned out to be starting a Junior Achievement Club where he helped the kids manufacture and sell products in the community! Case closed? As far as I'm concerned, yes!

In thirty-eight years, in literally tens of thousands of cases, throughout the world, with people of many different walks of life, neither I nor any of my colleagues in the People Management networks in any part of the world has *ever* seen a fundamental change in a person's MAP. Follow-up studies of particular individuals have fully confirmed this apparently universal fact.

The bottom line is this: Our design is a marvelous gift that cannot be exchanged. It does not, *cannot* become something else, no matter how hard we try, no matter how hard others try.

Part Two

The Person You Were Created to Be

Had God not endowed us, we would be animals sniffing in wonder at the embers of a fire triggered by lightning. Even girded by purpose, passion, and power to achieve great things in our lives, we, the image of God, need God to protect and lead us and keep us from self-destruction.

Chapter Seven

Finding and Following
God's Plan for Your Life

God seeks to inhabit the minds and hearts of his children and lead them into his ways and purposes for their lives. God is the Creator and Designer of human beings, who wants to mix in our lives; who is personal, available, and trustworthy; who seeks to use his creation to rebuild the world on a foundation of love, mercy, and justice.

To start off on this pilgrimage, I would like you to become convinced of, or at least open to, the truth that God has designed each person with certain competencies and passions. In other words, God is responsible for your MAP.

Take a look at this list of some of the characteristics of our giftedness, our design, our MAP:

- Universal: *Every* person has giftedness.
- Inherent: Giftedness is inborn in each person; it is not the result of personal effort.
- Precocious: Giftedness expresses itself in infants.
- Unique: Each person has a different pattern of giftedness.
- Unconscious: Giftedness functions regardless of awareness.
- Purposive: Giftedness seeks a certain outcome.
- Stable: Giftedness is not subject to fundamental change.
- Irrepressible: Giftedness always seeks expression.
- Undeniable: Giftedness is demonstrated over a lifetime.
- Dynamic: Giftedness is a driving force in each person.
- Holistic: Giftedness captures the whole person in action.
- Amoral: Giftedness can be used for good or evil.

- Pervasive: Giftedness governs thinking, feeling, and actions.
- Predictive: Future behavior will be like past behavior.
- Systemic: All elements of giftedness operate cohesively.

The list can be made even longer. But when we look at all of these characteristics of giftedness and design, it is difficult not to add one more to the list:

- Predetermined: Giftedness is decreed beforehand.

Let me be clear here: We arrived at the concept of giftedness, design, and motivated abilities after many years of collecting, analyzing, and interpreting data—a process that can be followed and duplicated by anyone, regardless of religious or ideological persuasion. The concepts as such are not contingent on belief in God.

GOD AND OUR GIFTEDNESS

But—if we believe in God, then it is impossible to escape the conclusion that God is the originator of our individual giftedness. So much in our life is determined by our giftedness that it is impossible to believe that God, who according to the Bible cares about what happens to each one of us and has a purpose for each one of us, is not involved in our design and our giftedness.

Besides, it is what Scripture teaches. Here is a summary of what you find in the Bible:[1]

- God has created you.
- God has designed you in order to fulfill his purpose for your life.
- God's Spirit can dwell within you and actively seek to work his purpose out through your design.
- God will hold you accountable for fruit produced from your giftedness.
- God intends that you use your giftedness in work appropriate to its nature and within its boundaries.
- God requires you to love him and those you serve, with excellence and with passion (qualities only available through your design!).
- God promises he will bless you and complete his intention for your life.

---

1. You will find the biblical basis for these statements in appendix C.

- God has instructed us to build his kingdom on the earth as it is in heaven, using the giftedness with which we were endowed.

These daunting expressions of God should fill you with excitement and fear and disbelief and hope—all at the same time. God is serious about you and your life. God has a game plan for your life … if you are willing.

THE IMPORTANCE OF FINDING YOUR GIFTEDNESS

If all we have said thus far is true, then it is clear that finding your giftedness is not something you do out of curiosity on a rainy Sunday afternoon when there's no baseball on television. It is a quest that is supremely important.

But one point needs clarification before we go on. Many Christians see no or very little connection between our natural giftedness and the spiritual gifts that God gives to each person in the church.[2] But there seems to be no clear biblical basis for the assumption that the spiritual gifts—given for the edification of the church—are given without any regard for the natural giftedness of the individual.

God doesn't simply scatter his gifts (the "spiritual gifts") more or less randomly through his church. He "gives them to each one, just as he determines" (1 Corinthians 12:11). There is forethought and purpose behind the gifts. Even the "rebellious" are gifted by God (Psalm 68:18).

Would it make sense for God to give two gifts that somehow are incompatible? True, God can do anything he decides to do. He *can* give someone two gifts that are utterly unrelated to each other and even contradictory. The question is, does he? There appears to be more evidence for the view that the gifts of the Spirit tie in with one's "natural" (but equally God-given) giftedness than for the two to be contradictory.

Take the apostle Paul. No one can question the fact that he was gifted by the Spirit. Yet when we look at Paul before and after his conversion,

> There seems to be no clear biblical basis for the assumption that the spiritual gifts are given for the edification of the church without any regard for the natural giftedness of the individual.

---

2. See Romans 12:6–8; 1 Corinthians 12:8–11, 28.

God most definitely can and will guide us through a growing understanding of our individual, God-given design and giftedness.

it is clear that his energies and his giftedness didn't change. Rather, they were freed up to function as God intended them. I think that the difference we often observe between a person before his or her conversion and afterward is not a fundamental change in giftedness or a gift of the Spirit that somehow negates or even ignores that person's natural giftedness, but rather a joyous freeing up of the person to finally be what God intended him or her to be. Ultimately it is the Holy Spirit who enables us to be who we are, in full freedom. The Spirit guides us into all truth—not just into theological or doctrinal truth, but into *living the truth* in honesty and humility, which includes living in harmony with the truth about our giftedness.

FINDING AND FOLLOWING GOD'S PLAN

When we talk about "finding God's will" or "finding God's plan for us" we are tempted to think that God will somehow tell us in a special way what his will is for us—perhaps in a dream, or in a sudden insight or revelation, or through some other clear and unmistakable way. And God sometimes does use very special means—ask Moses; ask Paul. But God

Following God's will and plan for your life means ordering your life around his gift to you—your design and giftedness.

very often leads us gently through the details of everyday life, and we must simply trust him to guide us. He can guide us using common sense and practical insight. And he most definitely can and will guide us through a growing understanding of our individual, God-given design and giftedness!

Following God's will and plan for your life means ordering your life around his gift to you—your design and giftedness. It means finding and remaining in a calling that God has given to you—sharing through *all* your gifts, bearing good fruit in your day-to-day life, and producing good products worthy of praise.

That is true whether you are a sanitation worker, a bank president, a homemaker, or severely limited by physical illness or handicaps. God's yardstick for measuring the quality of the fruit we bear is how faithful we are in using and applying our giftedness. It is a yardstick that levels all differences in class, status, IQ, race, abilities, and whatever else people measure. You are not responsible for what or how much or how little (by human standards) God has given you—only for what you do with what you have been given.

Following God's will and plan means working for God in whatever part of the world makes sense in light of our giftedness. We are to bring his presence into the place where we labor, delighting in the work of our hands, even as we delight God by functioning according to how he has designed us.

> Work . . . should be the full expression of the worker's faculties, the thing in which he finds spiritual, mental, and bodily satisfaction.
>
> —Dorothy Sayers

Dorothy Sayers says it well:

Work is not, primarily, a thing one does to live, but the thing one lives to do. It is, or it should be, the full expression of the worker's faculties, the thing in which he finds spiritual, mental, and bodily satisfaction, and the medium in which he offers himself to God.[3]

What follows are some insights and suggestions to help you along the way to finding and following God's will and plan for your life.

REORDERING YOUR LIFE

First off, what you do for a living should increasingly conform to your design. Opportunities for promotion and any other changes should be examined very carefully to make sure your strengths will be much in demand in the new job. If there is pressure from family, friends, or your employer to take an unsuitable position, stand firm. It is your life and God's design you are considering. Whether and how you invest your life in God's design of you is the second-most important decision you will ever make.

Money and status are usually the stumbling blocks to a sound decision. If you are gifted at meeting the demands of the present job, you should be paid accordingly. If that isn't enough money to properly

---

3. Dorothy Sayers, *Creed or Chaos* (New York: Harcourt, Brace, 1949), 53. This is also what the apostle Paul says in Romans 12:1: "Therefore, I urge you, brothers, in view of God's mercy, to offer your bodies as living sacrifices, holy and pleasing to God—this is your spiritual act of worship."

support your family, look around for another job suitably matched to your MAP, one that is paying what you believe you need.

We all want and can use more, but that's not the point. And I'm not with those who urge you to eat and live "on the cheap" so you have more to give away. I believe that in *all* areas of your life you should live in accordance with God's design of you. If you, like Solomon, are motivated and competent to acquire and manage lots of things, do so and give generously from your abundance. If you need a hair shirt to fulfill your pattern, buy one and wear it, but not so others can see it.

Whether and how you invest your life in light of God's design of you is the second-most important decision you will ever make.

Whether your home is common or unique, very large or modest, filled with precious antiques or rummage sale items, it should reflect you and your family's needs and reasonable wants, considering how God has constructed you. If you need extra room for all your books, your exercise equipment, or for all the visitors (human or canine) who seem to end up at your door because you are so gifted at building relationships and meeting needs—have it.

If you and your spouse yearn for the city or suburbia or the country, and your vocations allow it, do it. When the kids grow up, they can make their own choices. Their educational needs are a high-priority item, but beyond that it's your choice.

What kind of a car you drive, again, should reflect your MAP. I drive in lots of weather and traffic from fairly distant airports over country roads, so I need a very reliable (I'm moronic mechanically), surefooted, well accelerating, strong automobile. How it looks is not unimportant. No? Now why is that?

And the food you eat, how it's prepared and presented, can it also be an important aspect of living in accordance with your MAP? Yes. And clothes and fabrics and fashion and style, and how it frees you to function in the world you occupy because of your giftedness? Yes, I was thinking of that too.

And what about sex and how a couple can be mindful and accommodating of one another's MAPs—like being facilitative, or meeting needs, or being innovative? Yes, that too. And how and to what extent you deal with relationships and being intimate and one-on-one, and things like being a good interactive conversationalist, and being sensitive, and "the man is the head honcho and the teacher and the ruler of the home" depends on the marbles God has given you? Yes, once again!

God insists that you love him and others in everything you do—and that you love with your whole mind and your whole strength and your whole heart and soul.

From what I have seen, the only way it is possible to love so completely is through using your giftedness. If you can't be filled with such love in building a relationship with another person, or in evangelizing activities, or counseling an alcoholic or a pregnant teenager, or a coworker who has "gone off the rails," you simply do not fill your life up with such activities. You also do not feel guilty about it. Understand that *you are God's idea. You will be held accountable for using what he gave you to work with, not for pursuing someone else's agenda or MAP.*

> **You are God's idea. You will be held accountable for using what he gave you to work with, not for pursuing someone else's agenda or MAP.**

What do you do about those "voids" in your life, when personal relationships aren't an important part of your MAP? Point one, they aren't voids from your perspective. Point two, if the person you're married to, or one of your children, is highly relational, that person is perfectly able to carry the burdens of building his or her relationship with you, and bringing you into that relationship. That is the gift he or she has received from God, and it opens up an aspect of loving that is important.

There is one other way you can express love (although not with your whole heart, mind, and soul) and that is for you to encourage the important persons in your life to express their giftedness and to grow in its expression. What I've learned is that you can really do that without being phony—*if* you are making substantial use of your strengths *outside* of your relationship with them, so that you do not have to look for them for a motivated payoff they may not be able to deliver. You can be, in that sense, a rich resource and encourager to other members of your family, at home or at work.

You probably are wondering how I can describe as godly activities so much that seems to be indulgent. *How do we integrate faith with hot fudge sundaes?* Here I am indebted to my friend Ralph Mattson, who taught me and lots of others about God as the author of pleasure. I realize it violates much Christian culture, but it is right in line with Holy Scripture.

God intends to derive pleasure from his creation, including humanity. Our fulfilling his design of us, under his management, gives pleasure to God. God wants us to enjoy him. The main way we enjoy God is by enjoying the use we make of the giftedness with which he endowed each of us—in service to others and in love, praise, and adoration of God. The things of life we personally and uniquely enjoy are there because of our God-designed giftedness. We can enjoy mountains, and lakes, and music, and laughter, and hot showers. He gave us the ability to enjoy them. We were meant to enjoy his provisions. It is good for us to do so.[4]

> How do we integrate faith with hot fudge sundaes?

WHERE THE RUBBER MEETS THE ROAD

Jesus told his followers (and us), "If anyone would come after me, he must deny himself and take up his cross daily and follow me. For whoever wants to save his life will lose it, but whoever loses his life for me will save it."[5]

Losing your life means striving toward the motivational payoff that is so important to you—but to be able to live without it, and still be at peace. It means that we quit trying to protect what we regard as "our turf," our exclusive right to whatever rewards come when we do our thing. Instead, we lay our gifted efforts before God for him to do with as he will.

Again, the place where we most need to deny self and take up our cross each day is in the workplace, be it an office, a factory, a university, a hospital, or at home. Whatever the setting, our drive to glorify and protect our "self" reaches its peak in our vocation. It is in that arena that our faith will either wilt or prosper. Therefore, consider adopting the following articles of faith.

1. God Doesn't Support Worrying

"Losing your life" also means you *stop worrying* about the outcome of your efforts. Sure, go ahead and do your homework. Give it your best

---

4. 1 Timothy 6:17.
5. Luke 9:23–24.

shot. Pour your energy into whatever the task requires. Seek to hit a home run, but don't *require* it for you to be at peace. Never let go of the fact and faith that God has given you the gifts to do the things you do, and to do them well. He will carry you through. I call this condition of attitude and intention "detached intensity." Memorize it!

Losing your life means striving toward the motivational payoff that is so important to you—but to be able to live without it, and still be at peace.

God is the Author and Finisher of the work he began in you. Taking up your cross means giving up the right to have everything work out exactly as you would wish; deny the impulse to force things: let go of the worry about whether things will work out and of the anxiety after they don't.

Countless books and articles have been written about yielding our concerns to God. But I want to stress the importance of giving over to him the worries, anxieties, and fears we face in the marketplace. Obviously, work is vitally important to our sense of worth, so it is no surprise that workplace issues pose a major challenge to our faith.

But if we intend to follow God in our vocation, we *must* leave the ultimate results to him, because so much is outside of our control: the choices of our superiors, the whims of our customers, the shifting tides of the economy, changes in technology, even the weather. But nothing is outside the Lord's control. Having called us, he has promised that all things will work together for good. So, even though we must pay attention to the results, ultimately we leave them to him.

Detached intensity: Give it your best shot, but stop worrying about the outcome.

Of course, if our anxiety stems from being in the wrong job—a job for which we lack the necessary gifts—that is another matter. In that case, we need to do whatever we can to place ourselves where we will be more productive—and less stressed.

2. Act in Faith

Stop playing it safe with your life; act in faith. Not only does God want you to be well-matched with your job, faithful in your efforts, and trusting in his oversight, he wants you to be willing to take risks where your own skin is involved. That's really part of taking up your cross daily.

> **Taking up your cross means giving up the right to have everything work out exactly as you would wish.**

By taking risks I don't mean investing your life savings in some scheme. I mean being open to new and better ways of functioning, given your giftedness. It means listening to others who are similarly gifted and therefore in a position to advise you. It means embracing change and leaving behind your security, if following your dream requires it. It means, in your heart of hearts, a willingness to invest *your life* and *your living* in the gifts God has given you—not burying your talents in the ground because you prefer to keep things safe and secure.

Stop trusting yourself more than you trust God to bless you. I have found, in my own experience as well as the experience of those close to me, that most of our anxieties and fears are rooted in a handful of common, deep-seated convictions:

- Deep down, we don't believe that God is all that concerned about our lives.
- If he is, we don't believe that he really intends to bless us.
- If he does, we're convinced that he's not doing a very good job of it—no better than we could do ourselves.

Of course, these are silly lies. But most people plan, decide, and act based on these suppositions—particularly in their vocations. As a result, many spend their lives in jobs and roles that in no way match their design.

It isn't that they never think about looking for a "better" job and getting out of their misery. But they are afraid. They can't—or won't—trust God to bless them.

3. Stay on the Rock

Get the "right" job—one that makes good use of your giftedness—and stay in it. Many people start out in suitable jobs and callings, but

> **Stop playing it safe with your life; act in faith.**

yield to the temptation of climbing to a higher position when one is offered. Sometimes, they keep accepting promotions until they finally end up in a position that simply does not match their giftedness (the Peter Principle).

Please don't misunderstand. Aspiring to more responsibility or a greater challenge or a different task may be part of how God has put you together. Indeed, he has used people with these kinds of strivings to build world-class leaders, artists, inventors, and whatever. But it is *wrong*, it is *sin* to accept or remain in a position that you *know* is a mismatch for you.

Perhaps that's a form of sin you've never even considered—the sin of staying in the wrong job. But God did not place you on this earth to waste away your years in labor that does not employ his design or purpose for your life, no matter how much you may be getting paid for it.

It is *sin* to accept or remain in a position that you *know* is a mismatch for you.

Unfortunately, it is rare for someone in that position to say, "I made a mistake. I need to get off this treadmill and do something to which I am suited." Why? Because most of us have placed our security and prosperity more in the hands of an employer than in the hands of God.

Let me point out a related sin, or at least a dangerous temptation. Some people are properly pursuing their callings in demanding, high pressure jobs—for example, as a highly visible CEO. God's gifting has enabled the person to successfully climb to those exalted heights.

But then one day he starts to forget that fact—that *God* has endowed him and placed him where he is. He develops myopic narcissism, a preoccupation with himself and, consequently, with his own inadequacies. He looks at the enormity of the task he has taken on and begins to doubt that he is equal to it, or that he can sustain his performance. In short, he forgets God and thinks that everything depends on himself.

To control his growing anxiety, he may start seeking destructive outlets and pleasures. Ultimately, if he continues in this vein and fails to repent of his lack of faith, he is liable to ruin his vocation and fall into a spiritual crisis. Having forgotten that his gifts were not only given him by God, but were to be empowered by God's continuing grace, the self-reliant star loses his self-reliant nerve.

The same fate could happen to any of us if we lose the confidence that God is in charge and intends good for us. Trust God. Allow God to shape your life.

4. Get Intimate with God

The path to getting in step with God is to cultivate a *personal relationship* with him through the means you have been given to express love: your designed giftedness.

There is a tendency among many people to think that drawing close to God requires a person be thoughtful and reflective, with a distinct ability to relate one-to-one with others. Never mind that there are many saints in Scripture who were not inclined this way. But it's a holdover from a bygone era that godliness is marked by monkish meditation and deep, empathic concern. Now, if this were true, there would be many who are gifted to be explorers, farmers, tool-and-die makers, cost accountants, spectroscopists, scientists, entertainers, designers, and even preachers who could not effectively live the life of faith. *If* it were true. But it is not. There's nothing wrong with thoughtful reflection and one-to-one relationships. Those who are gifted that way play a vital role in fulfilling God's will.

> Most of us have placed our security and prosperity more in the hands of an employer than in the hands of God.

But God's will goes far beyond reflection and one-to-one relationships. That's why he has distributed gifts that will accomplish other purposes. So we do a tremendous disservice to the explorers, farmers, tool-and-die makers, and the rest by telling them, either explicitly or implicitly, that they ought to set aside their gifts and live by another pattern. If we want them to *personally* relate to God, we ought to encourage them to pursue the unique purpose for which he has fitted them, whether that involves people, or vegetables, or animals, or concepts, or machines, or space, or numbers, or color, or music, or birds, or ants. Ants? Yes, ants!

But what if one's motivational makeup does not incline him or her toward personal relationships? How can a person like that cultivate a personal relationship with God? Well, you may be the most stoic, grim-faced teamster who ever drove a twenty-two-wheeler, a man who merely grunts in response to your boss, your mother, or even your wife. But with God, it's a different story. After all, God is the One sitting next to you in that blizzard. He's the One waking you up just before you head across the median. He's the One restraining you from renting that video or visiting that old girlfriend. He's your Rock, your Guide, your Life. So with him, you get personal. You talk to him. You argue. You thank him. You complain. Whatever. The point is, you get *personal*—however you can.

The same holds true for the rest of us. Each one of us must relate to God *personally*—in whatever way we can. Of course, that means that the one gifted to be a warrior relates to God differently than does the one gifted to be a dreamer; the one gifted to be a farmer relates differently than the one gifted to be a civil engineer; the dancer relates differently than the theoretical physicist; the homemaker than the designer; the treasurer than the fisherman; the garbage collector than the police officer; the rare-coin collector than the auto mechanic; the retailer than the process engineer. You get the point.

This is vitally important if we intend to claim God's promise to work within us as we seek to live out our calling. *There's no sense in asking him to empower us for a task he has not called us to.* On the other hand, when we match our giftedness with a suitable vocation, we need to invite God into every detail of it. "Guide me, Lord, as I discipline this child . . . troubleshoot this glitch . . . sell this tough customer." "Bless my patient, Lord . . . help me save this tooth . . . give me wisdom to make the correct diagnosis." "Use me to bring grace to the people on my route, Lord." "Help me find a more efficient way of processing claims." "Father God, help me to listen." "Lord of the universe, show me why this assembly operation keeps falling behind." "Holy Spirit, anoint us as we sort out this critical decision." "Father of all comfort, strengthen my resolve in terminating this employee." "Maker of all things, paint through me the glory I faintly see." "God in heaven, show me why this sucker won't go over that fitting!" "Master Teacher, keep my mind on blessing my students—not on my fear of them." "Dear God, please show me how I can reduce our costs of producing this product without losing our shirts." "Spirit of Christ, sing through me." "Holy Father, how can I resolve this dispute with management?" "Father of all truth, reveal your mind to us about these candidates."

> There's no sense in asking God to empower us for a task He has not called us to.

Do you see what *intimacy* with God looks like? It doesn't matter whether your design/calling involves unionizing teachers, performing as a talk show host, researching the corrosion of coated finishes, modeling brand-name clothing, promoting forest conservation, working as a dental hygienist—*nothing* you do lies outside your relationship with God.

So invite him in to share *all* of it. If you do, God will make his face to shine on all that your giftedness touches. Our prayer needs to be like that of Moses: "Let the beauty of the LORD our God be upon us: and establish thou the work of our hands upon us; yea, the work of our hands establish thou it."[6] Read that out loud, again and again.

5. Learn About God

You relate to God through your giftedness. You learn about the Lord—his nature, his character, his wisdom, his goodness, his faithfulness, his anger, his love for his creation—in the details of your calling. Not exclusively, of course, but mainly. Obviously, Scripture defines the objective truth of these areas. But your *experience* of these truths comes principally through your gifts, as you seek to express them.

For example, if you are gifted to function as a team member, your fruitful times "with the Lord" will come mainly when you are involved with others. By contrast, if you're an individualist, you will tend to meet the Lord in the privacy of your own domain. If you learn through reading, you will probably come close to God by poring over the Word. But if you learn by doing or experiencing a skill or a principle; or by observing someone do the thing you want to learn; or by listening and discussing—those will be the primary ways in which you will learn about the Lord.

6. Love God

The same fact applies to loving God: you love him through the means he has given you to love. If you are gifted at performing or researching or maintaining or assembling or selling or accounting—your way of loving God will center in your gifted activity as you do it as unto him.

We are each intricate specks of grace brought forth by God out of his infinite creativity. Therefore, the mystery of "Christ in [us], the hope of glory"[7] is a clarion call to express Christ in us through his gifts to us. It is how we love God.

7. Let It Shine!

"You are the light of the world. . . . Let your light shine before men, that they may see your good deeds and praise your Father in heaven."[8] If people in the world are to praise God because of your "light," then your light has to be praiseworthy, if not amazing, just to get their attention.

---

6. Psalm 90:17 (KJV).
7. Colossians 1:27.
8. Matthew 5:14, 16.

In practical terms, it means giving each customer the best you've got, no matter what. It means not cutting corners ethically, even if you can get away with it. It means standing behind your work, owning it, claiming it, being quick to admit errors, slow to get angry when people criticize it, ready to make amends and take preventative measures to keep the same problem from happening again. It means being trustworthy and reliable, someone who can be counted on in the crunch times, giving more than what is expected.

As for attitudes, it means not harboring resentment, envy, lust, or bitterness. As for communication, it means presenting externally what you are internally. As for how you see your work, it means adopting not a moralistic legalism, but a vision for your task that draws on the wisdom and creativity of God. It means expecting God to anoint your giftedness. As for relationships, it means standing up for (and sometimes even picking fights over) issues concerned with truth or justice. It means being known as someone who not only hears, but listens and responds. It means having a reputation for goodness.

It means handling every person with respect. And *it means doing what God would have you do even when no one else is looking or will ever know.*

Obviously, I am drawing a portrait of a saint-in-process here. None of us lives up to all these ideals. And because of our varied giftedness, each of us will excel at some qualities more than at others. But the point is that if people in our world are ever going to seek the One who stands behind us, they must first be impressed by what they see of him in us.

Reflecting a deep faith in God is not something you can just "put on" like a sweater, because phoniness is obvious to everyone. Faith in God allows us to be natural and unaffected about the results that flow from our efforts, without pride or false humility.

Sure, you bust your tail to get the job done, but you aren't driven by anxiety in the midst of your labors. You *love* your task. You love God for the delight he gives you in your labors. You love those you serve through his gifts.

You can do this because you have invited God to complete his work in you—a work that mainly revolves around your giftedness. You can do it because you have confidence that God is in you, working out his purposes. God is your strength.

You can do it because you have the experience of him working alongside you and through you; nudging you to make a decision; illuminating a complexity you were struggling to sort out; suggesting how to maintain a near impossible relationship; giving you a hunch for taking a different line of inquiry; encouraging you to stand up for what you believe to be sound policy; surprising you with a real-life miracle only *your* eyes would understand; convicting you of arrogance or hardness of heart that you have cultivated for decades; enfolding you with love when you face disappointment or failure.

Your work, its fruit and its witness, are in God's heart for your life. Jesus Christ wants your life to make a difference; wants you to fulfill your destiny. He wants you to allow him to work through you and the gifts he has given to redeem his world that he might present that work to the Father.

Increasingly, as you operate in gifted activities, you trust the Holy Spirit to drive your thoughts and deeds, particularly in critical times and issues. When that happens, your light will move the world you occupy. People will wonder, and begin to ask questions.

Once you have turned over the management of your life to Christ, he will reshape your relationship with him around his priorities in your life. Be they so small and hidden as to escape anybody else's scrutiny, or so bold as to take your breath away, he will be an active partner.

If you don't walk away, the Holy Spirit will delight you, surprise you, court you, confront you. His agenda may be hidden from your eyes, more often than not, but it is always clear to HIM—making you into what he dreamed you could be.

Chapter Eight

Resisting the Dark Side of Giftedness

Giftedness used as God intended is marvelous to behold. But our greatest giftedness has the potential for the greatest abuse—or, as the Bible calls it, sin. Sin is often understood as missing the mark, as something that is the result of investing our lives in trying to become something other than who we are. But the Old and New Testaments alike make it clear that our transgressions against God are not just passive or benign, but willful and deliberate. We are not victims of sin, we *choose* to sin. We *enjoy* our sin. And—unless God helps us—we *will* gravitate toward the dark side of our giftedness. And like every other choice in our lives, the *kind of sin* we choose is ultimately determined by our design.

We act according to our pattern when we love and serve God. Yet, we also act according to our pattern when we choose to turn away from him and serve other gods or seek another path to walk than the one destined by our design.

Time and again in our years of helping people identify their giftedness, delighted and even awestruck by the beauty with which God has crafted individuals, we have found it sobering, if not chilling, to see how people can seduce themselves into sin by abusing God's good gifts.

This is true for us as individuals, but it also true in institutional and corporate settings—and even in the church.

THE DARK SIDE OF OUR GIFTEDNESS

We want to be God. We want to make our own rules (not only for us, but for others as well). We want to control our circumstances. We want to do what we want to do when we want to. We want to be elevated in the eyes of others. And, if there is a God, we don't want him to mix in and muddy up our life—at least while things are going well. Essentially, we want to go it without God—at least until we know we can't survive the immediate crisis without somebody's help.

The most compelling evidence of this desire for independence is those who pursue and achieve success. Our nature is to claim credit. Our nature is to overlook the fact that our success is only possible through the giftedness with which we were endowed. The tragedy of our pretension is that sooner or later we weaken, begin to fear, doubt, and unravel. Think of the superstars who have effectively destroyed their lives because they couldn't handle success in their own strength. Forget the superstars. Think of people you know of who have been brought down because they couldn't make it on their own.

God showers on us riches that stretch beyond our imagination. And yet, grand and glorious as these treasures are, they contain a "but," a looming qualifier that must never be forgotten, or else we are buying into a false paradise.

God himself has built a catch into the nature of humanity, and that catch is this: In his sovereignty he has determined that we *must* live our lives in relation to him. As his creatures, our very being derives from him. Each of us—precious in his sight as we are—is but a speck of his self-expression.

> The dark side of giftedness means inflating its payoff beyond its intention until it has assumed the place of God.

There is no escaping this reality, and it is here that we lose our way. God has made us to enjoy a lifetime of bringing honor to him and an eternity of sharing glory with him. His gifts predestine us to that end. But what if we should exercise those powers for anyone but him? What if we should turn them to our own glory, our own will, our own ends? In that case, the seeds of our destiny become the seeds of our destruction.

Sooner or later, each of us develops a sense of entitlement as we strive to achieve our motivational payoff. It may be to have others adore us, exalt us, envy us, see us as special, or submit to our will. It may be to accomplish things that others would find difficult to achieve, or to see and experience things that no one else has discovered, or to be unique, or to build monuments to ourselves. There are many possibilities.

None of these payoffs is inherently wrong. Indeed, at their root, payoffs were intended to provide legitimate thrust and purpose to people's lives. But *the dark side of giftedness means inflating the payoff beyond its intention until it has assumed the place of God.*

Sin is giftedness run amok.

Sin is giftedness run amok. Blinded by a false view of ourselves, we become compulsive about seeking our preferred outcome. Never mind that we are able to do what we do only because God has given us the means to do it. We make our gifts an end in themselves, employing them, not to love others but to render others subservient to us as we build our own kingdom. We want power and control. We want to be worshiped. This perverse demand can hijack our soul, whether we are six years old or sixty.

The drive for achievement is not sin. God designed us for achievement. But when we turn away from a relationship with our Creator that was meant to empower *and restrain* our strivings, we sin. We deny God his rightful place as Lord of our lives and become rebels against his government and grace.

This is something God will not abide. His sovereign character is unambiguous: He will not be displaced by *anyone*, including you and me. He has made our human frame such that if we attempt to live apart from him, we will fall into disaster. One way or another, the dynamics of our giftedness, along with our fears and insecurities and our terrible lust for self-determination, will ultimately lead to self-destruction.

Ultimately, the light that redeems the world is the love of God expressed *in action*, in human lives that reveal his glory.

We see this scenario played out by countless people in our world. Some who are "successful" become filled with themselves and suffer the inner torment of protecting and maintaining their treasures, or status, or track record, or material gains. Others do well for a while but, having no connection to the Source of Life, and with confidence in no one but themselves, lose their nerve, falter, and fall short of what they might have been. The vast majority of people seem to just bump along in life, barely aware of the latent powers within them. Theirs is the strategy of playing it safe, clutching at false securities. Sin dominates their lives all the same, for they are unwilling to trust God by investing in the gifts he has given them.

Tragically, this last category describes many religious people who view "secular" careers in the world as mere distractions to the things that "really count" for God. Among them are the sincere, but misguided, evangelists who invade the workplace with the aim of using their jobs as a platform (that is, pretense) for evangelism. Little do they realize that their "testimony" is suspect, and that their witness of a victorious life rings hollow because they are not living one. They think that the world will be won through talk, but it will not. Our society is drowning in words. Ultimately, the light that redeems the world is the love of God expressed *in action*, in human lives that reveal his glory—"that they may see your good works, and glorify your Father which is in heaven."[1]

> Our sins are almost more dangerous than those of a convicted felon because they tend to be socially acceptable.

Unfortunately, that light is often dimmed, if not extinguished. Each of us has a unique way of intercepting the glory that belongs to our Father in heaven. Just think of the ways in which the gifts of God can be used for evil purposes. History tells of raging monsters in every century whose gifts undoubtedly fitted them for gaining and exploiting power. And more than enough cases are publicized each day of people using giftedness to bilk widows, rob banks, distribute drugs, defraud governments, cheat customers, peddle influence, and oppress the poor.

Let's not play games. Even the saintliest among us is just one step removed from tripping. In fact, *our sins are almost more dangerous than those of a convicted felon because ours tend to be socially acceptable.*

As you read through the lists of examples below, you will probably shake your head and wonder how a Christian could ever do some of these things. But if you think you are a better Christian than that, think again. The reason you shake your head at some things is that they fall outside your area of giftedness! Which is exactly what happened to the religious man (the Pharisee) in the story Jesus told. The religious man prayed, "God, I thank you that I am not like other men—robbers, evildoers, adulterers—or even like this tax collector."[2] We can only compare ourselves favorably with other people as long as we fail to realize that our temptations and their temptations are not the same, because our giftedness is not the same as theirs. Our greatest temptations always come in the areas of our greatest strengths!

---

1. Matthew 5:16 (KJV).
2. Luke 18:9–14.

If we are gifted at making money, we can employ a variety of legally clean but spiritually corrupt things to make money. We can, for example,

- give out a false impression to make a sale;
- overreach for profit when the traffic will bear it;
- substitute a cheaper but unreliable or unproven part or ingredient;
- promise what we know we cannot deliver;
- make late payments to a small, struggling supplier, knowing he won't complain (or it won't matter if he does);
- shade financial statements to hide more than they reveal;
- avoid making overdue but costly safety expenditures.

We can only compare ourselves favorably with other people as long as we fail to realize that our temptations and their temptations are not the same, because our giftedness is not the same as theirs.

If we are gifted at meeting the needs of others and gaining a response thereby, we might

- indulge in what amounts to slander about a coworker who won't let us into his life;
- use our charm to "open up" a vendor's or customer's representative so that he reveals information we can use to our advantage;
- put someone on our "black list" who has received our help, but has not responded as we would like;
- let work pile up for someone else to do because we are preoccupied with needs where a response is likely;
- do harm to a subordinate by accepting and even apologizing for his drinking problem;
- and, on the home front, not respond to the bright, independent child and her achievements who has few apparent needs we can meet.

If, as the mother or father of a household, we are gifted at exercising dominion over a family, we can

- be vicious about a suitor who seeks to marry our daughter and move away;

- knowingly sabotage a spouse whose calling requires that he resign from a "secure" job and take up a less prestigious position;
- conduct a character assassination of another homemaker who is choosing to embark on a professional career;
- deeply envy the "picture-perfect" family that has a superb marriage and children who have "turned out so well."

If we are gifted at excelling, we can

- lust after a higher position;
- put down others as a way of highlighting our own achievements;
- demand attention in group settings;
- become self-absorbed (and boring) with stories of our own accomplishments;
- manipulate others into becoming stepping stones for our own agenda;
- become so obsessed with perfection that we attack anyone who stands in the way of our goals.

If we are gifted at competing, we can

- cut the ground from under a rival;
- humiliate someone who is not interested in competition as weak and unworthy;
- take advantage of people's humanity, all in the name of winning;
- turn all of life into a win-or-lose proposition;
- berate our spouse or children when their actions or choices threaten our ability to "get ahead";
- destroy our opponents by ensuring that they are not only down, but out.

If we are gifted at creating an image, we can

- viciously attack someone who ruins our presentation by asking an embarrassing question;
- build myths that cannot be sustained by reality;
- cover over genuine problems with smoke and mirrors, rather than address them squarely;
- fool ourselves into believing our own press reports;
- lead people into believing things that ultimately do them harm;
- become so obsessed with how others perceive us that we go deeply into debt to buy or maintain an image.

If we are gifted at managing, we can

- deceive a potential (and threatening) successor by delaying a promised promotion;
- run roughshod over people's needs and feelings in a campaign to upgrade efficiency;
- torpedo suggestions for change because they might cost us control, or just because we find change uncomfortable;
- fight so hard to protect "our people" that we forget about the larger needs of the organization;
- become so concerned with systems, numbers, and schedules that we become insensitive to people;
- withhold an allowance from an artistic, independent daughter because she so resists being managed.

These are but a handful of the countless possibilities. The point is that for *every* pattern, and for the person owning it, there is a dark side.

What is yours? Think about the thoughts and actions that recur again and again in your life that you regret. Do you realize that they, like the rest of your life, are expressed through your giftedness? The areas of your strength and passion are fertile ground for the good and the bad.

This raises particular dangers in your vocation, for it is there that you are most likely to pursue your bent. When you put your heart, soul, mind, and strength into your labors, you have an opportunity to fulfill the first and second commandments. But you also always have the temptation to stop laboring out of love and, instead, become driven by self-interest, playing God.

There are so many wonderful possibilities for a rich expression of sin in the use of our divine endowments: We can display every kind of wickedness, evil, greed, and depravity; envy, murder, strife, deceit, and malice; gossip, slander, insolence, arrogance, and boasting. We can become senseless, faithless, heartless, ruthless, unloving, unforgiving, unmerciful. (I'm not done!) We can display or cause hatred, discord, jealousy, fits of rage, selfish ambition, dissension, factions, and envy.[3] We can do all these things in a way consistent with our giftedness and *using* our giftedness.

People commit these things, people like you and me; individuals endowed by the Creator with unique strengths and passions that fit them for a unique purpose. Again, sin is giftedness run amok.

---

3. Romans 1:29–32; 2 Corinthians 12:20.

THE DARK SIDE OF CORPORATE AND INSTITUTIONAL GIFTEDNESS

Sin can operate not only at the individual level, but at the institutional level as well. That's why it is so dangerous to ignore giftedness. Unchecked, giftedness is powerful enough to subvert entire systems to the darker purposes of the human heart. This is the real source of systemic evil. Let me offer two disturbing cases in point.

Corporations

If people today feel that they are losing control over their lives, then who or what is gaining control? Certainly not Big Government which is slowly, but inevitably being whittled down. No, if any one institution is gaining control, not only over individuals, but over entire nations and economies, it is Big Business. One has only to revisit the 1996 U.S. presidential campaign to catch a whiff of the anticorporate resentment and distrust that smolders in the hearts of many.

> Unchecked, giftedness is powerful enough to subvert entire systems to the darker purposes of the human heart. This is the real source of systemic evil.

More and more people have come to feel that huge, multinational corporations represent everything that is wrong with democratic capitalism. This is ironic, because, as Professor Ralph Estes of the American University reminds us, corporations were originally chartered by sovereigns, and later by nation-states, for the express purpose of *carrying out public purposes to promote the general welfare.* Historically, corporations were intended to serve the broad public interests of the state and its people.[4]

Yet, increasingly, large corporations appear to be far more concerned about serving their own interests than that of the public. To be more precise, they appear to be serving the interests of those running the companies much more than the interests of those who work for, buy from, or even those who invest in the companies. Indeed, if anyone is doing supremely well today in the free market economy, it is the senior management of large corporations.

---

4. Ralph Estes, *Tyranny of the Bottom Line* (San Francisco: Berrett-Koehler Publishers, 1996), 30–31.

Why should that be? How is it that the average corporate chieftain enjoys power, perks, and amenities of which the average citizen can only dream, including compensation that in 1992 averaged *157 times* that of the average worker's?[5] The answer, according to Estes, is that corporations have succumbed to the "tyranny of the bottom line," a fixation on, and even obsession with, the impact of every development and decision on bottom-line profits. This tyranny well illustrates what can happen when the dark side of giftedness becomes institutionalized.

> The "tyranny of the bottom line" well illustrates what can happen when the dark side of giftedness becomes institutionalized.

As Estes documents, the real power in large corporations today rests not with stockholders, boards of directors, markets, or even governments, but with corporate managers. Citing research from Edward Hermann of the Wharton School of Business, Estes writes that

> management control of large corporations has been growing throughout this century, from some twenty-four percent of large companies in 1901 to forty-one percent in 1929 to ninety-two percent in 1974.
>
> With the torrent of leveraged buyouts in the 1980s and the recent rash of mergers and acquisitions, management dominance has certainly grown further and larger. The trend is clear: Management control of large corporations is virtually complete.[6]

Who are these people who run these vast, multibillion-dollar enterprises? What drives them in their pursuit of ever larger market share, greater corporate assets, and bigger companies—along with more power and prestige for themselves? Estes describes their motivation in moral terms, viewing them as people who are basically "good" in their private lives, but who succumb to compromise when faced with the demands of the bottom line.

"Business people, when functioning outside the corporate world as individuals, are responsible to themselves and their conscience, their

---

5. Ibid., 71.
6. Ibid., 67–68.

sense of morality, their families, and their religion: all of these act as a check on their personal behavior."[7]

But inside the corporation, a different morality obtains. "The corporation, without a religion, a guiding parent, a personal philosophy, a soul, or a conscience, receives its moral standards from the balance sheet. This becomes the soul of the corporation. In accepting their position in the corporation, and their rewards from it, managers often feel bound to put their personal morality aside and to act on the corporation's moral standards—at least while they are acting in their capacity as managers of the corporation and not separately as individuals." In this manner, corporations cause "good people to do bad things," in Estes's estimation.[8]

> The corporation, without a religion, a guiding parent, a personal philosophy, a soul, or a conscience, receives its moral standards from the balance sheet.
>
> —Ralph Estes

The dark side of the gift of maximizing profits and enlarging capital is that money can become not only a primary focus, but effectively the exclusive focus, and ultimately an idol to whom everyone and everything must bow. The dark side is that regardless of their pietistic policies and mission statements, companies become dehumanized so that people become expendable and little more than interchangeable parts in the machinery of business. They are no longer viewed as persons, but as exploitable commodities.

This is why every person, including our esteemed CEOs, CFOs, COOs, and so forth, needs to understand his or her design. Doing so helps to lift the veil on our entrenched tendencies toward sin. As always, C. S. Lewis summarizes the situation so well:

> The only way I can make real to myself what theology teaches about the heinousness of sin is to remember that every sin is the distortion of an energy breathed into us—an energy which, if not thus distorted, would have blossomed into one of those holy acts whereof "God did it" and "I did it" are both true descriptions. We poison the wine as he decants it into us; murder a melody he would play

---

7. Ibid., 74–75.
8. Ibid.

with us as the Instrument. We caricature the self-portrait he would paint. Hence, all sin—whatever else it is—is sacrilege.[9]

Education

We find a similar pattern in educational institutions. Education is based, not on the individual giftedness of students, but on the motivational makeup of the educators and administrators and politicians.

For education to be of value to the students, it must engage *what* they are motivated to learn, *how* they are motivated to learn, and *why* they are motivated to learn; with or without a teacher; alone or in groups. As it is, education only works well for those students whose learning dynamics (what-how-why) match the dynamics of the educators and the curriculum in place— probably less than twenty-five percent, at best. And educational success is measured by tests that, again, reflect the motivational makeup of the educational establishments.

The sad thing is that success on these tests bears no noticeable relationship to career success or life fulfillment. Seen from the perspective of a decade later, the educational experience reported by most people does not remotely support the costs and time that have been expended.

> **Every sin is the distortion of an energy breathed into us—an energy which, if not thus distorted, would have blossomed into one of those holy acts whereof "God did it" and "I did it" are both true descriptions.**
>
> **—C. S. Lewis**

Of all the thousands upon thousands of achievement experiences we have drawn from those considered reasonably "successful," few relate to an academic experience. Learning saturates what they do report as exciting and worthy of detailed recall, but the achievement described is rarely the mere study of some subject. Something must be accomplished of personal significance to the student. And grades don't quite make it—at least for most.

Can this be considered institutional sin? Yes! Education that fails to recognize individual giftedness not only fails to teach those children whose motivational pattern does not fit in with the academic requirements, it actively hurts them in several ways, each of which has the disturbing potential to leave a long-term negative impact on the student.

---

9. C. S. Lewis, *Letters to Malcolm: Chiefly on Prayer* (New York: Harcourt Brace Jovanovich, 1964), 69.

- Being "taught" by a person not motivated to cause learning can have a chilling effect on the interest of the student, even in courses that had potential value to the student. (Seventy percent of the delivery system is a rote, sometimes grueling experience, without a personally meaningful payoff.)
- Being graded with the mark of a "klutz" in subjects that have no personal significance to the student achieves nothing of value to the institution except to prove that it has screwed up one more time. Besides diminishing confidence and self-esteem, its value to the student is the elimination of one more subject area from vocational or avocational possibilities. (Who knows what might have happened if the same subject was taught in a way and with rewards compatible with the student's learning dynamics?)
- What is most tragic about the dark side of education is that it does not care about the life and fortunes of those students who don't fit the system. Education is so full of itself, it cannot even see the students for who they are and what they need. You would think in the thirteen years between kindergarten and the senior year of high school, someone could spend enough time with each student to find out what, how, and why the child is motivated to learn and then help the same kid develop skill in making use of his learning dynamics to attack at least some accessible subjects. You would think so.

There is a difference between corporations and educational institutions. A CEO whose leadership does not lead to bottom-line profits is held accountable for his or her failure to produce. In education, the failure to equip students to find productive, satisfying careers is blamed, not on the educators, but on the students. Wrong. At the very least, schools who equip students for failure or marginalized lives should be deconstructed. Let's start over based on what society wants.

THE DARK SIDE OF GIFTEDNESS IN THE CHURCH

If you ask a pastor to describe the purpose of the church, he will likely talk about an institution serving the families and community within some geographical boundaries.

Whether he talks about the church and its members as a worshiping community, as a center for fellowship and prayer, as a source for outreach into the community, or whatever he and his MAP perceive to be the primary mission of the church, you will usually end up sensing that however he defines the church, you and your normal life are not in its sights—except of course in the case of death, illness, disability, and maybe unemployment. The church seems interested in you mainly to become part of its life as an institution and to minister to you in time of dire need.

The tragedy of what you have just read is that the minister not only has defined the church in terms of itself, but he has defined what it means to live as a Christian. Practically, the church understands Christian living to center around the institutional church. The church concerns itself with itself—spiritually, financially, physically. This seems true regardless of denomination. Even on the issue of gifts of the Spirit, the church is focused on itself rather than on being released into people's real lives. And, again, the "gifts" are cloaked in sacred garments, to be distinguished from "natural" gifts from God that are to be used in the rest of our life.

Christians do not understand how to live or work as Christians. Except as related to the church, they do not understand how their faith and their life relate to each other.

Christians do not understand how to live or work as Christians. Except as related to the church, they do not understand how their faith and their life relate to each other. They don't understand why they're here. They don't understand what difference it makes to God whether they are accountants or engineers. They don't have a sense of purpose or meaning to their life. They don't have the faintest idea whether they are in God's will for the life they have apparently chosen. The things that excite them or engage them or worry them seem as far removed from a life of faith as does what they eat for breakfast.

Consequently, their real life and their faith grow further and further apart. Significant times with God are limited to experiences at or sponsored by the church—in worship, retreats, soup kitchens, fellowship activities. The bottom line, so to speak, is that they don't see any connection, except for the obvious issues of immorality, between their day-to-day life as an actuary or pipe fitter, and God.

The church exists for many purposes that it fulfills admirably. Where it does fall down is in its holy task of equipping lovers of God to find and embrace their calling to love and serve the world. As a high priority, the church should be "producing" working saints.

> All too often the church, while acknowledging in theory its need for the giftedness of all its members, ends up in practice being the place where one particular area of giftedness is made normative, whether it be evangelism, or political activism, or the study of prophecy, or whatever.

What happens instead is all too often that the church, while acknowledging in theory its need for the giftedness of all its members, ends up in practice being the place where one particular area of giftedness is made normative, whether it be evangelism, political activism, the study of prophecy, or whatever. This one-sided emphasis usually reflects the giftedness of the leadership in a particular church and is reinforced by it. Those whose giftedness does not fit in with the norm will feel guilty for not being "spiritual," become discouraged, and simply leave.

There are many institutionally sanctioned ways in which the church can express the dark side of its giftedness:

- by not allowing people to experience God as their giftedness allows them and even dictates;
- by not allowing people to disagree. The more we live outside our giftedness, the more energy it takes to maintain the illusion, for ourselves and for others, that all's well. And the more easily we are threatened by those who disagree or see things differently;
- by fostering a "spirituality" of principles and virtues that can be observed superficially and that leads too many people in the church to pray with the Pharisee in Jesus' story, "God, I thank you that I am not like other people," and too few to pray, "God, have mercy on me, a sinner";[10]
- by making one form of spirituality normative—whether it be Bible study or meditation or speaking in tongues—while disdaining the many other kinds of spirituality;
- by fostering a false humility that is based on the *denial* of our giftedness in order to fit into some inappropriate notion of what we should be. True humility is found in the grateful *acceptance* of our giftedness, of who we are, as a gift from God, to be used for him

---

10. Luke 18:9–14.

and for others—while joyfully accepting the giftedness of others as well.

Sadly, the list is actually much longer than this. But the one thing that stands out is this: *The church, to the extent that it fails to recognize individual giftedness as from the hand of God, fails to be the church.*

The church, to the extent that it fails to recognize individual giftedness as from the hand of God, fails to be the church.

Part Three

The Transforming Power of Human Design

Consider this fact, true of hundreds of millions in this century alone: Each person has a virtual destiny and the drive to achieve it. Yet that person is "educated" by an institution that is not interested in that fact, employed by a company that is too busy to worry about it, attending a religious institution that couldn't care less.

We have to change all that. If education would equip students for a calling suitable to their giftedness, if business would employ people in accordance with their strengths, if the church would disciple believers to overcome the dark shade on their light, then we would overcome those forces in our society that prevent life, liberty, and the pursuit of happiness, justice, and mercy for all people.

Chapter Nine

Transforming Work

Widespread appreciation for giftedness would lead to rapid improvement in the way industry operates. But human design is not a technique; it is a way of looking at life. It is a way of understanding the nature of people and how they want to function. So the crucial question is not, "What is the next formula for success?" but *"Is what we are doing or planning to do consistent with the way people are put together?"*

The failure to embrace a realistic and usable model of human nature has been the underlying cause of the failure of the many attempts to compete more effectively in the marketplace, whether national or international. None of the great new ideas and schemes hatched to revolutionize how we do business—reengineering, quality circles, teams, customer awareness, learning organizations, core competencies, performance management, globalism, change management—has been built on (or even informed by) a reality check as to the actual nature of the people involved. All have fallen far short or failed because they made assumptions about the people involved that were wrong—terribly wrong and terribly hurtful and destructive.

> The failure to embrace a realistic and usable model of human nature has been the underlying cause of the failure of the many attempts to compete more effectively in the marketplace, whether national or international.

Whether it is business-as-usual or grand new systems or tools or techniques, success is plausible and likely *if* you make sure your executives, managers, professionals, and workers are doing work that engages their strength. Once again: *You cannot achieve excellence in any function—at any level—except through people well-suited for their work.*

If you are a manager of people (as contrasted with a staff person), you may agree with me in principle. But then comes the realization that you do not gather and keep records on what your people (executives, managers, and so forth) are good at and motivated to do. Because you don't, you can't make sure your people are well-suited to their jobs. And no amount of training or development can bridge the gap between what people bring to the table and what you need in terms of motivated, turned-on working skills.

> You cannot achieve excellence in any function—at any level—except through people well-suited for their work.

And it is precisely this absence of data on the strengths of employees at all levels that is the reason job mismatch is epidemic in most organizations: conservatively speaking, one out of two—but more likely two out of three—are in "wrong" jobs.

If you recognize your company in what I have described, take the following series of recommendations seriously. They will transform your organization, its profitability, and the deep sense of satisfaction and levels of productivity enjoyed by your most important asset: your people.

GIFTEDNESS IN THE WORKPLACE: THE KEY TO PRODUCTIVITY

The key to workplace productivity and employee satisfaction is matching people's giftedness with the demands of their tasks. This is not particularly difficult or expensive to do for the benefits obtained, but it can make a spectacular difference in the results. I recommend the following steps.

Identify the Giftedness of Every Employee

> In many ways, people are the *only* renewable resource that continues to create wealth.

Identify the giftedness of every employee from the top to the bottom of the organization. Companies speak of people as "human resources." In many ways, people are the *only* renewable resource that continues to create wealth. They are the means by which value is added to raw materials and services are provided to customers. The strengths that workers bring to the job are the true strength of a company. Stewardship of the human asset of a company is being increasingly recognized as critical to its ability to compete.

Therefore, it makes sense for employers to identify the strengths their people have to offer. Quite often, company executives are amazed to discover how *little* of their people they are actually employing. They have workers assigned to jobs that maybe use twenty percent of their giftedness. By assessing people's strengths and deploying them accordingly, the company can up that effectiveness quotient to seventy percent.

> **By assessing people's strengths and deploying them accordingly, a company can more than triple their employee's effectiveness quotient.**

Employers often talk about how much they value their people. If so, they ought to find out what each employee is good at and motivated to do. I guarantee that for many employees it would be the first time that *anyone* has bothered to do that. I can think of nothing that would better communicate to employees that the company recognizes their worth as human beings.

Imagine a company investing one million dollars in a new piece of equipment. For that kind of money, company buyers would check out the specifications and performance of that equipment pretty carefully. Yet almost every employee is an asset worth at least one million dollars, and usually much more, in cash outlays over the life of his or her career.[1] In light of a capital expense like that, wouldn't it make sense for businesses to demand more "due diligence" from their investments in people?

Make No People Decisions Without Identifying the Giftedness of the Candidate and Matching It with the Work Involved

What is true for new hires is at least as true for promotions, transfers, assignments to teams and projects, and other decisions where people make a critical difference in the outcome. Whenever management has

---

1. An employee making eight dollars an hour today would earn almost $600,000 over a thirty-five-year career in constant dollars—considerably more in inflated dollars. Add to that expense the company's share of Social Security and Medicare, health insurance, and other costs, and the total "cash value" of that employee to the company easily tops $1 million. (The costs are far greater to recruit, transfer, train, and maintain salaried employees and senior management.)

You can take this reasoning further by estimating the value an employee adds to (or subtracts from) the company's product or service. Suppose that for every dollar a worker costs the company, he creates $1.25 of value. That might seem like a fair exchange—a 125 percent gain in value—until we learn that the company is employing only about thirty percent of the person's ability. But suppose we could identify the individual's strengths and help management place him in a spot where his effectiveness doubled. Then it is reasonable to double the estimated value of what he adds to the company to $2.50. An employee like that would be, quite literally, worth gold!

to make a "people decision," it should compare what the job requires as make-or-break competencies with the comparable strengths the employee does (or does not) possess.

A MAP ought to be the first document in an employee's records, because it tells the employer (and the employee's supervisor) how to read the rest of the file. When the employee's name surfaces as a candidate for a new position or assignment, the MAP provides the decision maker with the *crucial* information he needs, namely, how the employee will perform in the job, and therefore whether the person matches the opportunity.

Likewise, data on employee strengths ought to be put on performance appraisal forms, to be used by the supervisor and the employee in discussing achievement of performance goals, performance improvement, goal-setting, problem areas, and possible reassignment of duties.

MAPs are extremely helpful in finding solutions to operating problems where people are the probable root cause. By comparing the patterns of those responsible, managers can usually detect the source of the problem. Typical examples would be someone's lack of planning ability that is wreaking havoc on deadlines, or a worker's failure to take initiative because the heart of his motivational nature is to respond.

Encourage Workers At Every Level to Share Knowledge of Their Giftedness

This is especially true in any kind of career or development planning. Sports teams are well known for flaunting the assets of their players. They want everyone to know who their stars are and what unique talents they bring to the game. And the more enlightened owners recognize that financial success in a multimillion-dollar franchise tends to correlate with having the right players in the right positions.[2]

---

2. The comparison of business to sports deserves a whole book. Every day, in every newspaper in the country, countless columns of statistics appear in the sports sections detailing the performance of professional athletes. This is a tribute to how seriously sports teams, their fans, and bettors take individual and team performance. Why do businesses not do the same with their "players"? I know of very few businesses that "keep book" on their people—at least, not in terms of data that have relevance to performance.

Yet for many businesses (and their investors), the stakes are much higher than most sports franchises. A wealthy individual can buy a professional sports team for anywhere from $35 million to $135 million (a few exceptional franchises would command more). Meanwhile, many companies are worth ten to one hundred times that, and a few large corporations one thousand times that! One would think that for that kind of money, the level of relevant detail kept on employee performance—and used to position employees to greatest competitive advantage—would far surpass anything known in sports. Instead, ignorance tends to rule! I daresay some companies probably know less about their employees than they do about their customers.

Businesses could stand to adopt that posture. They should encourage employees to clarify what their strengths are for the benefit of their fellow workers. In fact, anyone who works on a cross-functional or self-managed team ought to be informed about the gifts and motivations of the other players. That way, everyone will know what to expect from each other and therefore what to demand. They will know how to organize their work and how to keep each other motivated.

Companies have a responsibility to ensure that their work teams are effective, that real diversity is assured through coupling complementary MAPs. That doesn't necessarily mean that everyone has to like each other. It means that teams have to be put together for productivity. There has to be a fit between the workers as well as a fit between each worker and his or her task.

> **Managers might approach their decisions for hiring, promotion, and transfer differently if they knew that the company was going to evaluate the wisdom and effectiveness of their choices!**

A "company coach" might be useful here, showing the team how to use each other's strengths and how to allow each other to give what each team member has to give at the appropriate time. The coach could also help the group understand and deal with conflicts that naturally grow out of differences among their gifts.

Hold Managers Accountable for Their People Decisions

How differently managers might approach their decisions for hiring, promotion, and transfer if they knew that the company was going to evaluate the wisdom and effectiveness of their choices! I suspect that managers would be far more interested in a way to predict whether someone was going to "work out" in a new assignment.

Managers should be held accountable for these decisions because making them is part of what management is all about. Unfortunately, if a manager makes a poor people decision, it is the employee(s) who tends to suffer most, then the company, then the employee's family, then the employee's coworkers. The last person to be affected—and often least affected—may be the manager.

This situation could be reversed, first by giving managers the right tools for making people decisions, namely, a summary of an employee's Motivated Abilities Pattern and a statement of the critical requirements of the task in question. Using those data, people who are gifted at management ought to be able to discern appropriate job matches.

These tools would also provide a basis for holding managers (and their supporting staff experts) accountable for selection and promotion decisions, as well as the overall management of their human resources.

Obviously, a manager cannot be responsible for the performance of an employee. But he or she is responsible for his decision to place the employee in the position—a choice that plays a causative role in the employee's performance.

The kind of accountability I have in mind is biannual review of people decisions by a "job fit" audit committee of line and staff management. They could review the job fit of each employee reporting to middle and upper management. Where mismatches are identified, a plan and timetable could be developed to adjust the employee's work—either by a change of assignment, transfer, or outplacement. Whatever action is agreed on, it could be monitored to see that it is carried out.

> The priority of a human resources department should be to assure job fit by identifying the critical requirements of all the company's open positions, and then helping it recruit people whose giftedness fits those functions.

This suggestion will no doubt seem far too threatening to some managers in corporate America. But it need not be. If I truly have skills as a manager, then I *want* to be held accountable *for using those skills*. In fact, I want help in improving them, so that I do my job better and better. The accountability process, coupled with the tools mentioned for identifying job fit, will help me in that regard.

On the other hand, if I fundamentally lack the skills to be an effective manager, then I don't want to be a manager. (I realize that others may, for whatever reason; but I don't want to waste my life doing what I am not cut out to do.) In that case, I may need a review of my people decisions to show me that I am not good at making those decisions. Then I can start answering the question, what am I good at?

Reorganize the Human Resources Function

Many human resource (HR) departments carry out noncore tasks made necessary by the demands of employing human beings.

I would change the function, requiring HR to be responsible for influencing management to make sound decisions in regard to workers. Its priority would be to assure job fit by identifying the critical requirements of all the company's open positions, and then helping it recruit people whose giftedness fits those functions. HR would act as a consultant to managers on their people decisions, so that employees are deployed strategically and effectively, and managed appropriately. It would offer to MAP employees who are being terminated, quitting, retiring, or otherwise leaving the company, so that they have an informed basis for taking next steps.

> **The key question for a company is: "Is what we are doing consistent with the way our employees are put together?"**

The HR department and its key players should be *held accountable for building close relationships with operating management, and for the quality of the information managers are given by HR for making people decisions.* It should also be expected to develop expertise in job fit, monitoring and reporting to senior management on those that exist, and anticipate those that might come about in the future.

All HR functions concerned with control and pure administrative tasks I would transfer to the accounting or legal department. All the HR functions concerned with communications to employees and employee social activities I would transfer to a marketing function concerned with relational issues: public, customers, community.

Build Giftedness into the Fabric of How You Do Business

As mentioned earlier, giftedness is not a technique but a way of looking at life. It is a way of understanding people—in a company's case, its employees. So the key question for a company is, "Is what we are doing consistent with the way our employees are put together?" In other words, "They are the ones who must reach our goals; therefore, are we taking into account our people's giftedness in everything we do?"

Asking these questions at every level of the organization will begin to make employee giftedness part and parcel of the way a company operates. For example:

In Hiring

Fashion recruiting techniques to attract suitable candidates. Take a lesson from marketing: advertise not descriptions of your company and your product and technology, but what the right candidate looks like and would find exciting.

Initially screen in or out mainly on the basis of who possesses necessary gifts, not factors such as length of education or "experience" or seniority.

In Placement

Think strategically by positioning people with particular strengths to meet critical operating needs or problems. You need innovation in a particular department? Assign Isaac the Innovator to that department for a year.

> All giftedness is transferable; no strength is ever job-specific.

Require that people's giftedness be identified and verified before making any organizational changes. Never change supervisors or work without counting the cost. Ask, "How will this move be affected by the giftedness of the people involved—and how will it affect them?" If you change from directive supervision to a facilitative type, or vice versa, realize you create new "fit" problems.

Build flexibility into your workforce by identifying people's gifts apart from job labels: "José is our 'results' man," *versus* "José is our line supervisor"; "Peggy is a person driven to prevail," *versus* "Peggy is a lawyer." *All giftedness is transferable; no strength is ever job-specific.*

In Making Assignments

Define jobs in terms of critical strengths and results rather than generic descriptions of tasks performed.

Continuously improve the match between people's work and their strengths. Shuffle work around to match available strengths, as necessary. See what the employees think about cutting up the pie.

If you are making an assignment to "develop" an individual,[3] do it in a way that stretches abilities already present. Don't try to develop what a person doesn't have. You can't remake the person!

---

3. Because I have said that giftedness is unchanging, you may have assumed that I think people can't change or be developed. They can—but only in terms of the elements of giftedness they already possess. For example, the individual with a knack for solving complex problems might start out troubleshooting a relatively minor accounting discrepancy or explaining a simple chemical reaction. But by tackling larger and more complex problems, the person can hone his skills so that twenty years later he makes major contributions to financial management or research and development.

What you can't do is "train" the person to be someone else. You can't say, "I know you are good at solving problems, but what we really need is someone who can come up with new products. So we're going to send you to a specialist in creativity and help you develop some inventiveness." It won't work—not unless the person happens to have some inventive ability already.

In Forming Teams

Build compatible teams. (Don't assume that everyone can or should play on a team.)

Build groups, teams, and staffs that complement each other in terms of giftedness. Don't clone yourself; that only reinforces deficiencies, even if it does make for smoother relationships. Strive for a complementary group of people whose gifts work together to achieve productive outcomes.

Encourage everyone in the organization toward mutual reliance on one another's strengths. Require that people share and use information on each person's strengths. It's the answer to the conflict generated by building diversity in your teams.

In Managing

Actively manage the gifts that are already available to you. Anticipate employees running out of motivational gas: they are who they are, so take that into account. Require HR to keep book on MAPs and surface likely need for new assignments.

If you want to improve performance, improve the match between the person and the position. Telling employees to "work harder" is almost never the answer.

Overmanage areas of employee "weakness." Don't assume that good intentions will do the job.

Track down and confront poor performance using principles of giftedness as your guide. Performance problems are almost always rooted in a job mismatch somewhere. You can't afford to ignore it!

When trying to resolve disputes and conflicts and to deal with stress in workplace relationships, look carefully at the gifts of the people involved for clues as to what is going on. Don't assume that it is explainable by personality, "chemistry," or the notions of pop psychology.

In tracking people's long-term performance, limit the information to content-rich data about their motivated competencies. Eliminate data that have no demonstrated relationship to performance.

In Promoting

Promote people on the basis of whether they possess the giftedness required by the new job. Don't automatically promote the best performer because of excellence in his present job.

Require employees to deal with the career implications of their strengths. Stop encouraging everyone to climb some mythical ladder of "success"—least of all by making appeals to their presumed "potential." It's cheap, and in the long run creates many job fit problems. However, if you work with them to define their MAP and its many implications, you achieve solid future growth.

Attack the problem of "plateaued" or dispirited employees as an unnecessary evil, by investigating people's motivational payoff and how their work is failing to engage it. If you have no ideas for how to redeploy a valued worker, present his MAP to a top-level committee for suggestions of new directions and assignments. (See p. 144 about job-fit audit committee.)

In Pursuing the Company's Core Mission

Integrate the objectives of the organization with individuals' motivations. Don't assume that employees will automatically "buy off" on a stated corporate mission. They work more for their own reasons than they do for yours. Relate the two.

Measure Mismatch

Business has been taught to measure, measure, measure. For it is only by measuring precise outcomes that you can measure performance and know what has to be worked on to get to where you're trying to go—or some similar and more artfully or technically phrased aphorism.

What is true of a manufacturing process is true of job fit. How do you measure the extent of the match between the work and the motivated abilities of the employees? Here are some suggestions. Gather and publish data about the

- percentage of employees who believe the company is making good/adequate/poor use of their strengths;
- number of promotions in the company, and the kinds of data used to consider candidates; number of promotions refused and stated reasons;
- names of managers responsible for hiring and promoting an employee into a position where he or she has failed or has been wildly successful;
- number of employees who have requested a transfer within the past twelve months, and the action taken;
- amount of voluntary turnover and the most frequently expressed reasons for resignation;

- absences by number of employees, frequency, length, and reasons given;
- number of employees who report regular stress on the job severe enough to impact their efficiency, the most frequently expressed reasons for that stress, and measures the employer is taking to deal with those reasons.

CREATE VALUE—AND PURPOSE

It does no good to accept the premise that every employee has a unique, valuable contribution to make if you are not going to take practical steps to ensure that each one is making his or her contribution. That's like ordering equipment or supplies and leaving them on the loading dock, unwrapped!

Fortunately, the means exist to unwrap the gifts your people have and install them where they will do the most good.[4] Indeed, companies can make SIMA® a *core technology* by which they will vastly improve their productivity in *every* area of their operation. It's easy to see why. Discovering a person's design takes a lot of the guesswork out of getting the job done. It offers a reliable way to put the right person in the right position at the right time to produce the right results.

> Discovering a person's design offers a reliable way to put the right person in the right position at the right time to produce the right results.

But it does something else, something far more valuable than any product or service your company could ever offer: it provides a way for workers to contribute mightily to the company's welfare and to find meaning, dignity, and value in how they spend their lives.

It means transforming work from duty and drudgery into a bright opportunity for fulfillment—the kind of fulfillment that can only come from energetic, meaningful effort. Workers who are working at tasks that make effective use of who they are have a sense of destiny about their labors. Believe it or not, they get *excited* about their jobs! The work *matters* to them—because *they matter!* They feel worthwhile doing the thing for which they were placed on this planet. Nothing in the world quite compares to that.

---

4. System for Identifying Motivated Abilities (SIMA®).

HOLD COMPANIES ACCOUNTABLE

Institutional investors and stockholders must take one additional step that is critical if we are to achieve these makeable outcomes: *Hold companies accountable for their selection and management of people*. If the employees prosper, so does their company. If the employees do not prosper, an audit is made of the detailed basis for the selection or promotion; particularly issues around whether critical requirements of the job and strengths of the employee were clearly established. Confidential surveys of employees, not unlike those regularly used today for other purposes in many corporations, would provide assurance that people and jobs were matched—and if not, why not. Get away from attempts to probe whether or not people are "happy." Who would admit they weren't? Go after issues that involve use of their talents: Do they have enough of a challenge? How could they be more productive?

Measurements of mismatch would not be difficult to develop and maintain. Survey results would be published for all to see. Confidential procedures could be established for people to (figuratively) raise their hand because of a serious job match issue (for example, they've run out of motivational gas), and be given thoughtful attention. Job performance measures, gaining so much emphasis nowadays, would prevent any managerial tendency to overlook marginal performance by employees.

> **Who will hold executives accountable for making productive use of the strengths available to them?**

So who will hold executives accountable for making productive use of the strengths available to them? What could work is a council of natural leaders, selected from within each organization at various levels and functions, who would ride herd on the system that was established to enforce the accountability for productive use of employee strength. Not a union as such, but leaders empowered to inspect and adjudicate and require corrective action—from *all* levels.

An enforceable requirement for accountability will not only provide greater health and productivity among the managed. It will also function to flush out executives and managers unsuitable for their jobs who have been able to maintain their positions because nobody has looked at their job fit. Once you examine job fit of the subordinate, the strengths and weaknesses of the boss become apparent because they are a crucial factor in determining the fit of the subordinate.

THE POWER OF SELF-INTEREST

A strong case can be made for the improvement of productivity, quality, and profitability by a concerted and continuing effort to make productive use of the strengths available in the workforce, and their management. But little of any of the foregoing will be accomplished unless those managing the company believe such steps are in their personal self-interest.

Lacking a commitment on the part of top management, even if significant improvements can be made in profitability and investment return, I would recommend the mobilization of the forces available in a free society to bring about change by appealing to self-interest.

We see some of this happening today. Even as some corporate executives act in ways that prove destructive to other members of society, a vast cadre of voices and forces—the press, the government, academia, cities and states, the courts, employee groups, small business, even markets themselves—has sprung to a counteroffensive.

Ralph Estes has called for a new "corporate scorecard" by which corporate performance should be measured and reported. "We should ask how well and in what ways the corporation has served, and how it has harmed, the public interest," he says. Estes's book provides detailed lists of items for measuring corporate accountability to customers, workers, communities, and society in general.[5]

He is joined in this effort by a growing number of groups that take an active interest in broader, nonfinancial measures of corporate performance: the press and media, industry watchdog groups, environmental groups, health and safety concerns, religious organizations, think tanks, policy analysts, lobbyists, shareholders, and investor services. More and more the Internet is making the information that these groups provide immediately accessible—and noticeable—worldwide.

If such expressions from society do not have the desired effect, then other more confrontational steps should be considered. One such step is political: one of our main parties, or a brand-new one, builds an appeal to voters and ultimately a legislative program to correct the mismatch between people and education, work and a share of the economic pie, which provides a more level playing field for democratic capitalism to govern the affairs of private industry. Associated with such a potential

---

5. Ralph Estes, *Tyranny of the Bottom Line* (San Francisco: Berrett-Koehler, 1996), 30–31.

movement would be enabling statutes to encourage the emergence of collective and individual "bargaining units," not unlike those we see in professional sports.

Such steps could move industry from a short-term, bottom-line fetish to building profitability through giving employees and their managers the opportunity to be both highly productive and richly fulfilled.

Chapter Ten

Transforming Education

Critical to the suggestions made in the last chapter is the fact that the vast majority of people in the workplace today have suffered through an educational system that ignores giftedness—except in the exceedingly narrow sense of "academic giftedness." If we want to see long-term changes in the workplace, we must make foundational changes in our educational systems and philosophies.

The time may be ripe for experimenting with education based on giftedness, if not yet on the level of public schools and universities (where many have a vested interest in the status quo), then certainly in those educational programs—charter schools, parochial schools, home schooling, and so on—that in effect are sounding the charge in opposition to the institutions that are failing our children and young people.

> If we want to see long-term changes in the workplace, we must make foundational changes in our educational systems and philosophies.

Especially in this chapter it is important to remember that when I talk about "giftedness" I mean *giftedness in the all-inclusive sense* described in part 1—*not* in the narrow sense of "academic giftedness."

STUDENTS: THE MOST IMPORTANT PART OF THE CURRICULUM

Giftedness cannot be taught or developed. Students arrive with their unique pattern already formed. The job of the schools (ideally) is to honor the person and prepare him to use his giftedness in society.

153

That makes the individual himself the most important part of the curriculum. Indeed, of all the subjects a student is asked to study, nothing is remotely as important as the study of himself. Nothing.

In a bygone era, self-understanding was deemed just as important as understanding the world. Today, kids are on their own when it comes to figuring out who they really are and what they have to offer. The result is that most of them waste *years* of their lives, many thousands of dollars, and untold misery groping for an answer.

> Giftedness cannot be taught or developed. The job of the schools (ideally) is to honor the person and prepare him to use his giftedness in society.

If they chose to, schools could alleviate this problem by supporting a serious effort to help students identify and employ their giftedness. This initiative need not be at the loss of any other part of the curriculum. If anything, it would make the rest of the curriculum far more effective, because it would bring to light what causes each student to learn.

In addition, an intentional focus on giftedness would do more than any other part of the curriculum to contribute to a student's success in society and satisfaction throughout life.

STEPS FOR BUILDING EDUCATION ON GIFTEDNESS

To put it even more strongly: Schools and other educational environments will have success in educating students only to the extent they make use of students' and teachers' giftedness. What, how, and why teachers are motivated to teach, and learners to learn, depends on the MAPs of the teacher and the learner, respectively. Learning will take place to the extent that the unique learning styles of the students and the unique teaching style of the gifted teacher are engaged.

To that end, I recommend the following:

1. From a child's earliest days in the educational system, identify—and help him or her recognize and value—aspects of his or her unique design, particularly those aspects related to learning.

Some of my associates work in this way with children as young as six. They seek clues about the children's giftedness by means such as storytelling, asking a child to explain a drawing he has made, observing the child's preferred activity when exposed to a variety of alternative situations and objects, making note of songs and stories that contain some of the child's "favorite things," looking at the child's favored roles in playacting, and asking the child to tell about his favorite heroes and sports or television personalities.

In addition, they ask the child's teachers to report on behavior observed in the learning environment and the parents to report on observable behavior in the home. (Teachers and parents can usually be shown how to observe motivationally significant behaviors.) Another technique that has proven fruitful is to ask children who have suitable giftedness to record achievement interviews with others children.[1]

> **Schools and other educational environments will have success in educating students only to the extent they make use of students' and teachers' giftedness.**

2. At each level of schooling (elementary, junior high, high school, postsecondary, graduate school), further identify the student's giftedness and refine both the student's and the institution's understanding of it, as follows:

- Ages 10–14. Building on the earlier record, if available, a trained specialist should spend time with the student, interactively seeking a more detailed telling of achievement stories, incrementally adding facts and knowledge.

At this stage, a much greater emphasis should be placed on identifying learning dynamics. The objective is to gain clarity about motivated learning and investigative abilities, and how those affect the child's education, both now and in future years.

- Ages 15–18. During the sophomore year in high school, an ideal approach would be to provide a two-semester course in career matching, meeting two hours per week. During the first semester, students would work in triads to identify approximated patterns of giftedness for one another.[2] In the second semester, they would be

---

1. "Achievement interviewing" involves asking a person to recount the details of how he went about doing something he enjoyed doing and did well (see chapter 2). Some children have remarkable facility at eliciting highly useful information of this kind from other children, and so they can be used as achievement interviewers.

2. The triad is an effective way to conduct peer interviews. It consists of the person who tells his or her achievement story; the interviewer, who asks questions and probes for detailed data; and the observer, who takes notes and makes sure that the interview stays on track.

given the results of a computerized job match comparing their motivational patterns with the critical requirements of various jobs.[3] Under the guidance of a trained specialist, they would explore the importance of job fit and other issues related to careers for which they seem suited. Extensive career information is already available in school and community libraries for use in this endeavor.

Another tool to develop during this stage of life is a formal "learning strategy"—a written summary description of a student's unique approach to learning and the implications of that approach for future course work. A useful learning strategy would show one's preferred kind of teacher, manner of teaching subjects, methods of evaluating work done, and opportunities for special projects, independent study, or team study.

- Ages 19–22. During vocational school, in the freshman year of college, or between freshman and sophomore years, the school should provide a two-semester career course, two hours per week.

During the first semester, students would develop a more complete picture of their motivational patterns—or, if necessary, be introduced to the concept of giftedness for the first time and have their motivated abilities patterns assessed. As with the high school course, this assessment could be accomplished through a group process, using triads. The first semester of the course would also reexamine and revise, if necessary, the students' learning strategies (see above).

During the second semester, the course would look at the implications of the students' patterns. This is to prepare them for deciding on a major, to envision themselves working in likely careers (in general terms), and to select appropriate courses and professors. The course would have the further benefit of providing students with insight as to the motivational reasons behind strong emotional reactions they have to situations or people, as well as the motivational dynamics of their relationships with others. It would also afford them an opportunity to examine their values and spiritual development.

---

3. This is not the same as the approach taken by certain skills inventories, which compare a person's responses to a questionnaire with the responses of people already employed in various occupations. A job match compares the unique motivational pattern of an individual with the critical requirements of a particular position, seeking to determine how much "fit" there is between person and position. It does not compare the person with others because whether or not someone else would fit the job is of no relevance to whether the person in question would fit the job.

College students in the last semester of their junior year have many crucial decisions looming. They would benefit from a two-hour-per-week course in which they use their MAPs to research their most likely careers. This would include an examination of the implications of those careers for possible graduate study; the identification of likely job families, possible employers, and even preferred geographical locales; tentative "crossroads" determinations that affect one's future career, such as whether one is a generalist or a specialist, a manager or contributor, an operations or a staff worker, and so on. It would include the writing of an "ideal fit" statement; making plans for field interviews with people already working in job families and careers to which the student is drawn; and instruction in the techniques of job hunting, interviewing, résumé writing, evaluating job offers, and negotiating the terms of employment.

- Adults. Provide ready access to instructional and counseling resources for alumni whose careers become derailed. This requires schools to maintain active and involved contact with their graduates. But they need not see the task as theirs alone. They could encourage alumni to seek help from each other by providing administrative and technical services supporting an alumni network. They could also network with employers.

3. Build each student's education around his motivated abilities. In other words, focus on strengths rather than abilities that are lacking. If a child excels in writing, give him as many opportunities to write as he can handle. If a teenager is motivated to excel in music, increase her opportunities for instruction in music. Decrease the expectations for areas in which a student has little motivation or aptitude.[4] *Require teachers to elicit an achievement experience from every student in every course.*

---

4. There are certain basic skills that every citizen obviously needs in order to function in and contribute to society: reading, writing, figuring, expressing oneself clearly, among others. We can debate the threshold of what is acceptable in each of these areas. The point of my suggestion is that beyond basic functioning and knowledge, we should start asking whether demand for increased skill or proficiency in a particular task or knowledge in a particular field is motivationally appropriate to the individual. That is, are we asking him or her to produce results that he or she fundamentally is not "wired" to produce? If so, we are doing neither them nor society any favors by browbeating them to "apply" themselves. In fact, we are probably doing damage. We may be creating a bad taste in their mouth for learning, plus we are forcing them to concentrate their attention and energy from things that they *do* do well and enjoy.

Some people look back on their schooling and say, "I didn't see the value of what I had to learn at the time, but now it's become valuable to me." That's wonderful! It's a testimony to their gift for making use and seeing the meaning of information acquired long ago. Many others, however, look

4. Encourage students to celebrate their knowledge of their giftedness; to stand behind it and be identified with it; to use it productively in day-to-day life, both in and outside of school; to seek help when they encounter difficulties living out their pattern; to take responsibility for the use of their gifts, including the improper or excessive use of them in ways that are harmful; to provide papers, stories, or descriptions about the careers they imagine pursuing, given who they are, and what use those careers might make of their giftedness.

Plan and evaluate overall educational effectiveness on the basis of how it contributes to the life of the student after their educational experience. To that end, establish a central operating principle that students' giftedness and learning dynamics will guide the development of new curriculum. Course effectiveness should be judged by whether or not it provides achievements reported as experienced by its students.

5. Hire new teachers on the basis of whether they actually have giftedness for teaching—by demonstrating that they have caused learning to take place in the past. (An alternative is to require them to demonstrate the ability in the classroom. People with genuine giftedness for teaching will display it almost instantly. Even those for whom there are lingering questions will show in a matter of days whether they can cause learning to take place.)[5]

6. Provide outplacement resources for teachers who lack the ability and motivation to teach. Naturally, this would include an assessment of what the person actually is gifted to do and help in matching the person with a suitable job.

7. Appoint supervisors, department heads, administrators, and executive personnel on the basis of their giftedness for their responsibilities.

8. Revise compensation plans to encourage increasing expertise at causing learning and eliciting achievements from the greatest number and variety of students.

9. Make substantial use of student and parent giftedness in supporting students-in-need educationally. This could include both one-on-one tutoring and organizing teams of students who are motivated to learn as part of a team.

---

back and say, "Ninety-five percent of my education was a waste of time. I didn't learn a thing until I got out of school and started living in the real world." That, too, is a testimony to giftedness—only it reveals that the schools almost never tapped the way these people learned.

5. A new teacher whose ability for teaching seems to be in question needs to have his/her motivated abilities pattern (MAP) assessed.

For example, highly creative students often learn in ways not accommodated by the typical classroom. They tend to learn by doing, observing, or experimenting, and learn in order to solve a problem, defend a position, prevail against others, or act out a role. These children may struggle academically when faced with normal methods of instruction. But often they can be reached by placing them in a brainstorming session where they come up with ideas for acquiring knowledge and skills according to their own preferred learning styles. Thus they make use of each other's giftedness.

ACHIEVEMENT-BASED LEARNING: WILL IT GET THE JOB DONE?

To some, education based on giftedness may appear to be lacking in the kind of discipline and effort that they think the conventional classroom could achieve. But actually, just the opposite is true. When a youngster's motivation is fully engaged, he learns with a passion that astounds most adults. Just think of the kid who gets turned on by tinkering with his chemistry set; or the girl who reads by the hour; or the budding actors who spend all day and well into the night focused on an upcoming performance; or the aspiring athlete who is still shooting baskets in the driveway long after night has fallen.

I know of educators who would give anything to tap the wellsprings of energy and effort like these that they know are in their students. Guess what? The students would give anything, too! The key that unlocks their motivation is giftedness. Giftedness tells the teacher where, when, and how to really lean on a student and require a prodigious effort. When the teacher calls on a student's area of strength, the response is liable to go well beyond the class standard—maybe even off the chart.

If the teacher keeps going with this demonstrated aptitude, pressing for more achievement and better results, he can take the student to ever higher levels of comprehension and expression—seemingly with no limits in sight. A student whose motivational pattern is turned on will not be constrained by the artificial boundaries of generic learning. He will keep striving, exploiting, and harnessing whatever is called for by the motivational payoff he seeks.

From time to time, we see this kind of intensive learning taking place even in the current school system. A gifted teacher will connect with the motivational bent of his students, and suddenly they come alive. Most of us think of this as an exceptional situation. I am suggesting that it need not be. If we paid more attention to the giftedness of students and their teachers, we might be shocked at how much learning takes place!

Schools can provide a continuum of services to determine and keep track of every student's giftedness. That information would be the student's badge of honor. We would celebrate it—and thereby honor the student. He would tell it to everyone: his fellow students, his teachers, his parents, his coaches, his counselors—anyone involved with his education. He would want everyone to know who he is, how he learns, and what unique bent he brings to our world.

> **If we paid more attention to the giftedness of students and their teachers, we might be shocked at how much learning takes place!**

And when he graduates from the system, we would help him share that information with prospective employers, so that they know where to place him, how to manage him, and how to keep him dedicated to the job.

If all of this sounds too ideal, that is only because we have become too jaundiced by the current system. We have come to accept that people just wander for about the first thirty years of their lives until (hopefully) they find their "place" in the world. But I have seen too many individual cases where the elements of what I am proposing have worked. If they can work in a few cases, there is no reason why they cannot be made to work for the majority.

How do we make it work for the majority?

Gifted Leadership

In his perceptive book *Visions of Grandeur*, my friend Ralph Mattson points out that every leader is an agent of change.[6] Leadership is not about stature—as if the world could be transformed if we were only blessed with enough Thomas Jeffersons, Winston Churchills, or Martin Luther King Jr's. for all the key spots.

No, leadership has to do with change. And change is a *condition*. A leader surfaces when someone with the right stuff is introduced into the right conditions and begins to produce sustained transformation.

---

6. Ralph T. Mattson, *Visions of Grandeur: Leadership That Creates Positive Change* (Chicago: Praxis Books/Moody Press, 1994), 18.

This goes a long way toward explaining why so many schemes for reforming society and its institutions have ended up collecting dust on a shelf. The ideas may or may not have merit, but that's not why they don't get implemented. They fail because no one with the motivated abilities required to implement them appears in the right place at the right time. In other words, they die for lack of leadership. Not just any leadership—a lack of *gifted* leadership.

Consider our schools. How long have people been crying out for fundamental reforms in our nation's educational system? How many bright, perceptive, knowledgeable experts have put forth creative ideas, bold visions, innovative programs, and new strategies in a bid to upgrade the schools' performance? Yet more often than not, change has proven elusive.

But if we pay attention to human design, we can see why. Those who run the schools—I'm thinking of administrators and policymakers—do so out of their unique motivational patterns. No one should expect them to do otherwise. But what if an administrator's pattern predisposes him toward maintaining the status quo rather than changing it? In that case, what others see as "reform" he will see as a nuisance and a threat and prove singularly intractable in implementing what has been called for.

> **Many schemes for reforming education fail because no one with the motivated abilities required to implement them appears in the right place at the right time. These schemes die for lack of leadership—a lack of *gifted* leadership.**

Oh, you can exercise political muscle and mandate change. But what you will get is grudging compliance, not genuine reform. That's because the administrator cannot change who *he* is. The leopard cannot change his spots. If by nature he resists change (which, in the right circumstances, is not a bad thing), then it is pointless (and unfair) to make him the point man for change.

I believe that the purpose of education is to equip students for life and work. I concur with noted educator Paul Gagnon that the schools' purpose is three-pronged: to have an impact on the future effectiveness of students in the world of work, in public affairs, and in their private culture.[7]

---

7. Paul Gagnon, "What Should Children Learn," *Atlantic Monthly*, (December 1995) 70.

Most schools today are doing nothing of the sort. But if we want them to, we have to import leaders into the schools who *by their own motivation* have both passion and potency for making education an equipping process leading to a productive and fulfilling life. We can't just convene presidential committees and governors' conferences and the like and legislate a set of high-minded objectives and then expect administrators to value that agenda and get it implemented. It won't happen, and hasn't happened, because it *can't* happen apart from people gifted at making it happen.

Nothing of consequence takes place in the world apart from inherent giftedness.

As far as possible we should reposition and redeploy personnel where their strengths will do the most good. Just because someone is not a change agent does not mean he has no contribution to make toward the education of young people. He should be reassigned—and not dishonored in the process—on the basis of his giftedness.

These are elements of giftedness that tend to fit people for leadership roles. You can't "train" people to have them, you can only identify people who already do, and then put them where they will be most effective. And one thing is certain: change cannot be managed apart from people with the giftedness to manage change. So it's not a question of "doing the best we can with the people we've got." The only way to accomplish any major objective is through people fitted to achieve that objective. As always, nothing of consequence takes place in the world apart from inherent giftedness.

Accountable Educators

If educators and administrators were held responsible for equipping students to pursue a quality of life and calling suitable to their design, our educational process and experience would change radically. How long it would take for such a transformation depends. Probably it would take at least one generation for entire school systems to change, but certainly some individual high schools and community and four-year colleges would catch and run with the idea.

Although the greatest beneficiary would be the student, gifted teachers would be recipients of the high reward of teaching mainly those students who are turned on by the teachers' favorite subject!

Who would build the educational effectiveness surveys and other feedback mechanisms looking back from age twenty and thirty to evaluate one's educational experience and its value? The same constituency or authority that allocates financial support, whether that be state legislator, school board, or parents' organization in the case of private secondary schools, colleges, and universities. Over time, measurements would become more accurate and able to pinpoint specific weaknesses in each school needing attention, whether in the faculty or the curriculum or the administration.

Society can break free from the crippling tautology that academic success is an end in itself.

Society could finally break free from this crippling tautology that academic success is an end in itself. The institution would be held responsible for education that makes a clear and obvious difference in the student's life as an adult.

If we hold them accountable so their jobs and compensation depend on acceptable performance, some will find a way to make it work. Others will have to find a suitable job for themselves somewhere else. There would be no room for tenure.

Policies Consistent with Human Design

Leaders are crucial, but as someone has pointed out, to be a leader you have to have someone following you. If you don't, you are not a leader, no matter what your title or pretensions may be. This can be a humbling realization. It suggests that leaders bring change only when people choose to change. Without that collective will behind them, so-called leaders end up as voices crying in the wilderness.

A group's collective will is expressed through policy. Policy may be formally stated in laws, regulations, and written guidelines, or informally known as "the way things are." Either way, policy both expresses and reinforces what the group wants.

Right now, many policies in the United States work against individuals and institutions making the best use of people's giftedness. For example, a moment ago I alluded to the political muscle and bureaucratic inertia that stand in the way of change in the schools. These are largely a matter of policy, what one observer has described as an extraordinary web of laws, regulations, and contractual arrangements that preserve the monopoly power of regional educators.

These impediments include

- state licensing laws that prevent people from teaching who haven't spent thousands of dollars and countless hours earning an obsolete education degree;
- laws preventing people with general management skills but without extensive training in an education school from attaining positions such as school superintendent;
- collective bargaining contracts that dictate class sizes and require all teachers to be paid the same, regardless of the demands and supply for their particular position and level of job performance;
- labor laws that make it hard to replace ineffective employees.[8]

It's easy to see how a climate like that could keep ineffective teachers and administrators in a school system and stifle the deployment of personnel according to their MAPs. So if society wants better schools, it will have to change the policies by which schools operate.

What kinds of educational policies are consistent with giftedness?

- Policies that demand *demonstrated ability* for the tasks required for teaching and other academic positions, not just a certificate showing completion of course work.
- Policies that encourage teachers to make the most of their unique teaching styles, not just adhere to a set approach to the classroom.
- Policies that put management functions in the hands of people with demonstrated capability for management, not just people who have survived attrition and moved up the ranks.
- Policies that reward employee performance, not just seniority.
- Policies that consider where each individual student will be five, ten, or even twenty years after leaving the institution, and the school's impact on that, not just students' performance on standardized tests.

Can policy changes like these really be enacted? Yes, but probably not painlessly. I am loathe to ever try to legislate change, but I doubt that

---

8. James H. Snider, "Education Wars: The Battle over Information-Age Technology," *The Futurist*, (May-June 1996) 26–27. Snider is a former school board member and a university fellow at Northwestern University. The point of his article is to advocate for more effective use of new technologies for educational purposes. However, the well-entrenched, interlocking policies that he outlines stand as an imposing barrier against that.

changing the policies by which schools operate can be achieved without swallowing the bitter medicine of a political fight. In fact, that battle is already underway and can be expected to heat up considerably in the coming years. No doubt some heads are going to roll. On the other hand, we may also witness a bloodless revolution in which new alternatives for education are allowed, forcing traditional schools to compete—and as a result, either learn to satisfy the "market" or go the way of the railroads.

Chapter Eleven

Transforming Religion

I love the church.[1] But change of a fundamental sort is necessary in the church's perception of why it exists—which, among other things, is *not* to do church. Instead of being at the front of society, it seems to be on the sidelines. The church has largely forgotten why it exists. It tends to define its purpose in terms of its needs and interests as an institution, and to organize its people around that purpose. But the institution is not where the action is. The Lord of the church is not in the institution, but in the people, and the people are out working in the world.

> Change of a fundamental sort is necessary in the church's perception of why it exists—which, among other things, is *not* to do church.

To that end, he has gifted and called each one to a life of sacrificial love, to be poured out through a suitable calling as a continuing act of worship and adoration. I believe he intends to transform the world through the work of his saints. And that is the church's mission—to produce working saints.

HOW TO PRODUCE "WORKING SAINTS"

How can the church—including denominations, local churches, seminaries, and parachurch ministries—accomplish that task? Only by engag-

---

1. I feel constrained to limit my comments to the institutions of Christianity, which is my tradition. But I hope leaders from other traditions will translate my thinking into the language of their own faith, and transfer my suggestions into the management of their own institutions.

ing and sanctifying the giftedness of its people to serve the world. Several suggestions follow.

Develop an In-Depth Theology of Human Design

This book opens the door on that endeavor. But people who have gifts for theological research and thinking need to investigate the biblical data on personhood so that the church's understanding accords with Scripture. They also need to study the history of giftedness and what Christians have had to say on this subject down through the centuries. In this connection, the subject of "spiritual gifts" needs an overhaul (see also chapter 7).

Teach the Subjects of Human Design in Seminaries

The issues of human design touch on nearly every aspect of theological inquiry.[2] They also find a place in the pastoral care curriculum, training pastors-to-be how to identify people's giftedness and how to use that as a primary tool in pastoring parishioners.

Admit People to Seminary on the Basis of Demonstrated Giftedness

Men and women need to be admitted to seminary based on a demonstrated giftedness for the critical demands of the prospective work they intend to do—not merely on the basis of a subjective "call" to the ministry. I won't quibble here with the idea of a specialized call to the ministry, but I will say that it is not enough. Just because someone says he is "called" to vocational Christian work should not in itself make him a candidate for training. The most important question is, has God fitted him with the gifts required to do that work? If not, he doesn't belong there. He has misunderstood his "call," because God never calls someone to do something without giving him the ability to do it. Indeed, ability is one of our primary clues as to what God's calling is for us.

By "mapping" students (assessing their motivated abilities pattern, or MAP) either prior to admission or at least once they have enrolled, seminaries could do a valuable service in deploying leaders for the

---

2. For example: the Person of God (theology proper); the design of Christ (Christology); the Holy Spirit's role in accomplishing God's work through human giftedness (pneumatology); sin and the "dark side" of motivation (hamartiology); the grace of God expressed through our day-to-day lives (soteriology); the ways in which design makes humans distinct from angels (angelology); the church's role in nurturing and resourcing the gifts of its people (ecclesiology); and the ultimate ends toward which our gifted efforts are aimed, so that God's will is done "on earth as it is in heaven" (eschatology).

> Just because someone says he is "called" to vocational Christian work should not in itself make him a candidate for training. The most important question is, has God fitted him or her with the gifts required to do that work?

church. They could direct students into work or ministries that fit who they are, vastly increasing their productivity and satisfaction.

If this sounds like too much trouble, consider how much more trouble comes from admitting a person who is not cut out for the ministry.[3] Consider, too, that knowing every student's motivational makeup could transform the effectiveness of seminary training. (To understand why, see my earlier comments on the implications of giftedness for work and education.)

Identify the Motivational Makeup of Current Church Leaders[4]

A moment ago I pointed out that the mission of the church is to produce working saints. Yet there is a growing body of evidence suggesting

---

3. Current seminary admissions processes tend to screen applicants on whether they can do the task of learning in a seminary, not whether they can do the tasks of vocational ministry. Like almost every other institution of higher learning, seminaries look at transcripts, undergraduate degrees and course work, letters of reference from college professors, and so on. These measures—inaccurate and/or irrelevant as they may be—supposedly tell the school whether the applicant is fitted to do the course work of a seminary education.

As a result, those admitted—and therefore those who graduate and end up in the better-paying, more influential jobs in the institutional church—tend to be people fitted to do the course work of a seminary education. They are often readers, concept-oriented, abstract thinkers, interested in words and languages, fascinated with societies and cultures, and most comfortable relating to groups (not individuals), among other common characteristics. Many of them make (or would make) excellent professors. But is that what parishes and parachurch ministries need?

4. I would guess that most ministerial positions have been well reviewed, and the particulars of their demands are easily obtained. Seminaries could collect these data into a simple database of positions and use it to screen or direct students into suitable career choices.

For example, it is well known that a key task for a senior pastor is usually to preach and teach. So, an admissions person could look at an applicant's achievement activities and ask: Are there any hints here that the person enjoys and does well at communicating verbally to groups? Are there any examples of his having taught someone else? Does he seem to possess any communication skills such as explaining, persuading, promoting, or inspiring? Is there any hint that subjects such as concepts, words, principles, values, and groups figure into his pattern?

One *cannot* make final judgments as to the person's MAP based on this exercise. A full-blown achievement history and motivational assessment would be required for that. But if the individual has any talents that destine him for preaching and teaching, they probably will be apparent to the trained eye even at this preliminary level of inquiry. If there is *nothing* among the achievements to suggest that this person can communicate effectively with groups, that doesn't mean he is not fitted for some form of vocational Christian work; but it strongly argues against admitting him with the idea that he will train to be a senior minister. To do so would be utterly dishonest. At the least, it says that he needs to be "mapped" before he graduates from seminary.

that working saints—people who are spiritually alive and personally effective in their day-to-day activities—are not being turned out by today's churches.

One recent survey found that less than one percent of pastors interviewed agreed that if Christ returned on earth today, he would characterize the church as doing "tremendous, highly effective work." Instead, fifty-three percent felt that the church is having "little positive impact on souls."

"I don't think any pastor truly committed to the gospel could look at America today and claim we're really revolutionizing this country," remarked one minister who was polled, the leader of a midsized congregation in Alabama.[5]

Why is that? Ephesians 4 is clear that God has given the church certain people with just the right gifts for equipping saints for their work. So if working saints are not being produced by a given congregation, that suggests that the giftedness to produce them must be lacking—perhaps because it is not present.

> Churches need pastors and other leaders who are gifted at causing spiritual growth to take place.

It is not a question of blame. It is a question of whether the right giftedness is present for the task. Just as schools need teachers who are actually gifted at causing learning to take place, so churches need pastors and other leaders who are gifted at causing spiritual growth to take place.

Again, though, the data show that many churches are served by clergy who do not have that giftedness. In his fascinating study entitled *Today's Pastors*, researcher George Barna reports that only fifty-two percent of senior pastors claim to have a gift for preaching or teaching. Six percent of pastors say they have no idea what their "spiritual gifts" are!

According to Barna, "The inference from these numbers is that the pastors heading churches today are looked upon to communicate and to interact on mass and personal levels with people but not necessarily with strategic considerations in mind."[6] How true! Too many clergy and their congregations appear to be just "doing church" in a rote, aimless way, with little if any passion or intentionality in what they are about, no burning sense of

---

5. George Barna, *Today's Pastors* (Ventura, CA: Regal Books, 1993), 57–60.
6. Ibid., 121–22. I find Barna's list of items that are not considered spiritual gifts interesting. It is true that these functions are not found among the New Testament lists of gifts. But in our assessments

> **Few evils are greater than job mismatch. For the church to permit it within its own institutions is doubly evil, because the church really ought to know better on the basis of Scripture.**

mission or intelligent plan of action to make a difference in their world.

Add to this the fact that *only six percent of senior pastors feel that they have a gift for leadership*,[7] and I think the case is made that the church could only benefit if its leaders had a clearer understanding of how God has fitted them for service.

As Christians, we are shooting ourselves in the foot if we place and keep people in leadership positions for which they lack the requisite skills and motivation. In light of this, the next suggestion is fairly self-evident.

Redeploy Ministers, Missionaries, and Other Church Leaders Who Do Not Have the Gifts to Accomplish the Ministries They Are In

Few evils are greater than job mismatch. For the church to permit it within its own institutions is doubly evil, because the church really ought to know better on the basis of Scripture.

All I am saying is that we should assess the motivational makeup of vocational Christian workers—the human design that God has given them. We should also assess the critical requirements of ministerial functions—the aspects of the job that must be done if the function is to be accomplished. Then we should evaluate whether the person fits the position in which he is currently serving. If not, we should make haste to find him a more suitable place of service, both for his sake and the sake of the kingdom.

It may be that he still belongs in vocational Christian work, just in a different spot. However, it may also be that the world is suffering greatly because we are hiding his light under an unsanctified bushel.

---

of people's giftedness, we have often found some expression of these abilities among people's motivational behavior.

So I am not surprised if a pastor feels that he has a gift for hospital visitation, or even cooking. He probably does, and he should use that gift.

What troubles me is not the rare individual who *knows* he has a gift for something not generally recognized as a "spiritual gift." It is the person who hasn't a clue as to *any* of his gifts; or worse, the fellow who thinks he is gifted in an area, or would like to be, but clearly lacks that endowment.

7. Ibid., 122.

Preach and Teach on Human Design in the Local Church

I almost hesitate to suggest preaching on human design, lest anyone turn it into an academic sort of thing. Pastors who lean toward the theoretical can do that, you know!

Still, there is a body of theological truth and its practical application concerning human design that every Christian has a right to know *and celebrate*. So if I were a pastor, I would keep the theme in front of my people that God takes a *personal* interest in them as unique individuals. I would explain that he has fitted them for a purpose, showing them many examples of people in the Bible and throughout history whose lives were gifted for a particular task. I would name or point out gifts displayed by people in my congregation—not to put anyone on the spot, but to praise God for his handiwork and to affirm what is good. I would come back again and again to those passages of Scripture that speak of God's craftsmanship in forming us as individual human beings, and the implications of that truth (see appendix C, "The Biblical Basis of Giftedness").

> If, as a pastor, I understand a person's giftedness, I have a lot of clues as to how he relates to God, person-to-Person. I even have insight into the sins that will tempt him most.

Identify the Strengths and Motivational Patterns of Church Members, Then Use Those Data As a Strategic Tool for Pastoral Care

If, as a pastor, I understand a person's giftedness, I have a powerful tool with which to meet his or her spiritual needs. I know how he learns. I know what matters to him. I know the dynamics of his motivation. I understand how he relates to others. I recognize what he is passionate about, what triggers his energy, and what he needs to sustain it.

I have a lot of clues as to how he relates to God, person-to-Person. I even have insight into the sins that will tempt him most.

In fact, if I put all of this information together with his life story, I can anticipate the overall direction of his life.[8] I can help him define and articulate his purpose. I can help him interpret the events of his life, so that

---

8. Bill Hendricks gives about two dozen examples of this principle in his book, *Exit Interviews: Revealing Stories of Why People Are Leaving the Church* (Chicago: Moody Press, 1993).

they have meaning. I can almost predict where his "breakdowns" will come—as well as his successes.

Of course, this pastoral care requires that he be treated as an individual. Does that mean a staff person dealing with him one-on-one? Not necessarily. It could also mean a gifted layperson carrying out that function, as well as the person participating in a small group designed for individual spiritual development (led, of course, by someone possessing some giftedness for causing spiritual development).

Place Volunteers in Church-Related Ministry Positions on the Basis of Their Giftedness

Having identified people's motivational patterns, it ought to be fairly easy to find people whose MAPs match volunteer service opportunities (if the critical requirements of those service opportunities have been properly identified).

I am not saying that everyone in the church ought to be a volunteer in the church program. I am saying that there are obviously tasks to be done that relate directly to the purposes and programs of the institution. Volunteers for these positions ought to be recruited on the basis of giftedness for the task (not through guilt or goodwill).

> Volunteers for church positions ought to be recruited on the basis of giftedness for the task—not through guilt or goodwill.

Every church-related function ought to be handled by a person fitted for the task. Use gifted readers to read the Scripture, people to whom words and their expression matter. Use gifted teachers in Sunday school, people who can cause learning to take place. Turn over the books to a numbers-lover, someone who delights in a neat row of accurate figures.

Everywhere, in every function, everything should reflect the glory of God—yes, even something as "mundane" as maintenance or the making and serving of the coffee. God deserves excellence, so recruit people who by nature will take the job seriously, albeit joyfully.

And if you are a pastor, *stop* doing what your congregation or staff don't have the gifts to do—or at least stop emphasizing it. If it really matters to God, if he really wants it done, then trust that he will supply someone with the right bent for making it happen. Do not bore God or each other with dull, lifeless, or ineffective efforts. Encourage what is lively and fresh and God-honoring.

Tear Down the Walls Between the "Secular" and the "Sacred"

There is no distinction between "sacred" and "secular" in the New Testament. That dichotomy is of pagan origin. The Lord of Scripture is Lord of all. Nothing falls outside his concern or sovereignty. Therefore, the issues and activities that take place outside the four walls of the building—"secular" things such as business strategy and planning, conflicts with a supervisor, the ideas of a college professor, dirty diapers—deserve just as much consideration as those that take place inside the structure— prayer, missions, Communion, hymns.

For many church leaders, this requires a new way of thinking. One way to foster that would be for pastors and teachers to spend more time in the "secular" work world to appreciate what people face there and to better understand what it means to live out one's calling there.[9]

> If you are a pastor, *stop* doing what your congregation or staff don't have the gifts to do—or at least stop emphasizing it.

Consider the Varieties of People's Giftedness in Applying Spiritual Truth

Preachers are fond of ending their sermons with some form of a call to action. Quite often, they have some specific behavior in mind.

However, they need to recognize that what they perceive as an ideal way to practice the truth is heavily influenced by their motivational makeup. I guarantee that the majority of their people would apply the truth differently, if it were up to them.

Provide a Variety of Ways to Learn in Church, Because Not Everyone Learns in the Same Way

May I speak bluntly? Many pastors were admitted to seminary and did well there because they learn by listening to lectures. By contrast, the majority of laypeople do not learn by listening to lectures. Most learn by experiencing, doing, discussing, or observing. Yet it is their lot to sit week after week and listen to a pastor trained to speak in lecture format.

---

9. Ironically, the pastor's own world contains similar problems as those experienced by his people. The challenges he faces in areas like attendance, budgeting, conflicts, building repairs, employee management, leadership recruitment, people problems, and personal effectiveness are not much different. The point is that he looks at and deals with issues from the standpoint of calling, and therefore as important matters to God, not from the standpoint of daily living.

Preachers need to recognize that what they perceive as an ideal way to practice the truth is heavily influenced by their own motivational makeup. The majority of their people would apply the truth differently if it were up to them.

So what do they do? The same thing they did in school: they let their mind wander; they daydream; some of them even fall asleep.

Pastors may criticize this inattention as evidence of a "lack of commitment." But the problem has nothing to do with people's zeal for the Lord.[10] It has to do with learning style: they simply don't learn by listening!

It also has to do with teaching style. Probably ninety-nine percent of senior pastors are expected to preach, yet Barna finds that barely half of them feel they even have a gift for it! (Who knows how many who feel they do actually do!)

Despite these facts, churches, particularly Protestant churches, have made the sermon their primary means of instruction. The results speak for themselves.

I love a good sermon. But it's clear that churches could be far more effective in helping adults learn if they provided a variety of ways to learn, even in the course of a Sunday morning worship service.[11]

Some churches that are trying to do just that have been criticized for offering entertainment rather than edification and worship. That may be true in some cases (it may just be envy in others). But how do we evaluate that? As always, the question when it comes to the effectiveness of education is whether the learners learned anything. Do they demonstrate

---

10. Barna reports that thirty percent of pastors blame a "lack of laity commitment" as their greatest frustration in ministry. By this they mean "a lack (on the part of laity) of commitment to the faith, a failure to accept the responsibility of believers to minister, confusion over what it takes to interest people in pursuing their faith, disenchantment with long-term members who are the least enthusiastic of all about ministry, the difficulty of enlisting volunteers to help the church, and the challenge of sustaining long-term commitment."

By now you may recognize this "lack of commitment" as a motivational issue more than a spiritual one. However, because pastors tend to see things in spiritual terms, they assume a lack of spiritual commitment as the diagnosis of these ills.

11. One clue to consider in carrying out this suggestion: in our experience assessing tens of thousands of people during the last forty years, we have found that the vast majority of adults (more than sixty percent) favor learning by doing, trying, or experiencing something. For churches, that suggests that most parishioners need a far more interactive learning environment if anything is to "stick."

some knowledge or skill after the instruction that they did not demonstrate prior to it?

Whatever methods a church uses to instruct its people, whether through Scripture reading, traditional hymns, contemporary music, testimonials, drama, slide shows, video, liturgical dance, classroom lecture, discussion groups, service projects, field trips—the possibilities go on and on—it *must* use people who possess gifts in those areas if it expects to cause learning to take place. Otherwise these attempts will come off as gimmicks.

Troubleshoot Conflicts and People Problems by Looking at Giftedness As the Causative Element

Invariably overlooked in the relational spats that thrive in every congregation is the fact that people relate to each other on the basis of who they are. They relate out of their MAPs.

Trying to resolve conflicts by labeling people "right" and "wrong" is inevitably counterproductive. I'm not saying that there is no such thing as right and wrong. Of course there is, and sometimes people are flat-out wrong. But people behave toward others on the basis of their MAP, and if we fail to consider who they are and how God has made them, we do nothing to help them get along with others. We only condemn them.

> When people problems surface in a church, leaders need to resist the urge to look immediately for "spiritual" causes. Instead they should ask, What is the motivational bent of these people who are having trouble?

When people problems surface in a church congregation, pastors and other leaders need to resist the urge to look immediately for "spiritual" causes. Instead they should ask, What is the motivational bent of these people who are having trouble? What ends are they driven to seek in all of their endeavors? How do people fit into those intentions? What mismatches are there in this relationship between the giftedness of the people involved?

Taking this approach, many conflicts can be resolved simply by rearranging the players so that their motivational needs are satisfied rather than frustrated. In fact, the conflict may actually lead to better and deeper relationships in the body because people are able to appreciate and value each other as persons. And if there are spiritual factors involved, paying attention to giftedness is the fastest way to get at them, because it will reveal whether someone is succumbing to the "dark side" of his pattern. Which leads us to the next point.

Challenge People to Be Aware of How Their Gifts May Be Used for Evil

Every pattern has a dark side (see chapter 8). The very strengths that fit us for useful service become the means whereby we sin against the Lord and other people. It is common to think of sin as an expression of moral weakness. But I think if you analyzed the most egregious sins that people commit, they almost always are corrupted forms of the very gifts that ordinarily produce great good. Just think of the passion and energy with which a trial lawyer may defend a criminal. Then imagine that same firepower trained on his family, whom he may abuse in the worst possible ways. Think of the overwhelming charisma a gifted actress may employ to hold an audience spellbound. Then consider how she may use that charm to manipulate and connive her way to the top of her profession.

> If you analyze the most egregious sins people commit, you find that they almost always are corrupted forms of the very gifts that ordinarily produce great good.

Churches need to place a warning label on giftedness. They need to caution their people about the temptation to use strength in the interest of sinning. They should teach people to bring their gifts under the mastery of Christ and to exercise them with a sacrificial spirit. Part of dying to self involves *refraining* from the use of one's talents when doing so would be inappropriate or inconsiderate. Along with the rest of life, we have to put our gifts on the altar as part of the "living sacrifice" that the New Testament calls us to be.

Encourage People to Form and Participate in Small Affinity Groups, Especially Around Their Vocational Interests, Experience, and Problems

The value of small groups has long been recognized as an effective means of nurturing personal and spiritual growth. What has not been recognized is why these groups can be so helpful: they reach people's personhood. In small groups, individuals have a much greater chance of expressing their unique bent and benefiting from the contribution of others.

Through discussion, celebration, confrontation, prayer, accountability, problem solving, and learning together, group members tend to become much more in tune with each other's giftedness.

There are many more ways in which human design affects the life of the Christian community. But I think these will be more than enough for any church leader to chew on—and, I hope, implement. In considering these suggestions, I want you to notice that nothing here violates any central belief or doctrine of orthodox Christianity. Admittedly, this may seem like a novel approach to working with people. But I see it as a return to a sound understanding of persons, not a departure from it. If ever the church needed such a return, it is now, because our world needs people of spiritual vitality more than ever.

Consider these benefits which would accrue to the church and its people:

Good job fit for the pastor(s) and staff bears much fruit in achieving the spiritual, financial, and administrative goals and objectives of the church and its leaders.

Laypeople (and professional staff) are bonded and committed to active and involved church membership because they

- have found their purpose in life;
- have integrated their faith and all of their life;
- have connected to knowing and loving God in a way they can live with and cultivate;
- have solved nagging and destructive relational, financial, and vocational problems haunting their peace;
- have called out and dealt a death blow to root sins and evil thoughts and actions driven by misuse of their giftedness;
- have been given the courage to start new lives, new callings, new relationships, new priorities;
- have built effective families and productive, satisfying careers;
- have found an engaging work of service and ministry in the church and have taken an active role in the local body of Christ.

Chapter Twelve

Starting the Transformation Process

Changing the pillars of society in the foundational ways described in the last three chapters is a long, hard road—"unlikely and impractical" if you're a pessimist (or consider yourself a realist). I've been told that we need a "hook," a reason rooted in the self-interest of those currently in charge, to get the kind of action I've proposed. One such "institution" that has an inherent and live interest in this matter of endowed giftedness is the family, whether headed by both a mom and dad, or by either.

THE FAMILY AS A FORCE

Families with school-age children can be readily enlisted in the common cause of reforming education. In fact, the family could be the *only* unit in our society that has an inherent interest in the welfare of their kids and a commitment to their getting what they need to succeed in life.

In every part of the globe, when I have presented our findings, men and women come up after the session to ask about help for their kids (preteens to young adults). Clearly, there is a serious and abiding concern on the part of parents about their kids' schooling and absence of a career focus. As often as not, requests for help come from single parents. Criticism and indictment of the career guidance given to their kids is frequent and withering.

This parental worry appears to be universal and could surely be engaged to drive change in existing educational systems. This would be true especially if the learning dynamics and educational needs of their kids had been identified and were awaiting a response from the school.

I realize that teachers often complain about the many parents who do not want to get seriously involved in reviewing the performance of their kids. But if the discussion were more responsive to the specific needs of the youngster, I believe more parental motivation could be engaged. In other words, if the parents had their own understanding of what, how, and why their kids are motivated to learn, I believe such parent-teacher sessions would be much better attended and more productive.

The key is always motivation: motivation of the teachers, motivation of the parent, and, of course, motivation of the student. If the family can clearly identify in reasonable detail the learning dynamics of their youngster, the family, and each of its members, has an agenda to actively pursue throughout the academic years. The trick is not to rely on the assumption that the teacher knows better and to actively resist the school's insistence that the student conform to the educational systems in place.

Perhaps the most effective strategy for a family to follow is to explain their student's history of achievements and pattern of giftedness to each teacher, and to ask the teacher to create an achievement opportunity for their youngster. Offering to work with the teacher to bring that opportunity about would, of course, be a good policy.

A family can take a lot of the mystery and uncertainty out of the educational maze by being a source of information about their youngsters, and by being a force seeking creative teacher performance. Ultimately, the family has big reasons to require the schools to produce meaningful education for their kids. Foundation for life is what is at stake—their kids' foundations and their kids' lives.

What is so significant about a focus on families is the spillover effect into the worlds of work and religion where family members also have a personal involvement.

Whether families can bring their understanding of giftedness and human design into their roles as employees and members of a church is likely, based on our experience in the industrial and church worlds.

But what about those members of a community who are not part of a family with kids? Where can we find a motivation in the community to help those outside the arms of the family?

THE COMMUNITY AS A FORCE

Most of the severe people problems in any community are rooted in a single cause: They are people who don't fit in our world the way it currently works. They have been broken. They are drowning. They didn't make it to first base or were thrown out trying to steal second. Their lives have no apparent purpose. They fell off the train (or were pushed off), and they don't know how to get back on, or they aren't sure if they want to, even if they could. For them, the community "sucks."

Consider

- hard-core unemployed
- school dropouts
- prevailing youth illiteracy
- violent youth gangs
- welfare society
- teenage pregnancies
- drug and alcohol addiction
- crime and recidivism
- rampant infidelity

Mismatch in school and work drives people of all ages to destructive behavior in their efforts to find some experience, some thrill, some power that would give their lives some meaning. Even here, patterns of giftedness prevail.

- Gang leaders are gifted leaders.
- Combative prevailers can be gifted muggers and trigger men and women.
- People motivated to meet requirements follow charismatic leaders who lead them into slavery of thought and ultimate destruction.
- Risk takers get caught up in gambling or drugs.
- Budding entrepreneurs can turn to pimping for big profits.
- Young women and men motivated to seek a response who are failing in school may end up in prostitution.
- Excellers can seek bigger, more, flashier, whatever.
- Strategists can pull off complex scams and heists.
- Those motivated to have an impact on and shape others can be an insidious, powerful influence to lead others astray.
- Pioneers can come up with ever new ways to frustrate authorities and get into trouble.

All these forms of aberrant behavior are striking in their revelation of giftedness gone awry. The realization that gifts are being used constantly, even in wrong ways, can be instructive if we but realize the power of giftedness in people that is available to be harnessed to legitimate life-giving pursuits and objectives.

Gang leaders are gifted leaders.

In every community you establish a cadre of gifted counselors and ombudsmen and women who will work with those in need; with the businesses who will employ them; with the banks who will loan them money to take steps towards greater health, happiness, and security; and with the religious organizations and agencies providing human and financial support, especially in times of crisis.

The emphasis of the programs would be on the people's giftedness—their potential. Beyond discovering their design, training would stress the practical implications of giftedness, such as determining suitable jobs, building job campaign-interviewing skills, confronting excesses and poor habits driven by their motivational patterns, building discipline around their competencies, and like activities.

The program would show participants a way out of the darkness by introducing them to the light they possess, by building the light into a fire, and by providing help at critical times through safety nets manned by counselors thoroughly familiar with giftedness and its practical implications.

What is possible in every community, based on an exploitation of human design, is to locate people who possess the kinds of strengths and motivations required in working with those in trouble and the institutions and agencies who would assist their recovery. Formed into teams, or "families," these gifted staff members essentially function as a private enterprise, continuously measuring the success of their "clients."

It is practically possible to enlist volunteers in the following efforts who have the "right stuff" as long as the core are paid staff, ideally compensated by salary and incentives (for the need includes hustlers as well as counselors!).

The first thing you do, the second and third thing you do, and the things you continue to do are to identify, educate, harness, and exploit the unique gifts with which those in need have been endowed and help them rebuild their lives on the basis of their giftedness. At every step of a helping process you must return to and build from the strengths of the person in need (and what better way to get a handle on those strengths than to look at the giftedness they displayed in their aberrant or deviant behavior!).

In school, you build a curriculum around what they need to learn in order to be equipped for the fields of work indicated by their strengths.

Outside of those personal "core" courses, you provide simple audit courses so they can function in normal life circumstances (e.g., grocery-store arithmetic).

At every step of a helping process you must return to and build from the strengths of the person in need.

But you approach their education on the basis of *what they need for a productive and fulfilling career*, not to satisfy some standards imposed by educational authorities (standards that are indefensible at the level of "core" courses).

Once you get into knowledge and skill requirements that lie at the center of this giftedness, you press for more work and greater discipline. You go as deep and as far and fast as their enthusiasm and abilities will allow. *You make sure they receive an abundance of whatever motivational payoff feeds their soul.*

As they advance, you become more and more focused on the career they will eventually claim as their own. As the right career emerges more clearly, so the higher-level expert knowledge and skills they yet need become the heart of their educational process.

Everything they attempt to learn should have an obvious and direct connection to their giftedness. How long they stay in a formal educational setting before they move to vocational settings and serve a formal or informal apprenticeship would depend on the trade, craft, or profession.

A similar pattern of help would be followed for adults whose lives needed to be put back on track. The process of identifying the unique pattern of giftedness is especially critical for people who haven't "made it" in society.

Giving them back a sense that they are of real value, that their endowment can serve as the center of a renewed, contributing life, and making sure the person really understands the fact of his or her giftedness and the kinds of jobs and career they could pursue, is a necessary foundation.

As social workers who have helped people move from being an inmate to life in the world know, the steps are incremental, basic, and tedious. But the process can be enlivened and related to the powerful dynamic of developing their giftedness in pursuit of their new life. A coordinated effort by the cadre of coordinators and counselors working in and with every church, institution, agency, and business that make up the host community is, of course, critical to success. There are models to draw from and copy in their best practices.

Essentially the same driving concept would be available for penal institutions to facilitate their efforts to repatriate prisoners and equip them to live productive and fulfilling lives after paying their debt to society. Work programs could assure the fit of prisoners and their work. Personal development plans that identified likely careers after release, and education or training provided by other gifted inmates or through correspondence courses to give them a needed head start, could be readily accomplished. Even hands-on work experience during their tenure in prison could be a possibility for many types of jobs.

Giving the prisoner a reason for making the large effort required would be a worthy, achievable objective. If a lot of assistance could be provided in the months following confinement so a suitable job is found and landed, the obscene rate of recidivism would be drastically lowered and the ranks of productive citizens expanded.

> **The process of identifying the unique pattern of giftedness is especially critical for people who haven't "made it" in society.**

What does the community do about those whose health is breaking down? Moving from "the down and almost out" to those at various steps on the ladder of life, served by one or another medical service, the issue of *why* the body is signaling "help" becomes a question to which the patient will surely pay close attention.

If, as part of a physical or psychological workup, the motivational and competency structure and dynamics of the patient could be included, long-term solutions to the medical problem would be available. As emphasized in this book, and increasingly in literature and studies from a variety of relevant fields, job mismatch drives killing stress, which results in breakdown, which in turn requires expensive treatment or leads to premature funeral expenses.

What we have learned from a third of a century of helping employees at all levels, is that in time of personal need, people are open to examining themselves, their motives and capabilities. We believe a similar phenomenon is at work when people become ill enough to need a doctor. It is not difficult to determine a likely cause for stress-related illness once the person's giftedness is identified, particularly in cases of severe mismatch.

If the paradigm urged in this book became part of the belief system undergirding societal understanding of the nature of humankind, lives doomed to despair could be saved. Education, work, and religion could provide the self-understanding of personal giftedness and rescue many who would otherwise be lost. Social service agencies (welfare, rehabilitation, therapy, unemployment) providing payments and supporting services could require those seeking benefits to undergo the discovery process and produce data with the help of counselors who could use that information to build a recovery program centering around the person's giftedness. Such a program would start with discovery and move to diagnosis of the causes of their present condition, then equip the people to order their life around their giftedness, initially aiming at employment or training/education necessary to achieve suitable employment.

> In time of personal need, people are open to examining themselves, their motives and capabilities.

Such could happen in any community that cared enough to change their own way of living. Once started in their lives, it would be most natural and obvious to extend it to those who never "made it" under the old systems.

COMPETITION AS A FORCE

Because the United States continues to be a melting pot that attracts foreign-born from every land, we enjoy the rich diversity of giftedness that the immigrants from diverse races and families of humankind bring with them. Because giftedness appears at least in part to be genetic, drawing from a wide range of gene pools gives us a potential competitive advantage over countries of less diversity. The big "if" is, *if* we can learn to identify and develop the variety of gifts available to us through our brothers and sisters from far lands.

If our employers are smart enough to begin making more productive use of widely diverse employee strengths, they will experience sustained improvement in their productivity and competitive edge. Not only does this conclusion follow in terms of worker productivity, but the U.S. should be able to compete with major industrial nations in spite of their admitted national advantages (e.g., German precision, Japanese marketing, Italian design, Dutch commercial sense, and so forth). If we have in the U.S. representative giftedness from these countries and can properly employ the carriers of those gifts within our workforce, we should be able to compete most effectively on all counts: more desirable and useful designs, products, marketing and packaging strategies, shrewd pricing structures, and customer-focused distribution networks.

This competitive edge we might gain in the international marketplace requires, in addition, that our nation encourage the development of small businesses built around the giftedness of a unique group of people with the necessary vision and capability. If state and federal taxation and services were to promote such business formation around the notion of complementary giftedness, we would both improve our competitiveness and reduce the excessive failure rate of new businesses.

If we would devote a tenth of the time in evaluating the key human resources of a new business that we spend in scrutinizing its numbers, fewer would fail and more would succeed.

To accomplish this front-end qualifying would require the lenders of money and providers of expert services to ask the unasked question of embryonic entrepreneurs: "In addition to your numbers and glowing description of your products and markets, include in your business plans a brief summary of the giftedness of your key players and where they have demonstrated what they are good at and motivated to do."

If we would devote a tenth of the time in evaluating the key human resources of a new business that we spend in scrutinizing its numbers, fewer would fail and more would succeed. *People and their job fit, or misfit, are the predominant reasons organizations succeed or fail.*

What is true of a small retail store is as true of a multinational giant deciding to acquire a potentially profitable company in a different but attractive field. Everything is looked at microscopically—except the people. Nobody really knows how the officers and other key managers will perform under the new "circumstances." Why? Nobody asked.

Vast improvements can be made in employment levels, productivity, and prosperity in small-town America as well. Areas that have suffered obscene levels of unemployment for a generation could be helped to pull themselves out of the hole. Inventorying the giftedness present in a town or small city among the unemployed, the underemployed, and the misemployed could provide town planners with a clear picture of what's available and what's needed.

Armed with such information, government and business leaders would then be able to talk about what kind of business or industry would harness the available human capability, could attract and land suitable investment, and buy whatever supplementary competencies were needed to make whole units for viable organizations.

THE INDIVIDUAL AS A FORCE

On this side of eternity, there is no force as unremitting, imaginative, and fierce as self-interest. Tapping in to that force by providing practical ways for people to advance their self-interest would go a very long way to getting this transformation train out of the station.

As a legup, industry has been declaring for some years now that employees are mainly responsible for their own development and have funded career workshops and various quick-and-dirty inventories or tests to aid in that career management process. Much more is needed and should be provided by companies, especially if they believed that employees pursuing their own self-interest would end up in a job more suitable for them, and therefore engage more of their productive power.

What is needed are practical mechanisms for employees to gain access to information about jobs they can investigate and go after. What would be helpful here would be an improvement in the depth and quality of self-knowledge gained through current instruments. It is not enough for an employee to know he is a certain type or how he compares to normative data. Employees need, at least once in their lifetime, to understand the unique powers and drive of their individual endowments. Everything else, regardless of how well it is marketed and packaged, is incapable of describing or predicting individual behavior.

> On this side of eternity, there is no force as unremitting, imaginative, and fierce as self-interest.

In any program to encourage employee-initiated internal job searches, the establishment by the company of practical, enabling procedures that all managers accepted as desirable in the long run, would be of help.

What if I could prove to you that your employees have twenty percent more to give you of what you're paying for but not receiving because you have them matched to the wrong jobs? What about thirty percent more? Fifty percent more? Would you then be interested in identifying the strengths of your people? Do you have any idea of the improvement in your competitive position if you got serious about your people and their potential for productivity when matched to suitable work?

But ultimately, and especially in America, the individual and self-interest need to be engaged and empowered to locate and land the right calling. Michael Novak says it well:

> Any political economy which wishes to be as creative as possible must try to invent a system which permits persons of talent in all fields to discover their talents, to develop them, and to find the social positions in which their exercise bears maximal social fruit. Necessarily, such a system must encourage massive programs of self-discovery and self-improvement.[1]

---

1. Michael Novak, *The Spirit of Democratic Capitalism* (New York: Touchstone Books, 1983), 85. The way to accomplish this is with SIMA®, our System for Identifying Motivated Abilities, the standard for "measuring" human motivated behavior. I have taken pains to avoid making this book into an advertisement for our services. See page 256 for the address of People Management International.

Appendix A

Why Psychological Testing Doesn't Work

Psychological testing has reduced the study of human beings to the *study of pieces or components assumed to be present in all human beings.* Because of that methodology, psychology has been called a reductionistic science. In other words, you reduce the study of people to small, discrete aspects or qualities of people and see how they relate to other such qualities and behaviors. The aim is always to uncover generally valid laws that govern human behavior.

Such a reductionistic approach is vital to psychology as a "wannabe" science, because it permits the use of statistical techniques of measurement and comparison, which in turn are assumed to be an absolute requirement—if you can't measure it with numbers, it isn't *science.*

Now, where psychological testing has gotten (and stayed) off the rails is its most foundational assumption that there really are universal qualities of people that can be measured and compared. This in contrast to our conclusions, and those of many other authorities, that each individual is a unique mix of traits, aptitudes, and intelligence. Furthermore, that individual mix may *or may not* include one or more of the so-called universal qualities *as significant in how it functions.* In other words, unless such a universal quality (e.g., dominance over others) was motivationally significant to the person, how that person measured on that quality would lack any real life significance.

Rather than inveighing against this fatal flaw in psychological testing, let me add the weight of others more knowledgeable. The article from which I draw is fifteen years old, but it is unusually well reasoned, clear and succinct. The following are just a few excerpts of particular value here (my emphasis).

- One basic limitation of measurement techniques is that *tests cannot measure unique characteristics*; they measure only traits common to many people.
- Perhaps the first lesson that everybody using tests should learn is that the highness or the lowness of a score is not a measure of an individual's worth or value. *Each person functions in a unique way.* Traits have been separated out from the vast complexity of human functioning as a convenience to us. *A person cannot be described as a combination of varying amounts of different traits.*
- The second major error that test users and the public fall into is to assume that tests measure innate characteristics. This has been particularly troublesome in intelligence testing, but it occurs in interpreting tests of aptitudes and talents, neurotic tendencies, interests, and many other traits as well. *The point is that no test measures these original endowments.*
- Finally, and perhaps most importantly, intelligence tests do not measure strength and persistence of motivation . . . Educators must realize that they cannot produce this quality of motivation in persons who do not already possess it, and although we can recognize it, we cannot measure it.
- One unwarranted belief is that scores on interest tests indicate how highly motivated individuals are to succeed in their chosen occupations or majors. Unfortunately, there is no basis for this assumption. Interest tests do not measure how much interest the person has in anything, but only what direction his or her interests have taken.
- One must be even more cautious in drawing conclusions from scores on personality inventories . . . the most serious problem is that most personality tests are not designed to reveal positive or admirable qualities. Those tests grew out of attempts to identify persons with psychotic or neurotic tendencies."[1]

Looking back on his own work as a psychologist, Abraham Maslow wrote,

My original question was: If I want to know a person, what is the best way to go about doing it? And now I can rephrase this ques-

---

1. For an excellent summary of the limitations of personality profiles, intelligence tests, and skills and interest inventories, see Leona E. Tyler, "Testing the Test: What Tests Don't Measure," *Journal of Counseling and Development* (September 1984) vol. 63, p. 48.

tion more pointedly. How good for this purpose are the usual procedures of normal physical sciences (which, remember, is the widely accepted paradigm for *all* the sciences and even for all knowledge of any kind)? In general, my answer is that they are not very good at all. As a matter of fact, they are practically useless if I want not only to know about you but also to understand you.[2]

Maslow says that the scientific method—the genuinely scientific method of the physical sciences—is useless for understanding persons. A different technique is required. Gordon Allport explains why:

> Now it is certainly true that we often *wish* to use universal and group norms. We want to know whether Bill, relative to others, is high or low in intelligence, in dominance, in affiliativeness. But although Bill can be compared profitably on many dimensions with the average human being or with his cultural group, still he himself weaves all these attributes into a unique idiomatic system. His personality does not contain three systems, but only one. Whatever individuality is, it is not the residual ragbag left over after general dimensions have been exhausted. The organization of Bill's life is first, last, and all the time the primary fact of his human nature.[3]

A prominent authority in psychometrics, which drives psychological testing and measurement, concluded that the validity and usefulness of such testing depended on the presence in all people of universal traits, attributes or characteristics which operate at the level of the 'essence' of the person's make-up and behavior.

> For some years now there has been a controversy as to whether or not general traits of personality exist. The controversy has been between those who espouse a *nomothetic* and those who espouse an *idiographic* point of view, the former referring to "general laws" applicable to all people, and the latter referring to a personalized approach. Essentially, the idiographic point of view is that each person is a law unto himself. In terms of factor-analytic approaches, this means that either there are no general factors among personality

---

2. Abraham Maslow, *The Psychology of Science: A Reconnaissance* (New York: Harper & Row, 1966), 10.

3. Gordon W. Allport, *The Person In Psychology* (Boston, MA: Beacon,1968), 87–88.

characteristics or those which do exist fail to capture the "essence" of the individual. . . .

The idiographists have an important point: To find general traits (factors) of personality, it is necessary to find correlations among specific traits (habits); but everyday experience suggests that such correlations frequently are either very low or absent altogether. For example, it makes sense to deal with a general trait of dominance only if there are positive correlations among tendencies to be dominant in specific situations; but there are so many examples of persons who are dominant with their wives but not dominant at work, dominant with men but not with women, dominant in intellectual matters but not in practical matters, and so on. . . .

Enough failures of this kind would eventually lead to the admission that the idiographist is correct: personality traits are 'scattered' among people in such a way that the only approach to understanding the individual is by tracing out the life threads of how he came to be the way he is. Then it would have to be admitted that there are no general traits of dominance, extroversion, or others; instead, each individual would need to be considered a unique configuration of specific traits (habits).[4]

No such universal trait, attribute, or characteristic has ever been found in our nearly forty years of studying the makeup and motivated behavior of tens of thousands of persons. Tests and inventories based on psychometric theories do not and cannot define and describe individual makeup and behavior.

After studying the work of numerous investigators, the authors stated that "nearly all of the nonintelligent trait measures failed to display either adequate predictive or construct validity . . . Moreover, measures of personality traits do not display any substantial stability over even relatively brief intervals of 2 to 5 years—despite years of study, the understanding of human individuality and differential behavior has advanced very little."[5]

---

4. Jim Nunnally, *Psychometric Theory* (New York: McGraw-Hill, 1967), 471–72.
5. Mumford, Stokes, and Owens, *The Ecology of Human Individuality Patterns of Life History* (Hillsdale, N.J.: Erlbaum, 1990), 23-24.

Excerpts from a MAP Report

In the following pages, we present excerpts only from a MAP Report forty-one pages long—seventeen pages of transcript, twenty-three pages MAP Report and Commentary. The report was produced in the 1970s when we supported each conclusion with evidence taken from the person's description of his or her achievement experiences. My purpose in retrieving a report from so long ago is that it shows the genesis of our current work as based on demonstrated capability and motivation, which we simply add up.

PART I: CHRONOLOGICAL LISTING OF ENJOYABLE ACHIEVEMENTS

Childhood

1. I had a Sunday paper route in which people seemed to like me—and I liked them—and earned spending money. I helped buy a new bike. My mother gave me a dime for each A and a nickel for a B in elementary school. I earned a lot of money that way.

"Somehow or other that interested me—that I could sell these papers—take as few back to the agency as possible—I just liked going up to the door and talking to people—I saw some other guys doing it I guess—seemed like a way to earn money—seemed like an enjoyable thing—in the winter I had a sled with a box on it—in the summer had a wagon—a sense of completion when you made your route and sold all your papers—I guess I was always conscious of money—my folks had very little—somehow my mother came up with the idea that if I would do well in school she would pay me—seemed like kind of a good deal to me—I think it motivated me some but I did do fairly well in elementary school—school was not very hard for me—I did what I thought was minimal work and got fairly good grades—I had an old bike—I wanted a new one—couldn't get it unless I helped earn it—remember going down to Sears and buying this red bike—that was a great accomplishment—I really treasured that thing—took care of it—a big thing to show the other kids."

2. I helped my uncles on the farm and earned money through a scheme they had worked out for my pay.

"My mother's brothers farmed a farm outside of town and I used to stay with them—I was their only nephew and they apparently really enjoyed having me there—they segregated little jobs that I could do— I could drive the tractor when they loaded the hay on the wagon—he had a scheme where I worked so many hours and got so much money— he encouraged me to make sort of a score sheet which I put up on the side of the barn—every time we brought in a load of hay I checked it off—then I'd get paid and Saturday night we'd go to town—I enjoyed one uncle particularly, and he's probably more influential on my personality—he was really a model to me—I made up my mind I didn't want to be a farmer—it's a lot of work—I did it because they were there."

3. I enjoyed building model airplanes and did well, but rarely wished to risk flying them.

"Model airplane building was a big thing when I was a kid—put all the sticks together and wrap paper over the glue—had several buddies I went around with and I thought I did pretty well compared to those guys—used to spend afternoons after school—for some reason I never liked to fly them—I didn't want to break this nice creation—I think I was a pretty good builder—I like to work with my hands—putting all those little pieces together—seeing how it all fit together—measuring— sizing—putting it all together and seeing a finished creation—setting it there and looking at it and saying, that's something I did."

Age 20–25

1. I achieved a teaching position in the school system I desired because of my record—and my desire to work immediately on a master's degree.

"It was very desirable for me to teach in Kalamazoo because I wanted to work on a master's—applied to all the teaching systems around—got selected for a very desirable spot—it was a new shop—it was kind of an accomplishment I thought—when I was in college I was a dorm proctor—I was the guy that controlled the hall and kept peace—did a little counseling and that sort of thing—for three years—I felt I was one of the better guys because I got selected early and continued on—enjoyed that—a lot of responsibility—guys looked up to you—you were in charge—kind of difficult sometimes—difficult personal situations—one time I caught the other proctor having beer in his room—because of that I could get a job as a counselor—got my room and board for that—had that in addition to my teaching job—then I could work on my degree nights and summers—that worked out pretty well—had a nice two-room apartment in the dorm—it was responsibility and counseling—a feeling of importance—a lot of hours—the guys coming in with course problems, personal problems—I was sort of coming into my own in Christianity at that time too—we had pretty serious religious discussions—I would sit every third weekend in the office on call—people would come to the desk with various needs—even being let into a room—that was pretty important—stick that master key in the door and let them in— every third night you'd be plugged into the switchboard—finished the master's in two years which I thought was kind of an accomplishment; night school and one summer—I think I was one of my counselor's favorite students—sort of prided myself on that—had my master's program all planned out—he said, you've got this pretty well mapped out; most of these guys come in here and they don't know—I did that on my doctoral program too—said these are the kinds of things I want to take, can I do it here—to me you shouldn't let education take you, you should take it—I studied the catalogs and the course descriptions—I tried to learn all I could about profs before I'd take them—had a fairly organized way to get a job and then do the job—when I made the calls I planned them out—when I did the counseling in the dorm I worked it so when I was at the desk on duty I would do my grading of papers so I was always busy and productive—did very little sitting around."

Age 31–35

1. Returned to OPM as a Personnel Manager for the Chemicals Product Department. I organized and developed a hiring and staffing system in which we competed very favorably with the rest of the company.

"This was a new job—they had not had a strictly personnel man do this before—they were having trouble getting people into their department—a lot of competition not only outside but within OPM—I developed good interview schedules within our department, in the chemicals department and I toured the guys to the labs—I think we competed very well—we got good acceptance and filled all of our requisitions—at one time we had twenty openings for technologist—so I talked to this guy who handled that over here—went out recruiting—in six to eight months we got all those—we have this Special Assignments Program where the guys would be on projects within the company—I figured out in order to get the guys in your department you've got to project them— I had at least as many as six guys projected all the time in the chemical department—that way we had a better chance of getting those top men—I competed well with the other departments—we got more than our share of Special Assignment guys who would select chemicals as their place—I enjoyed that—didn't have a good boss—I sort of existed—I think I did reasonably well in spite of that—he wasn't very much help— I gained more satisfaction from the people contacts, working with the managers, etc.—satisfaction in the organizing of the new function—the interviewing—keeping it all organized—so many personnel changes you couldn't keep up with it—I wound up with what I call the stats sheet— I was seen as a good source of knowledge of what's going on—I think I do well because I'm seen as a knowledgeable guy in the function—if you really want to know what it's all about, come and see me—the minority committee is in this week to talk—they want to know about transfer, separation, hiring—I get selected to go and talk to them."

2. We had a contractor build a home for us to our specs. My wife and I did all the painting and finishing to save money, but also to have the job done right. It was a lot of time and work but gave us a great deal of satisfaction.

"This was a big project—the first home we had owned—we planned and I worked on the blueprints—worked with the contractor—there every other night—I took afternoons on vacation and worked from noon until nine to ten at night—we did all the painting—staining—nail holes to be filled."

3. I began gardening as a hobby. I grow tomatoes second to none.

"I had tried growing tomatoes a few times but it didn't click—then I got some good plants and I talked to people about how to fertilize them—ask a lot of questions—figure out how people do these things— then one year I had some dandies—put up some stakes—I had tomato plants like six feet tall—I counted over fifty tomatoes on one plant—I brought them into the office and gave them to my secretary, supervisor—everybody raves how big they are—really makes you feel good— I figured out that I like to do things I can succeed at—if I think I can succeed at something and I like it, then I really try to excel—I like to plant the tomatoes—fertilize them at the right time—watch them—tie them up—help this creation along—see how many on there."

4. I enjoy a nice car and usually take great pains to have it clean and shiny.

"My wagon is nearly four years old and looks fairly new—I really take pains to wax it—keep it washed—the whole thing looks good—it's fun to drive."

MOTIVATED ABILITIES PATTERN

I. One Particular Result

As background to understanding this part of the motivational pattern, the reader should realize that in every achievement the person accomplished one particular result which was and is of paramount importance to him. In most cases, the person was not aware that obtaining this result was of such overriding importance. However, regardless of supervisory expectations, a job description, or even an objective determination of what is needed, he will seek consciously, or most probably unconsciously, to achieve this particular result. He should be in a job which allows him to do so. If he is not, he will not be motivated, productive, or satisfied.

What is the one primary result he wants to accomplish in his life? acquire/possess:

- money/material things
- status/reputation
- authority/control

His motivation in life is to acquire/possess money/material things, status/ reputation/standing, or control/direction over the affairs of others. The essence of the motivation is ownership, possession, and dominion.

He wants to be important in the eyes of others, to have standing, to be looked up to, to be admired, to be in a position of authority and control. He wants to acquire things and position that give him a standing with others and over others.

Gathering the similar manifestations of this motivation into group-
ings we see the following:

Where He Acquires Money or Material Things or Improves Their Value . . .

"I had a Sunday paper route—earned spending money—helped buy
a new bike—really treasured that thing/I helped my uncles on the farm
and earned money through a scheme—sort of a score sheet/model airplane building—never liked to fly them—didn't want to break them—
setting it there and looking at it and saying, that's something that I
did/like taking this dirty car, clean it up and make it look nice/I was
putting a lot of money into this college and I wanted to get my money's
worth/between my wife and myself we probably had the best income of
those in married student housing/we had a contractor build a home for
us to our specs/I enjoy a nice car and usually take great pains to have it
clean and shiny—four years old and looks fairly new/have received two
cash awards."

Where He Acquires Status/Position/Reputation . . .

"I enjoyed being voted 'most likely to succeed' in my senior class/I
often won first place in the shot put—and achieved second and fourth
place at state-wide meets/I was awarded the scholar-craftsman
award/dorm proctor—guys looked up to you—a feeling of impor-
tance/they never had an IA teacher who got so much enthusiasm going
with his kids/I wanted to be seen as a person of high ideals and
morals/only one in the immediate family to have completed college—
I'm seen as a knowledgeable guy in the function—if you really want to
know what it's all about come and see Johnson/I grow tomatoes second
to none/one of the guys—said, I can still remember your ABC's (points
in sermon)/elected an elder in my church/of the three speeches so far,
have won a first place and two seconds."

Where He Acquires Recognition/Visibility . . .

"Seeing it (plane) there and looking at it and saying, that's something
I did/I liked to see things in print and took two years of printing in high
school/did a beautiful job in putting on those seat covers—people would
say they looked sharp—the boss was proud/I would always make a model
as a standard—get those kids' projects down there with names on

them—a display in the main hall/the article was sent in to the journal of shop teachers and it got published—I like to see myself in print/ develop and write a PR manual on trades training—the boss spread it all over the company and outside/enjoyed writing a newsletter—satisfaction to see it in print/I feel I am an outstanding contributor—two more articles were published—I like to see myself in print."

Where He Acquires and Exercises Dominion Over People or an Organization ...

"I was business manager of the yearbook—we made the yearbook come out in the black/fruit market—waiting on them, adding it up and taking the money—I'd run the thing in the afternoon/dorm proctor— you were in charge—pretty important/industrial arts—organizing it, planning it and seeing it all unfold—I'd challenge the kids—had pretty good discipline—enthusiasm—paddle—I enjoyed their responsiveness to what I was showing them/I made a business of it, managed the program and professors, rather than having them manage me/I organized and developed a hiring and staffing system/ becoming manager of Professional Personnel—hired about fifteen guys—job performance reviews—orientation schedule—monthly reports—strategic counseling—I would be very thorough in trying to understand (each) man/my two kids are my pride and joy."

Summary

In summary, his central motivation in life is to acquire/gain a position of importance, things of importance, authority, standing, reputation. Critical to the motivation is that others recognize him, his work, his articles, his expertise, his car, his home, his family, his employers as special, to be admired. It's sort of a mother syndrome in that he wants to own it, mother it, take care of it, make sure it succeeds, looks good, does well, gives the right impression.

A central quality to his motivation is his perception of the potential of the thing/activity to make money out of, to take charge of, to make the most of. You can get some sense of this quality in the industrial arts teaching, the graduate study, dorm proctor—counselor, church-elder-evangelist achievements. He starts off like his contemporaries teaching a class, or doing some other ordinary thing, and before too long, everybody is talking about and trying to copy what he is doing, he has an established position and a growing reputation, and he has gone into print. He has so achieved his motivation time and again since his earliest achievements, and with the only help being mainly encouragement and support and some inspiration from others. The point here is he can take what others consider mundane and even fallow ground, and bring a perception, a freshness, an exploitive creativity which achieves the result that represents his motivation. He can be assured of such growth and vigor in any assignment/function he is given which would accommodate his motivational pattern.

Another important quality of his motivation is his way of working with others. The key ingredients are: (1) a strong desire to be in contact with others; (2) a responsiveness to the needs and desires of others where a mutual benefit will accrue (e.g., boss wants and you deliver, customer wants and you sell); and (3) where he takes over the other person(s) by controlling what they will do, how they will do it, and in general owning or managing the relationship and the activity involved (e.g., industrial arts students, doctorate program and professors, church and pastor). Regardless of where he starts in, he will end up in control of or gaining from the relationship and the activity around which the relationship revolves, or he will become disenchanted. He may ingratiate himself but he will get a response of some sort that meets his motivation.

In the two preceding points, you will note a progression in the nature of his activity, which is another quality typical of his motivation. He starts off serving and ends up owning and running. He starts off writing a paper and ends up with a theme-writing business. It is not only a normal development from a seed to a tree (which it is in part), his path of progression also leads him to become and to do something few would envision when he starts.

HIS MOTIVATED ABILITIES

As background to understanding this part of the motivational pattern, the reader should realize that in every achievement, each person used some or all of a particular group of abilities. He is motivated to use these abilities and will strive to use them in any job situation regardless of how a job might be performed. This seeking to use the abilities he is motivated to use is so dynamic a force and so controlling of his behavior that an understanding of them is essential to productive use of the man.

Plan, Strategize

"Had my master's program all planned out—he said, you've got this pretty well mapped out—when I made the calls I planned them out/planned it all out—I was prepared if a dad came in—I planned all through the summer getting ready for the projects/try to do it with the least effort—show him a good job/I went in with my courses pretty well laid out—I really tried to map it out—it was kind of a big plan that I had/I could show up a pattern—that it would look like I was doing it/we planned, and I worked on the blueprints/I had a grander concept for a manual/sort of strategize to spend time with them/coming up with a scheme where the kids could pay half down/we do goal setting—I've tried all different ways of goal setting—I try to do strategic counseling/I really whipped up a good evangelism program."

Able to plan in detail how he will accomplish a particular objective/project. Able to conceptualize what is essentially novel to him and others in enough detail so he is able to plan and move with some certainty. Able to plan a strategy for getting things done to accommodate the personalities/politics and other key variables involved. Is skillful at achieving impressions which may or may not be supported by what they purport to convey. Able and motivated to come up with schemes for getting done what he is motivated to accomplish.

Control, Manage

"I was the guy that controlled the hall and kept peace—a lot of responsibility—you were in charge—one time, I caught the other proctor—it was responsibility—even being let into a room/I would always make a model as a standard—I'd take them through it step by step—had pretty good discipline in the class—I'd try to let its principles pervade all of my life—I spend time and work at it conscientiously/managed the program and professors, rather than having them manage me/I developed good interview schedules—keeping it all organized—I wound up with what I call the status sheet/we had a contractor build a home for us to our specs/had increasing numbers of people reporting to me—I pride myself in personal organization—the first thing we do is get an orientational schedule going—we map out together an orientation schedule—make sure he gets everything he wants and I get everything I want—then I ask him to do monthly reports—I like to be organized as a manager—so much stuff, the guy can't help but grow/I did what I thought was minimal work/did this a few weeks, and got to thinking, I was walking an awful lot of extra steps just to punch this clock—it would take about twenty minutes to do the route—but figured a way—that I could run that route in five minutes—so for five years, I did it the short way—that was ingenious—figuring out how to beat that time clock/usually couldn't keep up with all five to six classes, so would figure out which class would be my slider, and try to get by with as little as possible and still come out with a C or maybe a B—so I was always busy and productive—did very little sitting around/I followed the manual very closely—they've got a Toastmasters pattern of things they look for/I had calling, contact cards."

Skillful at devising methods of control over those people and things for whom and which he is responsible. Will be highly directive and closely controlling if the people and circumstances lend themselves to it or he will be studiously indirect but still controlling through one or another device limiting the other man's ability to move except as he wants him to. He disciplines himself to no less and probably to a much greater extent than he requires of others. He is prudent about how he spends his time and what he gets in return. He gives no more than what is required to get out of or from the effort. Part of this ability is that of economizing, putting out the minimum required. He gives what he has to but no more. He is very efficient with his use of his time and money.

Subject Matter That Recurs

As background to understanding this part of the motivational pattern, the reader should realize that frequently, but not always, we find a subject matter that recurs with great frequency. For jobs that require in-depth knowledge of a particular technology or field, it is probably essential that the person find great satisfaction from working with that particular subject matter (e.g., accountants and figures). If the subject matter that recurs and the field of work do not match, job fit should be questioned. Where a subject matter does recur, you can be confident that the individual is very much at home and enjoys dealing in depth within the area described and within the limits described in his achievements.

What follows are examples of recurring subject matter from our sample MAP.

Words, Publications

"I just liked going up to the door and talking to people/I had a lot to say—had to give a speech/I like to see things in print and took two years of printing in high school—I took this printing class—set up the type—put it in the press and print it—see it in print/I really worked hard on that (term papers)—I think I got a C the first term in English, a B the second—I thought I really mastered this program/The Bible is a very important book in my reading—talking to kids/the article—was sent in to the journal of shop teachers and it got published—I've written some other articles—I liked to see myself in print—here again, the recognition of this article/had the freedom to develop and write a PR manual—enjoyed writing a newsletter—I enjoyed writing term papers—probably the highlight of that was this PR manual—enjoyed writing the manual—see the proofs and see it printed/newsletter—that was probably the most important thing I did out there—I read the 'Art of Readable Writing'—I read all his books—then I got hooked up with this prof at Penn State with a potential doctorate program—I not only had fun doing the newsletter—got a letterhead for it—satisfaction to see it in print—then I took this paper that I wrote for the prof and made it into an article for the ASTD journal—they published it/I knew I would have to write a dissertation—went to the library—looked at dissertations—began copying how you begin one, how they are organized—ran into a book that had a sheet for note taking—made up some of those sheets—all the time I was doing reading for any course work/I enjoy reading self-improvement stuff, how to be a better speaker—I read things—read about how to be a better speaker—practice that—I joined Toastmasters last year—feel reasonably comfortable in giving talks and presentations—would like to be more skillful in giving a message in church/two more articles were published—like to see myself in print/I've always had an interest in being a public speaker, so recently joined a Toastmasters club—of the three speeches so far, have won a first place and two seconds for the evening speeches—I like to get all I can out of it so I can be a better speaker at work and at church situations."

Money, Material Things

"Earned spending money—helped buy a new bike—mother gave me a dime for each A and a nickel for each B in elementary school—earned a lot of money that way—I could sell these papers—seemed like

a way to earn money—sold all your papers—I guess I was always conscious of money—my folks had very little—somehow, my mother came
up with the idea that if I would do well in school she would pay me—I
had an old bike—wanted a new one—couldn't get it unless I helped earn
it—remember going down to Montgomery Wards and buying this red
bike—really treasured that thing—took care of it—a big thing to show
the other kids/earned money through a scheme they had worked out for
my pay—he had a scheme where I worked so many hours and got so
much money—I'd get paid/I didn't want to break this nice creation—
seeing a finished creation—setting it there and looking at it/I was business manager of the yearbook—for the first time we made the yearbook
come out in the black—I did that by coming up with a scheme where
the kids could pay half down and half when they got the book—got more
people buying/taking the money—I'd earn money/I was putting a lot of
money into this college and I wanted to get my money's worth/had a nice
two-room apartment/just wasn't enough money/my wife and I did all the
painting and finishing to save money—the first home we had owned/I
enjoyed a nice car and usually take great pains to have it clean and
shiny—my wagon is nearly four years old and looks fairly new—I really
take pains to wax it, keep it washed—the whole thing really looks good."

How He Operates with Others

As background to understanding this part of the motivational pattern, the reader should realize that emerging from the achievements of
each person is a certain type of relationship he maintains with people.
Either he wants to work alone, or to work in harness with other people,
or to be the star, or to be the leader or some similar role. This fact is
revealed clearly in his achievements. It is quite significant vocationally
since the type of relationship he seeks to maintain indicates the level and
type of position in which he can be productively used and to which he can
logically aspire.

What follows are examples of this person's relationship to others.

Individualist Role: Director

"I helped my uncles on the farm—they segregated little jobs that I
could do—could drive the tractor/they loaded the hay on the wagon/I'd
take them through it step by step allowing them freedom so they could
be individual—they never had an industrial arts teacher who got so much

enthusiasm going with the kids—I'd challenge the kids to think about what they were doing—he wanted to get more kids in the class—I helped him—sent out cards—did some calling, specific talking to kids/felt that I was a pretty good classroom instructor with good relations with adult students—they wanted a manual to explain what trade training was all about at OPM—what are the classes, what do you have to do to get into them—managed the program and professors rather than having them manage me—think he recognized my purpose in this thing—it was satisfaction to figure out what the prof wanted—of course with the help of my prof and my wife she did all the typing/I figured out, in order to get the guys in your department, you've got to project them—had at least as many as six guys projected all the time in the dept.—we had a contractor build a home for us to our specs—my wife and I did all the painting and finishing—we planned and I worked on the blueprints, worked with the contractor/we did all the painting, staining, nail holes to be filled/my whole purpose was to tell them what I wanted to tell them—I really felt these things, but I also wanted to have it organized so they would understand and remember/had increasing numbers of people reporting to me and after six years, became manager of the function—the development of a staff, men and women, as manager, has been a great source of pride/I always do everything I can to help my boss succeed because if he does I will too—at one time, thought I would like to be in a position where I was the only guy doing that kind of thing—then I could excel—manager for about two years now—during this time I hired or personally worked the interview schedule of about fifteen guys—whenever I have a guy on a project or a subordinate, I really take pains to give him job performance reviews—try to do it up well—I have to be careful—I might oversupervise—want to give them a lot of latitude, recognition—when I begin with a guy—we map out together an orientation schedule—make sure he gets everything he wants, and I get everything I want—may even review it with my boss—I follow up to see how it's coming—then I ask him to do monthly reports—we do goal setting—I try to do strategic counseling as we go along—have an annual performance review—remember trying to help one fellow understand the way he was coming through—so went to see the psychiatrist and psychologist—I would be very thorough in trying to understand that man—try to see that they get to every development program that's available—so much stuff, the guy can't help but grow—I know probably better than anyone else where these guys were and where they are now/I really whipped up a good evangelism program—we had a new pastor and (I) got him educated and going on it—they may need somebody to do that—I think my wife and I can do this—they don't have a calling program—I want to get them going on that."

Summary

When in a position of command, he would direct others to perform as he believed they should perform. In this sense, he is more a director of others than a manager of them. However we characterize his way of handling those who report to him, the important quality is that he stays very close to them and assures himself that they are doing the detail of the job in a way he approves. He would tend to closely control his subordinates in what they did. However, he would seek to have them grow and develop, but as in growing tomatoes, he would want to do those various things involved with the person to assure their growth. He would want to stay in close while they were under is tutelage. He should be an excellent person under whom to work the early years of a career. He would bring you up right. He would always want to be in charge but an apprentice would learn the fundamentals well and build solidly.

To elaborate further on this quality of his relationship with others, the evidence indicates he can make use of others, but as in a play the director calls the shots and sees that the script is followed. He is the one who determines what will be done, how it will be done, by whom, and in what sequence. He exercises each critical judgment and decision. Any member of the cast can have an enriching experience as long as they play their assigned role well.

APPENDIX C

The Biblical Basis for Giftedness

EXPLANATIONS FOR APPENDIX C

In chapter 7, I referred to a rather voluminous amount of scriptural references in support of the thesis developed that God claims responsibility for us and our endowed design. That material follows.[1] I would urge that you study it intensely, whether you count yourself a believer or not. As much as I have worked with this sweet music from God's Word, I am constantly taken aback by its ability to refresh my spirit and bring me up short.

In a number of places, I have parenthetically added definitions of particularly key words taken from *Strong's Exhaustive Concordance*. Especially note "ways" as meaning "mode of action"—which is close to "motivation" or "motivated behavior" or "patterns of motivation." And the word "work" or "works" do not mean charitable deeds in the Scripture quoted, but mean "work work."

God Has Created You

> So God created man in his own image, in the image of God created he him; male and female created he them.   *—Genesis 1:27*

> And the Lord said unto him, Who hath made man's mouth? or who maketh the dumb, or deaf, or the seeing, or the blind? Have not I the Lord?   *—Exodus 4:11*

---

1. In appendix C, the King James Version is used as the primary reference. Other versions used are noted.

207

He who fashions the hearts of them all, and observes all their deeds.
—Psalm 33:15 (RSV)

Know ye that the LORD he is God: it is he that hath made us, and not we ourselves.   *—Psalm 100:3*

Thus saith God the LORD, he that created the heavens, and stretched them out; he that spread forth the earth, and that which cometh out of it, he that giveth breath unto the people upon it, and spirit to them that walk therein.   *—Isaiah 42:5*

Thus saith the LORD that made thee, and formed thee from the womb . . . Thus saith the LORD, thy redeemer, and he that formed thee from the womb, I am the LORD that maketh all things.
—Isaiah 44:2, 24

For thus saith the LORD that created the heavens; God himself that formed the earth and made it; he hath established it, he created it not in vain, he formed it to be inhabited: I am the Lord; and there is none else.   *—Isaiah 45:18*

But now, O LORD, thou art our father; we are the clay, and thou our potter; and we all are the work of thy hand.   *—Isaiah 64:8*

The burden of the word of the LORD for Israel, saith the LORD, which stretcheth forth the heavens, and layeth the foundation of the earth, and formeth the spirit of man with him.   *—Zechariah 12:1*

All things were made by him; and without him was not any thing made that was made.   *—John 1:3*

For by him were all things created, that are in heaven, and that are in earth, visible and invisible, whether they be thrones, or dominions, or principalities, or powers: all things were created by him and for him.   *—Colossians 1:16*

Hath in these last days spoken unto us by his Son, whom he hath appointed heir of all things, by whom also he made the worlds.
—Hebrews 1:2

Worthy art thou, our Lord and God, to receive glory and honor and power, for thou didst create all things, and by thy will they existed and were created.   *—Revelation 4:11 (RSV)*

God Has Designed You With Gifts to Fulfill His Purpose for Your Life

And let the beauty of the LORD our God be upon us: and establish thou the work of our hands upon us; yea, the work of our hands establish thou it.   *—Psalm 90:17*

When I was woven together in the depths of the earth, your eyes saw my unformed body. All the days ordained for me were written in your book before one of them came to be.   *—Psalm 139:15–16 (NIV)*

LORD, thou wilt ordain peace for us: for thou also hast wrought all our works in us.   *—Isaiah 26:12*

Before I formed thee in the belly I knew thee; and before thou camest forth out of the womb I sanctified thee, and I ordained thee a prophet unto the nations.   *—Jeremiah 1:5*

For in him we live, and move, and have our being.   *—Acts 17:28*

(For the children being not yet born, neither having done any good or evil, that the purpose of God according to election might stand, not of works, but of him that calleth;) It was said unto her, The elder shall serve the younger.   *—Romans 9:11–12*

Having then gifts differing according to the grace that is given to us...
—Romans 12:6

Now we have received not the spirit of the world, but the Spirit which is from God, that we might understand the gifts bestowed on us by God.... "For who has known the mind of the Lord so as to instruct him?" But we have the mind of Christ. *—1 Corinthians 2:12, 16 (RSV)*

Men have different gifts, but it is the same Spirit who gives them.... God works through different men in different ways, but it is the same God who achieves his purposes through them all.

—1 Corinthians 12:4–5 (PHILLIPS)

In whom also we have obtained an inheritance, being predestinated according to the purpose of him who worketh all things after the counsel of his own will.   *—Ephesians 1:11*

For we are his handiwork, created in Christ Jesus to devote ourselves to the good deeds [toil, occupation, work] for which God has designed us.   *—Ephesians 2:10 (NEB)*

But to each one of us grace has been given as Christ apportioned it. This is why it says: "When he ascended on high he led captives in his train and gave gifts to men."   *—Ephesians 4:7–8*

It is God for His own loving purpose who puts both the will and the action in you.   *—Philippians 2:13 (JB)*

God also bearing them witness, both with signs and wonders, and with divers miracles, and gifts of the Holy Ghost, according to his own will.   *—Hebrews 2:4*

God's Spirit Can Dwell Within You and Actively Seek to Work His Purpose Out Through Your Design

You gave your good Spirit to instruct them. *—Nehemiah 9:20 (NIV)*

But it is the spirit in a man, the breath of the Almighty, that gives him understanding. It is not only the old who are wise, not only the aged who understand what is right.   *—Job 32:8–9 (NIV)*

For God does speak—now one way, now another.... In a dream, in a vision of the night, when deep sleep falls on men as they slumber in their beds, he may speak in their ears and terrify them with warnings, to turn man from wrongdoing and keep him from pride....

—Job 33:14–17 (NIV)

For the work of a man shall he render unto him, and cause every man to find according to his ways [mode of action]. —*Job 34:11*

I will praise the LORD, who counsels me; even at night my heart instructs me. —*Psalm 16:7 (NIV)*

Who, then, is the man that fears the LORD? He will instruct him in the way chosen for him. —*Psalm 25:12 (NIV)*

I will instruct thee and teach thee in the way [mode of action] which thou shalt go: I will guide thee with mine eye. —*Psalm 32:8*

Thou hast ascended on high, thou hast led captivity captive: thou hast received gifts for men; yea, for the rebellious also, that the LORD God might dwell among them. —*Psalm 68:18*

You guide me with your counsel, and afterward you will take me into glory. —*Psalm 73:24 (NIV)*

In all thy ways [mode of action] acknowledge him, and he shall direct thy paths. —*Proverbs 3:6*

But the Comforter, which is the Holy Ghost, whom the Father will send in my name, he shall teach you all things. —*John 14:26*

For in him we live, and move, and have our being. —*Acts 17:28*

For as many as are led by the Spirit of God, they are the sons of God. —*Romans 8:14*

For ye are the temple of the living God; as God hath said, I will dwell in them, and walk in them; and I will be their God, and they shall be my people. —*2 Corinthians 6:16*

I pray that out of his glorious riches he may strengthen you with power through his Spirit in your inner being, so that Christ may dwell in your hearts through faith. —*Ephesians 3:16 (NIV)*

For it is God which worketh in you both to will and to do of his good
pleasure.   —*Philippians 2:13*

Now the God of peace ... make you perfect in every good work to
do his will, working in you that which is wellpleasing in his sight,
through Jesus Christ.   —*Hebrews 13:20–21*

God Will Hold You Accountable for Fruit Produced from Your Giftedness

Then hear thou in heaven thy dwellingplace, and forgive, and do,
and give to every man according to his ways [mode of action], whose
heart thou knowest: for thou; (even thou only, knowest the hearts of
all the children of men).   —*1 Kings 8:39*

Then hear thou from heaven thy dwelling place, and forgive, and
render unto every man according unto all his ways [mode of action],
whose heart thou knowest; for thou only knowest the hearts of the
children of men.   —*2 Chronicles 6:30*

God hath spoken once; twice I have heard this; that power belongeth
unto God. Also unto thee, O Lord, belongeth mercy: for thou ren-
derest to every man according to his work [transactions, productions,
deeds, business, things made, things offered, workmanship].
                                                            —*Psalm 62:11–12*

If you say, "But we knew nothing about this," does not he who weighs
the heart perceive it? Does not he who guards your life know it? Will
he not repay each person according to what he has done?
                                                            —*Proverbs 24:12 (NIV)*

I, the LORD, search the heart, I test the mind. Even to give every man
according to his ways [mode of action], and according to the fruit of
his doings [endeavor, work].   —*Jeremiah 17:10 (NKJV)*

Great in counsel, and mighty in work: for thine eyes are open upon
all the ways [mode of action] of the sons of men: to give every one
according to his ways [mode of action], and according to the fruit of
his doings [endeavor, work].   —*Jeremiah 32:19*

Therefore, I will judge you, O house of Israel, every one according to his ways [mode of action], saith the Lord GOD.   *—Ezekiel 18:30*

For the Son of man shall come in the glory of his Father with his angels; and then he shall reward every man according to his works [toil, occupation, work].   *—Matthew 16:27*

Then he that had received the five talents went and traded with the same, and made them other five talents. And likewise he that had received two, he also gained other two. But he that had received one went and digged in the earth, and hid his lord's money. After a long time the lord of those servants cometh, and reckoneth with them. And so he that had received five talents came and brought other five talents.... His lord said unto him, "Well done, thou good and faithful servant: thou hast been faithful over a few things, I will make thee ruler over many things: enter thou into the joy of thy lord."   *—Matthew 25:16–23*

Then he which had received the one talent came and said, Lord, I knew thee that thou art an hard man, reaping where thou hast not sown, and gathering where thou hast not strawed: And I was afraid, and went and hid thy talent in the earth: lo, there thou hast that is thine. His lord answered and said unto him, Thou wicked and slothful servant, thou knewest that I reap where I sowed not, and gather where I have not strawed: Thou oughtest therefore to have put my money to the exchangers, and then at my coming I should have received mine own with usury. Take therefore the talent from him, and give it unto him which hath ten talents. For unto every one that hath shall be given, and he shall have abundance: but from him that hath not shall be taken away even that which he hath. And cast ye the unprofitable servant into outer darkness: there shall be weeping and gnashing of teeth.   *—Matthew 25:24–30*

And all the churches shall know that I am He who searches the minds and hearts. And I will give to each one of you according to your works [toil, occupation, work].   *—Revelation 2:23 (NKJV)*

And I saw the dead, small and great, stand before God; and the books were opened: and another book was opened, which is the book of life: and the dead were judged out of those things which were written in the books, according to their works [toil, occupation, work]. And the sea gave up the dead which were in it; and death and hell delivered up the dead which were in them: and they were judged every man according to their works [toil, occupation, work].

—Revelation 20:12–13

And behold, I am coming quickly, and My reward is with Me, to give to every one according to his work [toil, occupation, work].

—Revelation 22:12 (NKJV)

God Intends That You Use Your Giftedness in Work Appropriate to Its Nature and Within Its Boundaries

And the LORD God took the man, and put him into the garden of Eden to dress it and to keep it. *—Genesis 2:15*

Potiphar put him in charge of his household, and he entrusted to his care everything he owned.... So the warden put Joseph in charge of all those held in the prison, and he was made responsible for all that was done there.... So Pharaoh said to Joseph, "I hereby put you in charge of the whole land of Egypt."

—Genesis 39:4, 22; 41:41 (NIV)

And it came to pass on the morrow, that Moses sat to judge the people: and the people stood by Moses from the morning unto the evening.... And Moses said unto his father-in-law, Because the people come unto me; ... and I judge between one and another, and I do make them know the statutes of God, and his laws."

—Exodus 18:13, 15–16

And I have filled him with the spirit of God, in wisdom, and in understanding, and in knowledge, and in all manner of workmanship, to devise cunning works, to work in gold, and in silver, and in brass, and in cutting of stones, to set them, and in carving of timber, to work in all manner of workmanship. *—Exodus 31:3–6*

He has filled them with skill to carry out all the crafts of engraver, damask weaver, embroider in purple stuffs of violet shade and red, in crimson stuffs and fine linen, or of the common weaver; they are able to do work of all kinds and do it with originality.

—*Exodus 35:35 (JB)*

Deborah, a prophetess, the wife of Lappidoth, was leading Israel at that time. She held court ... and the Israelites came to her to have their disputes decided.   —*Judges 4:4–5 (NIV)*

And the LORD said unto Gideon, Every one that lappeth of the water with his tongue, as a dog lappeth, him shalt thou set by himself.... And the Lord said unto Gideon, By the three hundred men that lapped will I save you, and deliver the Midianites into thine hand.

—*Judges 7:5, 7*

The trees went forth on a time to anoint a king over them; and they said unto the olive tree, Reign thou over us. But the olive tree said unto them, Should I leave my fatness, wherewith by me they honour God and man, and go to be promoted over the trees? And the trees said to the fig tree, Come thou, and reign over us. But the fig tree said unto them, Should I forsake my sweetness, and my good fruit, and go to be promoted over the trees? Then said the trees unto the vine, Come thou, and reign over us. And the vine said unto them, Should I leave my wine, which cheereth God and man, and go to be promoted over the trees? Then said all the trees unto the bramble, Come thou, and reign over us. And the bramble said unto the trees, If in truth ye anoint me king over you, then come and put your trust in my shadow: and if not, let fire come... and devour the cedars of Lebanon.   —*Judges 9:8–15*

Like a partridge that hatches eggs it did not lay is the man who gains riches by unjust means. When his life is half gone, they will desert him, and in the end he will prove to be a fool.

—*Jeremiah 17:11 (NIV)*

Whose boasteth himself of a false gift is like clouds and wind without rain.   —*Proverbs 25:14*

As for these four children, God gave them knowledge and skill in all learning and wisdom: and Daniel had understanding in all visions and dreams. . . . And the king communed with them; and among them all was found none like Daniel, Hananiah, Mishael, and Azariah: therefore stood they before the king. And in all matters of wisdom and understanding, that the king inquired of them, he found them ten times better than all the magicians and astrologers that were in all his realm.   *—Daniel 1:17, 19–20*

For the kingdom of heaven is as a man travelling into a far country, who called his own servants, and delivered unto them his goods. And unto one he gave five talents, to another two, and to another one; to every man according to his several ability; and straightway took his journey.   *—Matthew 25:14–15*

The gifts we possess differ as they are allotted to us by God's grace, and must be exercised accordingly: the gift of inspired utterance, for example, in proportion to a man's faith; or the gift of administration, in administration. A teacher should employ his gift in teaching, and one who has the gift of stirring speech should use it to stir his hearers. If you give to charity, give with all your heart; if you are a leader, exert yourself to lead.   *—Romans 12:6–8 (NEB)*

What, after all, is Apollos? And what is Paul? Only servants, through whom you came to believe—as the Lord has assigned to each his task. I planted the seed, Apollos watered it, but God made it grow. So neither he who plants nor he who waters is anything, but only God, who makes things grow. The man who plants and the man who waters have one purpose, and each will be rewarded according to his own labor.   *—1 Corinthians 3:5–8 (NIV)*

For no one can lay any foundation other than the one already laid, which is Jesus Christ. If any man builds on this foundation using gold, silver, costly stones, wood, hay or straw, his work will be shown for what it is, because the Day will bring it to light. It will be revealed with fire, and the fire will test the quality of each man's work. If what he has built survives, he will receive his reward. If it is burned up, he will suffer loss; he himself will be saved, but only as one escaping through the flames. *—1 Corinthians 3:11–15 (NIV)*

But we will not boast beyond limit, but will keep to the limits God has apportioned us, to reach even to you.*—2 Corinthians 10:13 (RSV)*

As a prisoner for the Lord, then, I urge you to live a life worthy of the calling you have received. *—Ephesians 4:1 (NIV)*

As every man hath received the gift, even so minister the same one to another, as good stewards of the manifold grace of God. If any man speak, let him speak as the oracle of God; if any man minister, let him do it as of the ability which God giveth: that God in all things may be glorified through Jesus Christ. *—1 Peter 4:10–11*

God Requires You to Love Him and Those You Serve with Excellence and with Passion

... scarlet yarn, with cherubim worked into them by a skilled craftsman. ... twisted linen ... the work of an embroider....Tell all the skilled men to whom I have given wisdom in such matters that they are to make garments for Aaron, ... the work of a skilled craftsman; ... the way a gem cutter engraves a seal.... Fashion a breastpiece for making decisions—the work of a skilled craftsman.... The sash is to be the work of an embroiderer.... make a fragrant blend of incense, the work of a perfumer.
—Exodus 26:1, 31, 36; 28:2, 6, 11, 15, 39; 30:35 (NIV)

Hear O Israel: The LORD our God is one LORD, and thou shalt love the LORD thy God with all thine heart, and with all thy soul, and with all thy might. *—Deuteronomy 6:4–5*

For I am full of matter, the spirit within me constraineth me. Behold my belly is as wine which hath no vent; it is ready to burst like new bottles. I will speak that I may be refreshed. *—Job 32:18–20*

My heart took delight in all my work. *—Ecclesiastes 2:10 (NIV)*

Whatsoever thy hand findeth to do, do it with thy might.

—*Ecclesiastes 9:10*

But if I say, "I will not mention him or speak any more in his name," his word is in my heart like a fire, a fire shut up in my bones. I am weary of holding it in; indeed, I cannot.   —*Jeremiah 20:9 (NIV)*

Master, which is the great commandment in the law? Jesus said unto him, Thou shalt love the Lord Thy God with all thy heart, and with all thy soul, and with all thy mind. This is the first and great commandment. And the second is like unto it, Thou shalt love thy neighbour as thyself. On these two commandments hang all the law and the prophets.   —*Matthew 22:36–38*

I am the true vine, and my Father is the husbandman. Every branch in me that beareth not fruit he taketh away: and every branch that beareth fruit, he purgeth it, that it may bring forth more fruit. . . . Abide in me, and I in you. As the branch cannot bear fruit of itself, except it abide in the vine; no more can ye, except ye abide in me. I am the vine, ye are the branches: He that abideth in me, and I in him, the same bringeth forth much fruit: for without me ye can do nothing

—*John 15:1–2, 4–5*

This is my commandment, That ye love one another, as I have loved you.   —*John 15:12*

Even if I preach the Gospel, I can claim no credit for it; I cannot help myself; it would be misery to me not to preach.

—*1 Corinthians 9:16*

But it is good to be zealously affected always in a good thing, and not only when I am present with you.   —*Galatians 4:18*

For this reason, since the day we heard about you, we have not stopped praying for you, and asking God to fill you with the knowledge of his will through all spiritual wisdom and understanding. And we pray this in order that you may live a life worthy of the Lord and may please him in every way: bearing fruit in every good work, growing in the knowledge of God.   —*Colossians 1:9–10 (NIV)*

Whereunto I also labour, striving according to his working, which worketh in me mightily. *—Colossians 1:29*

Whatever you do, work at it with all your heart, as working for the Lord, not for men, since you know that you will receive an inheritance from the Lord as a reward. It is the Lord Christ you are serving. *—Colossians 3:23–24 (NIV)*

Who gave himself for us, that he might redeem us from all iniquity, and purify unto himself a peculiar people, zealous of good works. *—Titus 2:14*

And above all things have fervent charity among yourselves ... If any man speak, let him speak as the oracles of God. *—1 Peter 4:8, 11*

God Promises He Will Bless You and Complete His Intention for Your Life

I will be his father, and he shall be my son. If he commit iniquity, I will chasten him with the rod of men, and with the stripes of the children of men: But my mercy shall not depart away from him. *—2 Samuel 7:14–15*

You have made known to me the path of life; you will fill me with joy in your presence, with eternal pleasure at your right hand. *—Psalm 16:11 (NIV)*

Oh how great is thy goodness, which thou hast laid up for them that fear thee; which thou hast wrought for them that trust in thee before the sons of men. *—Psalm 31:19*

Delight yourself also in the LORD, and he will give you the desires of your heart. Commit your way [mode of action] to the LORD; trust in him and he will do this ... He will make your righteousness shine like the dawn, the justice of your cause like the noonday sun. *—Psalm 37:4–6 (NIV)*

You guide me with your counsel, and afterward you will take me into glory. *—Psalm 73:24 (NIV)*

Moreover, when God gives any man wealth and possessions, and enables him to enjoy them, to accept his lot and be happy in his work—this is a gift of God. He seldom reflects on the days of his life, because God keeps him occupied with gladness of heart.

—Ecclesiastes 5:19–20 (NIV)

LORD, thou wilt ordain peace for us: for thou also has wrought all our works in us. *—Isaiah 26:12*

For, behold, I create new heavens and a new earth . . . . And they shall build houses, and inhabit them; and they shall plant vineyards, and eat the fruit of them . . . . for as the days of a tree are the days of my people, and mine elect shall long enjoy the work of their hands.

—Isaiah 65:17, 21–22

Let not your heart be troubled: ye believe in God, believe also in me. In my Father's house are many mansions: if it were not so, I would have told you. I go to prepare a place for you. And if I go and prepare a place for you, I will come again, and receive you into myself; that where I am, there ye may be also. *—John 14:1–3*

And we know that all things work together for good to them that love God, to them who are called according to his purpose.

—Romans 8:28

For the gracious gifts of God and his calling are irrevocable.

—Romans 11:29 (NEB)

Therefore, since we are surrounded by such a great cloud of witnesses, let us throw off everything that hinders and the sin that so easily entangles, and let us run with perseverance the race marked out for us. Let us fix our eyes on Jesus, the author and perfecter of our faith . . . . the Lord disciplines those he loves, and he punishes everyone he accepts as a son. . . . Endure hardship as discipline . . . . God disciplines us for our good, that we may share in his holiness.

—Hebrews 12:1–2, 6, 10

And I heard a voice from heaven saying unto me, Write, Blessed are the dead which die in the Lord from henceforth: Yea, saith the Spirit, that they may rest from their labours; and their works [vocation, labor, work] do follow them.   —*Revelation 14:13*

God Has Instructed Us to Build His Kingdom in the Earth As It Is in Heaven Using the Giftedness with Which We Were Endowed

The Spirit of the Lord GOD is upon me; because the LORD hath anointed me to preach good tidings unto the meek; he hath sent me to bind up the brokenhearted, to proclaim liberty to the captives, and the opening of the prison to them that are bound; to proclaim the acceptable year of the LORD, and the day of vengeance of our God; to comfort all that mourn; to appoint unto them that mourn in Zion, to give unto them beauty for ashes, the oil of joy for mourning, the garment of praise for the spirit of heaviness; that they might be called trees of righteousness, the planting of the LORD, that he might be glorified. And they shall build the old wastes, they shall raise up the former desolations, and they shall repair the waste cities, the desolations of many generations. And strangers shall stand and feed your flocks, the sons of the alien shall be your plowmen and your vinedressers. But ye shall be named the Priests of the LORD: Men shall call you the Ministers of our God: ye shall eat the riches of the Gentiles, and in their glory shall ye boast yourselves.   —*Isaiah 61:1–6*

After this manner therefore pray ye: Our Father which art in heaven, hallowed by thy name. Thy kingdom come. Thy will be done in earth, as it is in heaven.   —*Matthew 6:9–10*

Now there are varieties of gifts, but the same Spirit; and there are varieties of service, but the same Lord; and there are varieties of working, but it is the same God who inspires them all in every one. To each is given the manifestation of the Spirit for the common good.   —*1 Corinthians 12:4–7 (RSV)*

He has made known to us his hidden purpose—such was his will and pleasure determined beforehand in Christ—to be put into effect when the time was ripe: namely, that the universe, all in heaven and on earth, might be brought into a unity in Christ. In Christ indeed we have been given our share in the heritage, as was decreed in his design whose purpose is everywhere at work.

—*Ephesians 1:9–12* (NEB)

Wherefore he saith, When he ascended upon high, he led captivity captive, and gave gifts unto men. . . . For the perfecting of the saints, for the work of the ministry, for the edifying of the body of Christ: Till we all come into the unity of the faith, and of the knowledge of the Son of God, unto a perfect man, unto the measure of the stature of the fulness of Christ.   —*Ephesians 4:8, 12–13*

Even the mystery which hath been hid from ages and from generations, but now is made manifest to his saints: To whom God would make known what is the riches of the glory of this mystery among the Gentiles; which is Christ in you, the hope of glory.

—*Colossians 1:26–27*

Appendix D

Discover Your Design:
A Step-by-Step Guide

OVERVIEW

Identifying your design is an easy and enjoyable three-step process:

Step 1: Recall and Summarize Your Achievements. Look back on your life so far and remember the things you did that you believe you did well and that you found satisfying. Write down a short synopsis of each achievement.

Step 2: Describe in Detail What You Did. Select four or more achievements that were especially important to you.

Step 3: Make an Inventory of Recurring Themes. Inventory the themes that recur in the major achievements and record them into the Distinctive Design summary.

Now let's look at the three steps in greater detail.

STEP 1: RECALL AND SUMMARIZE YOUR ACHIEVEMENTS

Discovering your design involves a three-step process. The first step in the process is to list as many activities as you can recall that satisfy three criteria:

What have you done in your life that

1. you enjoyed doing?
2. you did well, as *you* define "well"?
3. achieved or accomplished something?

Activities that meet all three of these three criteria are called *achievement activities*.

Examples:

- "I put on plays for the other children in our neighborhood, using costumes, props, etc. The most successful project was transforming a shed in back of our house into a fairyland with lighting effects, decorations, princesses, etc."
- "I organized a collection of seashells that I gathered at the shore one summer."
- "When I was twelve years old I fixed a grandfather clock that hadn't worked for two years."
- "I established an evening routine of a quiet time of sharing and reading with our children that made bedtime an enjoyable end to the day."
- "I was a prime mover in starting a company. I saw the utility of the product concept. I had a lot to do with early market development. I also helped conceive basic manufacturing concepts."
- "I organized and ran a company-sponsored national conference with about one hundred participants. The conference was a resounding success."
- "I caught a design problem during prototype testing and saved the company over ten thousand dollars."
- "I won the support of my subordinates over a period of years by building strong relationships. I took an interest in developing careers, and always sent cards on birthdays, Christmas, and special events."

Note that in each of these examples the person did something that he or she enjoyed doing and did well, and that activity achieved or accomplished something. Do the same as you generate your own list of achievement activities.

Achievement Activities Are Achievements Rather Than Successes

As you recall your achievements, keep in mind that achievement activities are achievements rather than successes.

Success is often perceived as being Number One, finishing first, or trouncing the opposition. It can also mean measuring ourselves against others to see if we're bigger, better, smarter, wealthier, and so on.

But your design is not discovered by recalling what anyone else thinks of what you've done, only in what is *meaningful to you*, whether or not it seemed significant to others. There's nothing wrong with finishing first; indeed, some people are motivated to be the best or to gain recognition. But you need not have finished first to list something as an achievement.

Examples:

- NOT: "I was the valedictorian of my class." (This is not necessarily an achievement activity; it depends on whether you enjoyed the steps leading up to it and whether it was significant to you.)
- NOT: "I was voted salesman of the year by the company." (We'd rather know about specific achievements that you enjoyed doing and did well.)
- BUT: "I trained for several years and came in third in the Boston Marathon." (This is an exceptional achievement, even though you didn't win first place. But what's useful is your reference to the training—a specific achievement activity that accomplished a result that was meaningful to you.)

Note: We're not suggesting that you shy away from outstanding accomplishments that were truly significant to you. But don't put something down just because your parents or your peers thought it was impressive, even though it meant little to you.

Achievement Activities Are Activities Rather Than Experiences

We all have memories that we enjoy recalling—personal milestones such as becoming an Eagle Scout, graduation from high school, or getting married. Or perhaps an unusually meaningful experience such as receiving a timely letter from a friend, enjoying a particular song, or visiting a place that left a big impression on us.

However, none of these experiences is useful in discovering one's design. They don't involve activities but merely reactions to events that took place. Discovering your design is about knowing something you did to accomplish a meaningful achievement.

Examples:

- NOT: "I toured Europe with my wife. The Alps were beautiful." (This tells us only about the Alps, not about you.)

- NOT: "My wife had a baby." (This is not necessarily an achievement activity, though it could be if it involved activities that you found significant—for example, reading about childbirth, learning Lamaze techniques, setting up a college fund.)
- BUT: "I coached my wife through the birth of our son." (This incident involves an activity—coaching—that you did to bring about a result.)

A Few Tips

- Take your time. Enjoy the experience!
- Go for volume. The more accomplishments you can think of, the better. You need a list of at least a dozen.
- Write what was important and satisfying to *you*, not to your family or friends. If some honor or recognition left you cold, leave it out.
- Include activities from throughout your life, from early childhood to the present.
- If an activity occurred in a group setting and you did nothing different from the others in the group, describe what all of you did (for example, "I was part of a team that explored an underground cave").
- Don't be modest. These are *your* achievements.
- If you can't stand to write or are unable to write, dictate your list into a tape recorder and have it transcribed, or have someone do the writing for you. It doesn't matter how you record these achievements, but eventually they need to be reduced to writing.

STEP 2: FILL IN THE DETAILS

The next step in discovering your design involves going into detail about at least four of the achievements from the list you generated in Step 1. Start by choosing eight that were especially important to you—perhaps the ones that brought you the biggest smile or the warmest glow when you remembered them.

Then, for each of the four, explain with as much detail as possible

- how you got involved in the activity
- how you went about doing the activity, such as
  - what you actually did

- what skills you used
- what was going through your mind as you did the activity
- what your approach was to solving problems and overcoming obstacles
- what was particularly enjoyable or satisfying to you

As in Step 1, if you don't want to or are unable to write, dictate the descriptions of your achievements into a tape recorder and have them transcribed, or have someone write down your descriptions for you (just make sure they write *your* words, not theirs). But you *must* have written descriptions of at least four accomplishments.

How Long Will It Take?

This is an open-ended exercise. Spend as much time on it as you need to provide "good data." Remember, the more detail you can give, the better. Many people take anywhere from two to four hours to complete their descriptions. But work at your own pace. You may even want to get started and then set it aside for a day or two before coming back to complete it. Remember, this is not a test; this is a *description* of activities that were meaningful to *you*.

Enjoy yourself!

Providing "Good Data"

The details of how you went about your achievements are extremely important. Your descriptions provide the "data" from which conclusions will be drawn. So it's crucial to provide "good data." Here are some suggestions:

1. *Use concrete terms rather than abstractions.* Give specifics rather than generalities. The more you can break down the mechanics of what you did into individual parts, the better. A good rule of thumb is, *Would an observer be able to tell that you are doing the activity you've described?*
2. *Illustrate what you did, if necessary.* If an activity is complex or technical, give an example or two of what was involved.
3. *Probe your memory with the fact-finder questions: Who? What? When? Where?* and *How?* (Don't worry about *Why?* That's an analytical question. For now, just give the facts.)
4. *Use action verbs rather than passive ones.*

Examples

- NOT: "I researched"; "I coordinated"; "I planned"; "I helped." (What exactly did you do as a researcher, coordinator, planner, and so forth?)
- BUT: "I researched a speech for my boss by going to the library and looking up statistics, articles, and quotes; calling people to get additional statistics and quotes; and interviewing a person who could tell me what her audience would be expecting to hear." (Anyone could tell whether or not you were doing the concrete activities mentioned.)
- NOT: "I was the program director for a summer camp." (That's a title, no one would know exactly what was involved.)
- BUT: "One week we had a child who was extremely homesick and his behavior was disruptive to the other kids. I discussed the situation with his counselor and then met with him myself. I bought him some ice cream and we talked about how he had never been away from home before and how he felt about that." (This illustrates how you went about part of your job as the program director.)
- NOT: "I went"; "I saw"; "I thought about." (An observer would be unable to tell if you were doing these.)
- BUT: "I drove to . . ."; "I stood by and watched while . . ."; "I envisioned . . ." (These verbs involve more action and specific activity.)

Note the rich detail in the examples shown in the following boxed examples.

Achievement Activity. Wife and I took over as leaders of a cub pack that was failing and developed a successful group.

Details. After attending the first meeting we were very displeased with the program they had—started to rebuild the pack along with my wife—the pack grew from twenty to fifty boys—what a mess it was!—disorganized—went about reorganizing the thing—we set up rules that no boy could come to the meeting without his parents—had a swimming pool—invited parents over for a planning meeting—built the thing up from folding to a thing that was enjoyable to the children—had to be careful with the rules part—required coordination—check with parents—encourage them to get involved—have to sort of prod them a little to get them started—couldn't be pushy or they might pull their kid out—wanted to see the thing built up.

Achievement Activity. Set up a daily pending file for my employer.

How You Got Involved. Employer wanted me to get involved right away.

Details. I set up a series of follow-up letters—some were forms, some dictated by the boss, and others I handled myself. I enjoyed taking dictation, then being left alone to work out the final "product." There was a good variety of work with secretarial posting, payroll reconciling statement, making department spreadsheets—liked working with figures and details. I enjoyed going to work knowing that what I have to do and doing it—the pending file itself was my idea to work out—it was a good follow-up that allowed me to check up and make sure things got done and not lost in the shuffle.

Achievement Activity. I renovated/restored a Victorian mansion into a quality office space.

How You Got Involved. A friend and customer of mine took me for a tour after a business luncheon where the discussion was totally unrelated to real estate. He simply liked the house, but I saw what it could become.

Details. The next day I had an old friend, who is a builder, an expert in Victorian architecture and an ex-real estate agent, go with me and another friend who was licensed to show the property. I asked a lot of questions about the structure and the building, the plumbing and wiring, and how long and how much it would take to get such a beat-up old mansion habitable. Met with other potential partners/investors and persuaded them to kick in. I managed the project. Although we discussed each decision at every major step, I single-handedly sought out and hired a team of old craftsmen to restore the mansion to use as quality office spaces. We then advertised and leased space. I was involved in all the negotiations. I even opened my own office for personal investment consultation. We had an open house and made all the newspapers. It turned out that the old place had quite a history. I was even interviewed on TV by some experts from the historical society. So my career in real estate/property development had begun. I started first as a passive investor, then active investor and manager, then part-time lease agent, then seller of limited partnerships. I had to make some quick money since expenses were higher than expected.

What was particularly satisfying to you? Being able to take a run-down building and do something profitable and constructive. Plus, it was good business recognition and great for tax write-offs.

Achievement Activity. Playing scrub baseball (sometimes helped organize).

How You Got Involved. I think an older kid who had taught me how to pitch encouraged me to get a team together.

Details. Sometimes I played at school and other times just got in on neighborhood games we worked up. One summer I thought, *Why not have a first-class team?* So I went around to kids I knew who were really good and asked them to play. I chose the name ("Blackhawks") and was co-captain with another friend (had to share that with him to get him to join up), but I assigned most of the positions. At the beginning I also set up most of the games. Would decide a few days in advance, phone around and get others to phone—never did much to have real schedule.

An older kid had taught me to throw a fast-break and a sinker. I used to practice every morning just before breakfast and right after I got home from school by throwing balls into a fifty-five-gallon drum. I was good on change-ups and became known as a good control pitcher. Got to know how to "read" a batter later on when we got our own Little League team, and usually won. Also played first base (with the "Blackhawks") before I became a good pitcher—I had long arms and a good reach.

What was particularly satisfying to you? Liked winning—it proved my ability to play ball well. Enjoyed the recognition from friends and from parents—especially support of little league coach. Liked to know they were looking to me to win. Very important to come through so we could win the city championship.

Achievement Activity. I tutored a guy who had not passed the college entrance test in math and saw him graduate as a math major.

Details. I guess it all started when I saw him outside the lecture hall one Thursday; he looked a little glum, so I asked him, "What's wrong?" At first he said, "Nothing," but when he saw I really wanted to know, he told me he hadn't passed the math entrance exam and was in danger of not getting in. I asked him if I could help, and that's how we got started, with me helping him to understand the basics of math. It opened a whole new world to him. I used to make him explain to me just how he got the answer he did. I made myself constantly available to him.

What was particularly satisfying to you? Just to think that I helped someone to understand, and helped him to do something he really enjoyed. . . . You feel like you've really accomplished something that really helps someone.

STEP 3: MAKE AN INVENTORY OF RECURRING THEMES

How is it that a few personally interesting stories can yield anything significant? The answer is in the details of *how you go about doing* what you love to do and do well.

Over your lifetime many things change, such as your skills, your level of education, your interests, and your psychological condition. However, some things don't change. These recurring themes can be found in childhood and adulthood; in work or play; in good times and in bad. Together, these themes comprise your unique way of functioning—in short, your distinctive design. In fact, whether you are functional or dysfunctional, you will still evidence this patterned behavior. In a very real sense, it is the only way you know how to "do life."

What to Do

1. Place your written achievements in front of you for easy access.
2. Take a few minutes to highlight the key words, phrases, and themes you can spot.
3. As we go through the assessment together, try and make your judgments based on objective evidence from your achievements. For now, if you don't see it in your written achievements, don't include it.

Distinctive Design Themes

Our inventory surveys five distinctive design themes.

1. *Abilities you love to use.* They are the ones that you never tire of using and that bring you great satisfaction when you employ them. We call these your **Motivated Abilities.**
2. *Things you love to work with or through.* This could be anything from numbers to ideas, from policies to people, from gadgets to strategies. We call these your **Motivating Subject Matter**.
3. *Conditions of work; situations or settings that stimulate you to achieve.* We call these your **Motivating Circumstances.**
4. *The way you prefer to work together with others*, as well as the most comfortable way you relate to your supervisor. We call these your **Operating Relationships**.
5. *The goal you love to work toward.* We call this your **Payoff**.

Each person's combination of these ingredients gives his or her approach to life a unique stamp.

1. Motivated Abilities

Your *Motivated Abilities* are those you are drawn to, that you find most absorbing and engaging, that you gravitate to without thinking about it, and that come so naturally to you that you probably think of them as "common sense."

We divide these *Motivated Abilities* into five general categories:

How I Learn

How did you go about taking in, "getting the hang of," or learning the information you needed in your achievements?

- By reading
- By observing
- By trying
- By memorizing
- By asking
- By conferring/discussing

How I Evaluate

How did you sift through the information, and how did you decide what action to take, and in what priority?

- By analyzing
- By empathizing
- By weighing pros and cons
- By calculating
- By assessing worth
- By comparing against a standard

How I Prepare

Having taken in what you needed and decided what you will do, how did you prepare to take action?

- By picturing
- By setting goals
- By strategizing
- By organizing
- By practicing

How I Take Action

How did you go about actually getting the achievement done?

- By nurturing
- By creating, innovating
- By physically doing
- By producing
- By operating
- By maintaining
- By overseeing others

How I Influence Others

How did you influence others, cause others to take action, or inform them about what you did or knew?

- By bargaining
- By getting others involved
- By motivating
- By conversing
- By counseling
- By teaching
- By writing
- By suggesting
- By persuading
- By performing

Transfer your selections to "My Distinctive Design" summary sheet (p. 237).

2. Motivating Subject Matter

Your *Motivating Subject Matter* is what you enjoy working with or through to achieve your "Payoff."

Look at the categories of Motivating Subject Matter listed below. Which of these show(s) up *consistently* in your achievements as something you worked *on*, worked *with*, or worked *through?* Check all that apply.

- *Data* (e.g., details, numbers, words, money, information)
- *Things* (e.g., structures, tools, machinery, materials, physical phenomena)
- *Senses* (e.g., sound, light, color, texture, taste, form, movement)
- *Living* (e.g., people, groups, plants, animals, nature)

- *Ideas* (e.g., concepts, theories, principles, values, thoughts)
- *Mechanisms* (e.g., strategies, systems, techniques, expertise, procedures)

Transfer your selection(s) to "My Distinctive Design" summary sheet (p. 237).

3. Motivating Circumstances

Your *Motivating Circumstances* refers to the situations that turn you into a motivated person, or the conditions that stimulate you to achieve your "Payoff."

Look at the categories of Motivating Circumstances listed below. Do your achievements reveal that any of these circumstances are truly and *consistently* motivating to you? Check all that apply.

- *Trigger* (e.g., responding to problems, needs, opportunities)
- *Visible* (e.g., being seen or noticed, in front of others, status, reputation)
- *Difficult* (e.g., pressure, demanding, risks, obstacles, competition, challenges)
- *Structured* (e.g., clear requirements, well-defined, parameters, order, models)
- *Measured* (e.g., finished product, standards, numerical results, goals)
- *Different* (e.g., new, novel, unique, unknown)

Transfer your selection(s) to "My Distinctive Design" summary sheet (p. 237).

4. Operating Relationships

Your *Operating Relationships* refer to the way in which you prefer to relate to others, and the way in which you want your supervisor or manager to relate to you, as you try to achieve your "Payoff."

Which of the following best describes how you related to others in your achievements?

- *Contributor*—Alone or as a member of a team, you want to make a personal contribution to the work, without being concerned with your affect on others or being responsible for making others take action.

- *Influencer*—You want to have an affect on others and/or influence them to take action, but do not want responsibility for their overall management.
- *Overseer*—You take responsibility for accomplishing a goal or getting something done through actively directing, leading, coordinating, or managing the efforts of others.

Which of the following best describes how you related to authority in your achievements?

- *Hands Off*—"Let me do my own thing." You function most effectively under an authority who allows you to exercise independent control over your specific area of responsibility.
- *Collaborative*—"Let me work *with* you." You function most effectively under an authority who treats you as an equal, who works with you as though you were involved in a joint effort, and who has a genuine interest in your ideas and suggestions.
- *Supportive*—"Give me help when I need it." You function best under an authority who, at your discretion, provides you with direction and support at key points of your involvement in a task.

Transfer your selection(s) to "My Distinctive Design" summary sheet (p. 237).

5. Payoff

Your *Payoff* refers to the central outcome you seek to achieve when you use the other four dimensions of your distinctive design.

"The outcome or satisfaction in my achievements seems to focus on . . ." (Complete the sentence using only *one* of the following. Use your own words.)

- *Personal Performance*—Measuring your achievement by how you perform or how you compare with others or with standards.
- *Impact/Effect*—Fixing things, shaping things, improving results, improving the performance, causing a response, extracting potential, leaving your mark.
- *Dominion/Power*—Exercising power or influence over people or things—focused energy to accomplish, to own, to master, to overcome.

- *Achieve a Goal*—Reaching a target, completing the job, satisfying the needs, passing the test, fulfilling the requirements, making the grade, or meeting expectations.
- *Engage in a Processes*—Pioneering, discovering the new, building proficiency, advancing a technology, making ideas a reality, developing a product or process.

Transfer your selection(s) to "My Distinctive Design" summary sheet (p. 237).

MY DISTINCTIVE DESIGN

Fill in and check off the themes that make up your distinctive design.

1. **Motivated Abilities (insert the appropriate abilities)**

   I learn by _____.

   I evaluate by _____.

   I prepare by _____.

   I take action by _____

   I influence by_____.

2. **Motivating Subject Matter**
   __Data
   __Things
   __Mechanisms
   __Living
   __Ideas
   __Senses

3. **Motivating Circumstances**
   __Trigger
   __Visibility
   __Difficult
   __Structured
   __Measured
   __Different

4. **Operating Relationships**
   __To Others
   __Contributor
   __Influencer
   __Overseer
   __To Authority
   __Hands Off
   __Collaborative
   __Supportive

5. Payoff
__ Personal Performance
__ Impact/Effect
__ Power/Dominion
__ Achieve a Goal
__ Engage in a Process

DESCRIBING YOU AT YOUR BEST

To give a better and perhaps more useful understanding of your MAP, proceed to integrate the various elements into an idealized description of you operating at your best.

One way to develop the integrated description is to use the format outlined below where you insert words from your MAP. This format corresponds to example #1, which follows.

- A job working with ... (insert your subject matter) e.g., people, ideas, numbers, machines, etc.

  SUBJECT MATTER

- So that I can ... (insert your motivated abilities) e.g., investigate the facts, analyze their significance, create a product, improvise a solution, get others involved, etc.

  MOTIVATED ABILITIES

- Where the conditions of the work are (allow me to) require ... (insert your circumstances) e.g., project-oriented, operate under stress, be in the background, etc.

  CIRCUMSTANCES

- Where I can operate ... (insert your operating relationships) e.g., member of a team, in a defined role, in a leadership role, etc.

  OPERATING RELATIONSHIPS

- Which will lead to ... (insert your motivational payoff) e.g., finished product, improved process, greater responsibility, recognition from my superiors, etc.

  MOTIVATIONAL PAYOFF

After the next few pages, you will be asked to write a short paragraph describing the essence of your MAP. First, look at these examples.

These examples follow a structured format that is described on the previous page.

- A job working with machinery and its maintenance, using my abilities to learn how machinery works, set up a maintenance schedule, repair broken parts, improvise with what is available, and explain to operators how to properly use the machinery; ideally where the conditions of work make clear what is expected of me, and each job can be completed before going to the next, where I can work with others as part of a team; which leads to an opportunity to work with greater variety and complexity of machinery.
- A job working with people, merchandise, and money—using my abilities to evaluate people, make friends with them, sell them on myself and my product, keep my merchandise neat and orderly and carefully account for my sales and cost of sales, where the conditions of work are not too structured and allow me to tackle and solve problems that come up, and require me to keep a cool head in the face of a lot of pressure; where I can operate pretty much on my own; and which leads to opportunity for participation in the ownership or profits of the business.

The next sample is more free-flowing.

- I see potential and opportunity in things, particularly people, ideas and ways to excite people and get things done. I'm good at promoting, selling, initiating and getting things started. I'm very concerned with details and meeting the needs of others, particularly when I can establish my reputation and look good in the eyes of others. I'm good in things like sales, coaching, client relations, strategizing, and generating ideas.

DEVELOPING A "FREE-FLOWING" DESCRIPTION

If you find the preceding format limiting, then you can be even more free-flowing. You may find it helpful to review the samples below.

SUBJECT MATTER

Original

Personal expertise: people-groups, people-individuals; thoughts, expressions

Personalized

I like to get my ideas across to people using my personal expertise to translate those ideas into something understandable.

MOTIVATED ABILITIES

Original

Evaluating—by appraising worth, assessing value; conceptualizing—by conceiving ideas and concepts; doing—manually and physically maintaining; influencing—by initiating, suggesting, involving, and getting participation

Personalized

I'm good at making value judgments which lead to my coming up with profitable ideas that I carry out manually or physically, while I maintain the effectiveness of the process. I like to get other people involved in innovative ideas and get those ideas publicized.

CIRCUMSTANCES

Original

Creative; growth-developing situation; potential—possible, finished product; project, program; group, team

Personalized

I enjoy being in a project-oriented position in a creative environment working toward a finished product that extracts the potential from a growth situation where I can contribute to a group or team.

OPERATING RELATIONSHIPS

Original

Individualist/facilitator

Personalized

I like working on my own with activities that reflect my style and interest. When I interact with others, I like to be free to function in various roles that help others to be more effective and satisfied in their work.

MOTIVATIONAL PAYOFF ————————————————

Original

Impress; impact on, make mark; shape

Personalized

I enjoy making a lasting impression on people's minds, on structures, events and activities I'm involved with. I like to start from scratch on a project, coming up with all the details to meet the needs or solve the problems within my specialty or expertise.

Now integrate the various elements of your MAP into a description of you at your best by following the formula, or by taking a more free-flowing path, as illustrated on the previous page.

_____

_____

_____

_____

_____

_____

_____

_____

_____

_____

_____

_____

_____

_____

_____

_____

LEARNING HOW YOU LEARN

Now that you have some understanding of your MAP, let's get more specific and help you understand what, how, and why you are motivated to learn. This understanding is critical if you are a student and need to take advantage of opportunities available to you wherever you are in your educational journey.

There follows a series of questions to which you are being asked to respond. How you answer indicates the nature of your learning dynamics and defines how you should approach requirements or opportunities to learn.

In responding to these questions, we want you to draw form *your achievements only*, not other experiences. So before you start answering the questions, consider your database. Recall your achievement experiences and think through how you went about acquiring the knowledge or facts or skills involved.

In fact, it is a good idea to go back over the relevant part of your achievements as you respond to the question(s) on each page; particularly if you are unsure about your recollection of the facts.

Ponder a bit on these issues. Then answer the questions. Feel free to write down evidence from your achievements on each page which supports your conclusions. Feel free to ignore that suggestion if the exercise is too arduous for you.

1. How Are You Motivated to Learn?

For each of us, the way we like to learn is distinctive. Think back to those achievements when you learned the most . . . what was the process you were involved in during those times? How do you prefer to learn, given an option? Circle one or two at most.

A   By reading written or printed material
B   By personally doing, trying, or experiencing
C   By observing detail, watching carefully, perceiving
D   By practicing, repeating, memorizing
E   By experimenting, tinkering, innovating, and testing
F   By investigating, researching, questioning, inquiring

2. To What Depth and Detail Are You Motivated to Learn?

A In depth
B Enough to handle the matter at hand
C To a superficial level

3. What Are the Mechanisms Through Which You Learn?

Curiously, learning happens best when we receive, or process, or discover new things through particular mechanisms. On the surface perhaps, these may be seen as inconsequential—but as you think in greater depth, you may realize they are not. They are frequently quite critical to us. What about you? Circle one in each grouping.

A Through a teacher
B Without a teacher

C In the company of others
D By yourself
E Alone, until moderately able, then learn with others

F Where feedback is immediate
G Where feedback can be delayed

H Where learning is structured
I Where learning is fluid

J Where you will be measured for your learning
K Where there won't be any grading

4. What Are the Circumstances in Which Learning Took Place?

The fact that there is a circumstantial component to the dynamics of your learning is frequently known in part . . . it touches on such facts that, even though you knew the exam was coming, you didn't do anything until the very last minute, or that part of you that liked to pit yourself against someone else. Circle one in each grouping.

A Where you learn under pressure
B Where there is ample time to learn

C In a competitive setting
    1. Where you compete with others
    2. Where you compete against a target or grade

D   Where you don't know how others do

E   Where there are right and wrong answers
F   Where informed opinions are what count

G   Where your performance will be observed by others
H   Where no one but you knows what you are doing

I   Where the material is standard
J   Where the material is unique and new

5. Why Are You Motivated to Learn?

This is often the hardest thing to fathom about ourselves ... just why sometimes we can really get fired up, and why at other times we have no interest. The intention in asking you to think about this question is not to have you check the boxes in some superficial "Everybody wants to do that, don't they?" way, but rather for you to contemplate in depth the particular significance to you of your interest in learning. When you see it in the context of your achievements, one of these primary focuses should stand out to you. Circle one only.

A   To achieve mastery/dominion
B   To meet requirements/expectations
C   To excel over others/ gain recognition
D   To discover/learn
E   To improve/develop myself
F   To make the grade/reach the grade
G   To impress/influence others
H   To advance/get ahead

6. What Are the Learning Outcomes You Seek?

Learning is frequently not simply an *end* for people, it is often a *means*. Circle one or two outcomes you seek.

A   New knowledge
B   New creation
C   Problem solved
D   Impact on others
E   Finished product
F   Quantitative result
G   Meeting a requirement

7. What Are You Motivated to Learn?

As we review our lives, it's obvious that some things (or subjects) always seem to interest us, while others leave us cold and unmoved. What about you and your life? What shows up in your achievements? Circle one, two, or three.

A   Intangibles and Abstractions
B   Tangible Objects and Concrete Substances
C   Data, Symbols, and Language
D   People and Behavior
E   Scientific, Technical, and Mathematical Phenomena
F   Visual and Other Sensory Expressions and Sensations

CONCLUSIONS

If you have conscientiously and honestly grappled with the questions, you will now be in a position to pull together all these disparate elements into a summary statement, as in this example.

1. How am I motivated to learn?
- by experimenting and observing

2. To what depth am I motivated to learn?
- in great depth

3. What mechanisms motivate me to learn?
- without a teacher
- by myself
- where feedback can be delayed
- where learning is fluid
- where I will be measured for my learning

4. What circumstances motivate me to learn?
- where there is ample time to learn
- where I don't know how others do
- where there are right and wrong answers
- where no one will know what I'm doing
- where the material is standard

5. Why am I motivated to learn?
- because fundamentally, I want to discover/learn

6. What are the learning outcomes?
  - I love solving problems

7. What am I motivated to learn?
  - about machinery, finance, and engineering subjects

Reach your own conclusions in a similar fashion and format on the next page.

MY PERSONAL CONCLUSIONS

1. How am I motivated to learn?

   _____

   _____

2. To what depth am I motivated to learn?

   _____

   _____

3. What mechanisms motivate me to learn?

   _____

   _____

4. What circumstances motivate me to learn?

   _____

   _____

5. Why am I motivated to learn?

   _____

   _____

6. What are the learning outcomes?

   _____

   _____

7. What am I motivated to learn?

   _____

   _____

Now you should have a solid grasp on your learning dynamics so you can plan and manage your education in a way which is effective for you.

Pursue that major field of study, those courses, and those teachers who engage what, how, and why you are motivated to learn.

Discuss the specifics of your learning dynamics with each teacher and attempt to arrive at a learning strategy and mechanisms which can give you what you need, and satisfy what the teacher requires you to learn.

Appendix E

Other Voices

In this book, we have explained the facts and nature of human design and trust you have been able to accept the truth of our representations. If you aren't as yet completely convinced that people possess a mix of certain endowments that should guide their way through life, perhaps the words of people more esteemed for their wisdom than your authors could underscore the message.

Let us, literally, go back to the beginning. God created human beings with distinctive skills, powers of memory and ingenuity. Our ability to apply those distinctive skills to natural resources, to create things of use and value to ourselves and others, is God-given, part of His creation.

The Archbishop of Canterbury, the Reverend George Carey

Was this the basis of your distinction between the man naturally gifted for anything and the one not so gifted . . . that the one learned easily, the other with difficulty, that the one with slight instruction could discover much for himself in the matter studied, but the other, after much instruction and drill, could not even remember what he had learned . . . ?

But the natural capacities are distributed alike among both creatures, and women naturally share in all pursuits and men in all . . .

Plato (427–347 B.C.
Collected Dialogues Republic: II

... each man should stick to what is natural for his own character, provided that it is not harmful.

... nothing is more fitting than complete consistency of life and
individual actions, and this cannot be achieved if we neglect our
own natural inclinations and follow those which belong more
properly to others.

We should therefore apply ourselves to those fields in which our
greatest talent lies. ...

Cicero (106 B.C.–43 B.C.)
De Officiis, *On Moral Obligation*,
trans. John Higginbotham

Moreover, human life would seem to consist in that in which
each man most delights, that for which he especially strives, and
that which he particularly wishes to share with his friends ...

St. Thomas Aquinas (1225–1274)
Summa Theologia, trans. Blackfriars (OP)

We cultivate most those studies for which we have the strongest
natural bent.

If we find Nature herself, who has disposed the heavens, and stars
in their various orbits and courses, at God's will making us, as a
matter of course, for different functions, then who will dare go
over into another occupation than that to which he was born?

Gionanni Boccacio (1313–1375)
Boccacio on Poetry, trans. Charles G. Osgood

The last thing to be observed is, that the Lord enjoins every one of us, in all the actions of life, to have respect to our own calling. He knows the boiling restlessness of the human mind, the fickleness with which it is borne hither and thither ... Therefore, lest all things should be thrown into confusion by our folly and rashness, he has assigned distinct duties to each in different modes of life. And that no one may presume to overstep his proper limits, he has distinguished the different modes of life by the names of callings. Every man's mode of life, therefore, is a kind of station assigned him by the Lord, that he may not be always driven about at random.

John Calvin (1509–1564)
Institutes of The Christian Religion

That at each man's birth there comes into being an eternal vocation for him, expressly for him. To be true to himself in relation to this eternal vocation is the highest thing a man can practice. ...

Shakespeare (1564–1616)
in *Henry V* (Act 2, Scene 4)

Men outside their proper callings are like joints out of place in the body; in finding his proper place, each must examine both his "affections" and his gifts.

And that they may the better judge aright, for what calling their children are fit, they must observe two things in them: first, their inclination; secondly, their natural gifts.

William Perkins
Cambridge Puritan in a Treatise of Vocations (1502)

The employment or calling we choose must be suitable or fit. Rashness and negligence herein has often been the ruin of particular persons, and sometimes a public mischief. Those who have capacities and endowments above their callings grow uneasy and discontented in them; and those who have employments above their capacities, after weak and unsuccessful attempts, are discouraged: and if they are placed in more exalted stations of life, render their weakness the more conspicuous and prove a flame and reproach unto them ... Let therefore the abilities of mind and body be considered.

Richard Steele (1672–1729)
The Religious Tradesman (The Tradesman's Calling)

It is the first of all problems for a man to find out what kind of work he is to do in this universe.

Thomas Carlyle
Inaugural Address, Edinburgh (April 2, 1866)

No man is born into the world whose work is not born with him; there is always work and tools to work withal, for those who will.

J. R. Lowell (1819–1891)
A Glance Behind the Curtain, l. 202

There is another aspect of work viewed as participation in the creative purposes of God which particularly needs further consideration. Each person is called to discover and develop his special capacities which have been entrusted to him as gifts by the Creator, gifts both for enjoyment and service. There are diversities of gifts, and each person is summoned to live his own life to the full. The acceptance of this call enables all forms of work that are undertaken for the glory of God and rules out any hierarchical scale of values as regards the kinds of work performed.

E. Clinton Gardner
"Religion in Life," vol. XXV, *Rethinking the Protestant Doctrine of Vocation*

There was reason to fear, as we have said, that the introduction of Christian perspectives might seriously upset the ordering of human action; that the seeking after, and waiting for, the Kingdom of Heaven might deflect human activity from its natural tasks, or at least entirely eclipse any interest in them. Now we see why this cannot and must not be so. The knitting together of God and the world has just taken place under our eyes in the domain of action. No, God does not deflect our gaze prematurely from the work He Himself has given us, since He presents Himself to us as attainable through that very work. Nor does he blot out, in His intense light, the detail of our earthly aims, since the closeness of our union with Him is in fact determined by the exact fulfillment of the least of our tasks. We ought to accustom ourselves to this basic truth till we are steeped in it, until it becomes as familiar to us as the perception of shape or the reading of words. God, in all that is most living and incarnate in Him, is not far away from us, altogether apart from the world we see, touch, hear, smell and taste about us. Rather He awaits us every instant in our action, in the work of the moment. There is a sense in which He is at the tip of my pen, my spade, my brush, my needle—of my heart and of my thought. By pressing the stroke, the line, or the stitch, on which I am engaged, to its ultimate natural finish, I shall lay hold of that last end toward which my innermost will tends. Like those formidable physical forces which man contrives to discipline so as to make them perform operations of prodigious delicacy, so the tremendous power of the divine attraction is focused on our frail desires and microscopic intents without breaking their point.

Pierre Teilhard De Chardin
Le Milieu Devin

Most of our life is in large part a rationalization of our failure to find out who we really are, what our basic strength is, what thing it is that we were meant to work upon in the world.

Ernest Becker
The Birth and Death of Meaning

Far more fundamentally, vocation is that original divine call addressed to each individual at the moment of his creation and reiterated in all the circumstances of his life creation and reiterated in all the circumstances of his life. It is God's creative summons, calling forth from nothing the very being of the creature. It is that same divine love which continues to actualize the potential of the individual inviting him to become what he is meant to be; to realize that unique being which he alone of all creation can express.

[Regarding individual vocation] God has provided each individual with unique talents. These talents of mind and body signify God's call to the individual, indicating by specific function in the total fulfillment of the divine plan. Every human person is uniquely designed to "body forth each in his own way, God's being" . . . these talents are invitations to personal responses.

Sister Helen Marie
"A Phenomenology of Vocation: Personal Relevance,"
(on the life and expressions of Edith Stein—scholarly intellectual, convert from
Judaism, lecturer on feminism, Carmelite mystic, martyr to Nazi Persecution)

Each one of you must—without presumption, certainly without boastfulness—courageously appeal to those interior resources, must make use of those personal energies, that God the Creator has providentially placed in you as so many gifts . . . It is not a question of standing alone and egotistically closing in upon himself. It is only a question of fidelity to the truth of one's human nature—the carrier of an unrepeatable destiny.

Pope Paul VI
Populorum Progressio, Art. 15, AAS, 59 (1967)

In a nutshell, then, this book is about calling, about fate, about character, about innate image. Together they make up the "acorn theory," which holds that each person bears a uniqueness that asks to be lived and that is already present before it can be lived.

Reading life backward enables you to see how early obsessions are the sketchy preformation of behaviors now. Sometimes the peaks of early years are never surpassed. Reading backward means that growth is less the key biographical term than form, and that development only makes sense when it reveals a facet of the original image.

The acorn theory proposes, and I will bring evidence for the claim, that you and I and every single person is born with a defining image.

James Hillman
The Soul's Code, in Search of Character and Calling

But they tend to the fabric of this world, and their prayer is in the practice of their trade.

Ecclesiasticus 38:34

These ancient and modern voices of wisdom and authority—Greek sages, patristic fathers, prelates, reformers, humanist philosophers, writers, scholars, other thoughtful and esteemed men and women over a period of 2,500 years—concluded that human beings have inherent strengths and a disposition to use them in certain ways. Whether you believe these endowments come from God or from some other mysterious source, or even if you would hope for a mechanistic explanation that we do not as yet understand, I trust you are convinced by now that people really do possess a unique makeup of certain competencies and motivations.

> People Management International, Ltd.
> 322 East Main Street
> Wilmore, KY 40390
> Phone (606) 858-2500 • (2600 Fax)
> e-mail: josjua@pmijobfit.net

Because the People Management family has offices in many parts of the world, it is likely your request could be forwarded to an office reasonably near you.

PMI Network* (March 1998)

Atlanta, GA	Ottawa, ON
Wellington, NZ	Oxford, UK
Baltimore, MD	Philadelphia, PA
Bussum, NETH	Pittsburgh, PA
Chicago, IL	San Diego, CA
Dallas, TX	San Francisco, CA
Hartford, CT	Seattle, WA
Los Angeles, CA	Singapore
Madison, WI	Somerset West (South Africa)
Minneapolis, MN	Sydney, AU
Nashville, TN	Tampa, FL
New York, NY	Vancouver, BC

---

* Actual Location or Nearest City